LOVE
IN A
TIME
OF
HATE

ALSO BY FLORIAN ILLIES

1913: The Year Before the Storm

LOVE IN A TIME OF HATE

Art and Passion in the Shadow of War, 1929-39

FLORIAN ILLIES

Translated by Simon Pare

P

PROFILE BOOKS

First published in Great Britain in 2023 by
Profile Books Ltd
29 Cloth Fair
London
ECIA 7JQ

www.profilebooks.com

Originally published in German as *Liebe in Zeiten des Hasses* in 2021
by S. Fischer Verlag, Frankfurt am Main, Germany

Copyright © S. Fischer Verlag GmbH, 2021
English language translation copyright © Simon Pare, 2023

'23rd August 1939' by Durs Grünbein published with kind
permission from Karen Leeder and Seagull Books

Erich Kästner, 'Familiäre Stanzen' (trans. Simon Pare), from *Ein Mann gibt Auskunft* (1930)
© Atrium Verlag AG, Zürich, und Thomas Kästner reproduced with kind permission.

Every effort has been made to contact copyright holders of material
reproduced in this book. However, the publishers will be glad to rectify in
future editions any inadvertent omissions brought to their attention.

1 3 5 7 9 10 8 6 4 2

Typeset in Garamond by MacGuru Ltd
Printed and bound in Great Britain by Clays Ltd, Elcograf S.p.A.

The moral right of the author has been asserted.

A CIP catalogue record for this book is available from the British Library.

ISBN 978 1 80081 114 0
eISBN 978 1 80081 115 7

LOVE
IN A
TIME
OF
HATE

Contents

BEFORE

The moment the young Jean-Paul Sartre first gazes into Simone de Beauvoir's eyes at the École Normale Supérieure in Paris in the spring of 1929 is the only time his mind goes blank. When he finally manages to arrange a date with her a few weeks later, in early June, she doesn't show up. Sartre sits in a tearoom in Rue de Médicis waiting for her. In vain. Paris is lovely and warm that day, white clouds cavorting high in the deep-blue sky, and he has decided not to wear a tie – he plans to take her to the nearby Jardin du Luxembourg after tea, and sail model boats on the pond. He has read somewhere that this is what people do. When he has almost finished his cup of tea, after glancing at the clock for the fifteenth time and protractedly tamping and lighting his pipe, a young blonde woman comes rushing up to his table. She tells him she's Simone's sister, Hélène de Beauvoir. Simone can't make it today, sadly. She is very sorry. 'But how did you recognise me so easily among all these people?' Sartre asks. 'Simone told me you were short, wore glasses and were very ugly,' she explains.

Thus begins one of the twentieth century's strangest love stories.

In the late afternoon, when the sun peeks out again from under the low clouds and its rays angle into Auguststrasse, the poet Mascha Kaléko blinks and stops for a second, savouring the warmth on her skin.

She always knocks off at four on the dot and then runs downstairs to the office of the Jewish Workers' Welfare Centre, where she has worked for the past five years. Mascha pushes the door open and stands there motionless. She lets the sunshine warm her, lets her thoughts run wild, hears the trams screeching in the distance, the beer delivery carts bumping along the streets, the shrieks of children running around the courtyards here in Berlin's Jewish quarter near Alexanderplatz, and the cries of the paperboys hawking the latest edition at the top of their voices.

But then she blocks out the noise and simply soaks up the gentle warmth. The sun sinks behind the tall buildings around Friedrichstrasse, a few last rays catching the golden dome of the synagogue in Oranienstrasse, and twilight finally comes. Yet twenty-two-year-old Mascha isn't ready to go home just yet; she's attracted instead to bars in the west of the city, usually to the Romanisches Café – a popular meeting place for artists at the end of the Kurfürstendamm, Berlin's main avenue – where she sits and debates in her sonorous voice. The satirist Kurt Tucholsky, author Joseph Roth, actress Ruth Landshoff and others draw up their chairs when Mascha arrives. They love her mop of curly brown hair, her knowing laugh, the benevolent wit that sparkles in her eyes. They are often joined later at the café by her husband, quiet Saul, a scholar through and through who wears metal-rimmed spectacles and has thinning hair. This skinny man is a reporter for the *Jüdische Rundschau*, Germany's bestselling Jewish weekly, and a lecturer in Hebrew; he's also madly in love. He sees the other men watching his impetuous young wife and notes how she relishes being watched. From minute to minute, quiet Saul grows quieter and quieter, and he orders some tea while the others start on their first bottle of wine. After a while he politely makes his excuses, puts on his hat, picks up his briefcase, bids them farewell and goes home. He is asleep by the time Mascha gets back to their flat on Hohenzollernkorso in Tempelhof. She gazes at him, as his earnest features softly rise and fall in time with his breathing. She goes over to the kitchen table, takes a sheet of paper and a pencil and writes him a love poem – perhaps one of the most moving love poems ever written. It begins:

The others are the boundless sea;
You, though, are the harbour deep.

She scribbles, 'For a man', places it on his breakfast plate and is soon snuggling up next to him in bed. She'll sail away again at six the next morning to her office on the other side of the city. When

Saul feels Mascha's body against his in the safety of her home port, he stirs briefly, reaches behind him and, greatly relieved, caresses her tenderly.

No one in 1929 has yet invested any hope in the future, and no one wishes to be reminded of the past. This is why everyone is so recklessly absorbed in the present.

'Who would risk marrying a man for love? Not I,' Marlene Dietrich states with conviction in the spring of 1929. She speaks these lines on the stage of the Komödie am Kurfürstendamm theatre, in a production of George Bernard Shaw's play *Misalliance*, drawing languorously on her cigarette and lowering her eyelids in a consummate display of listless elegance.

After the show she drives home to the husband she hadn't married for love, Rudolf Sieber. They perform their own production of *Misalliance* on a daily basis at home. She calls him 'Daddy', he refers to her as 'Mummy'. Their daughter, Maria, is five years old. The nanny, Tamara, now shares the marital bed with Rudolf, much to Marlene's relief. At last she doesn't need to feel guilty about going out drinking every night, touring the bars and negotiating the shifting sands of sexual identity. After her stage performances or her film shoots at the UFA studios in Babelsberg, west of Berlin, she will often come home first, take a short tour of the marina, rearrange the flowers in the vase in the hallway, kiss the sleeping Maria on the forehead, change her clothes and drink a glass of water. Then, after applying a fresh dash of perfume, she will float out of the house on high heels with the first warm breath of night.

Klaus Mann has spent the twenties adrift. Though only twenty-three, he often seems washed up. He is desperate to be loved. Yet his father, stiff old Thomas Mann, can't bring himself to forgive Klaus for living out his homosexuality so happily when Thomas has spent his whole life so artfully repressing his own. He offers

Klaus no help. Once, back in 1920, he could still write that he was 'in love' with his son. Now, though, he hides this love from him and condemns him to a life in the shadows. Later, in *Disorder and Early Sorrow*, Thomas depicts his son as a 'good-for-nothing and a windbag'. Life can be one long process of withdrawal. Klaus writes a letter to his father, complaining that such mockery causes him 'hurt', but he isn't brave enough to actually send it. His patricide remains entirely literary. His novella *The Fifth Child* clearly depicts Mann family life in Bad Tölz. It features all his brothers and sisters but not the father, who in the book has come to a sad and pre-mature end. Yet murder cannot heal the wounds of love denied. In his autobiography Klaus writes of his father: 'Of course there was no one's applause I craved more than his.' But Thomas doesn't clap. He just clears his throat.

Pablo Picasso paints his young lover Marie-Thérèse Walter once reclining, once standing and once seated. Then he starts all over again. He's rented a small flat at 11 Rue de Liège in Paris especially for her so that he can paint her and make love to her in secret. He kisses her and hurries home to his wife and child. No one has noticed so far, but one day his paintings will give him away. The paintbrush is a magic wand, the last remaining means of enchant-ment in a disenchanted age.

The twenties were a terrible decade for Gottfried Benn. Everything in Berlin was too loud, too fast and too hedonistic for this lover of the half-light. He has moved into the graceless rooms of his surgery at 12 Belle-Alliance-Strasse, first floor on the right, which he calls his 'retirement home'. Gottfried Benn, only forty-three at the time, treats skin ailments and sexually transmitted diseases from eight in the morning to six at night, but very few patients darken his door. 'Rarely does the doorbell interrupt my most welcome twilight,' he writes to a lover.

In the evenings he has a beer and a smoked sausage at the Reichskanzler pub around the corner and occasionally he tries to write another poem, but they never quite come together. The verses always have eight lines, but the words are irredeemably leaden and no publisher will print them. At night he stands at the bedroom window, turns off the light and hopes that inspiration will return. He listens to the schmaltzy melodies coming from the terrace of the music café at the back of the courtyard. He hears couples laughing too loudly and too gratuitously in their determination that this night will end less depressingly than the last. He tries to drink enough coffee to give himself a caffeine rush, goes two or three days without sleeping, takes cocaine – anything to rouse the primal forces of poetry within. But they refuse to be lured out. His wife has died, he packed off his daughter to a childless lover in Denmark, he had to relinquish his enormous flat in Passauer Strasse, and his brother was sentenced to death for his part in an assassination. Those were his 'roaring' twenties. Of course, he kept having affairs, usually with actresses or singers – his preference was for widows – but his stiff manner, his bouquets of violets, his refined military bearing and his thin voice were not exactly attributes that made the wild young things at the Romanisches Café or in the bars of Schöneberg and the Kurfürstendamm swoon. He always bowed when entering or leaving; he couldn't help himself. Those women who sought an ounce of solace – in the form of a sensual or chemical narcotic – from the poet in the doctor's coat and his unshakeable melancholia were always in freefall, searching for a way out; they were only looking for some sympathy for the reed-fringed backwaters of their forlorn lives. Benn's Expressionist poems inspired by the pathology department and the 'cancer shed'* had caused a furore before the war, but that was fifteen years ago. Nowadays, everyone talks about death and sex as casually as he had back in 1913. In 1929, Dr Gottfried Benn is a man with a past and hooded eyes – a predecessor.

On 1 February 1929, his surgery telephone rings, and on the

---

*Benn's poem 'Man and Woman Go Through the Cancer Shed' was published in his 1912 collection *Morgue*.

other end of the line is Lili Breda, his current lover, an out-of-work actress and yet another falling woman, aged forty-one and drained by her unfulfilled hopes in Benn and in life. She says she is about to kill herself and then sobs, quietly at first, then louder and louder, grief pouring out from deep inside her. She hangs up. Benn dashes from his surgery and races to her flat in a taxi. When he arrives, Breda's shattered body is lying in the street; she has jumped from her bedroom window on the fifth floor. Firemen are mercifully laying a blanket over the dead body Benn has so recently caressed. He places a death announcement in the *Berliner Zeitung* and makes the funeral arrangements. None of the twenty mourners says a word as she is lowered into the cold earth of Stahnsdorf, near Potsdam. Although it is only half past three, the daylight is already waning. Benn presents his terse condolences to Elinor Büller, Lili's best friend, before putting on his black hat, turning up the collar of his coat and trudging off through the light snow. He reaches the station far too early; the next train doesn't leave for another hour. Back at his empty surgery in Berlin that evening, steeped in the odours of formaldehyde and hopelessness, Benn realises he has forgotten how to weep. 'Of course,' he writes to his close friend Sophie Wasmuth that night, 'of course she died from or because of me, as the saying goes.' That sobbing on the phone was the last sound he had heard Lili make.

But the next morning, after a dreamless night, Benn rings Elinor Büller, whose hand he had briefly clasped by the graveside. They are on the phone for a long time. She talks, he listens. Two weeks later they meet up, go to an exhibition of Chinese art and have a glass of wine at Café Josty. Afterwards they go to Benn's place and make love. He simply can't live 'without it', he says later. 'The pinnacle of creation, the pig, the man', as he once wrote in a poem.

Soon they begin to think about marriage – Büller for the fourth time, Benn for the second. She has some calling cards printed: 'Elinor Benn, née Büller'. She will never have the chance to use them, but for nine long years she remains Benn's lover. 'Dear child, let us not get married,' he repeats again and again to appease her, for marriage, he says, is 'an institution to paralyse the sex drive'. And that surely can't be her goal, can it?

'In many works of the Victorian era, not only in England,' the philosopher and cultural theorist Theodor Adorno writes, 'the force of sexuality and the sensuality related to it becomes even more palpable through its concealment ... there are passages of an overwhelming tenderness, such as could be expressed only by one who was deprived of it.' The hedonistic son of a Frankfurt wine merchant, Adorno had almost everything he could possibly want. As a student in the twenties in Frankfurt, Vienna and Berlin, he lived a life of plenty as far as his studies, his doctorate and his advancement towards professorship were concerned – and his relations with women were no different. In his free time he composed, and he wrote music reviews. The woman he has really fallen for is Margarete Karplus, the daughter of a Berlin industrialist and a PhD in chemistry. Their fathers made the match. Adorno senior supplied excess tannins from his winemaking to her father, who used them to soften the gloves he produced in Berlin. Throughout her lifetime Margarete Karplus – later Gretel Adorno – would soften the tannins in her husband's philosophy by challenging, improving and typing it up.

In 1929, however, things are far less straightforward, despite her engagement to Adorno the previous year. This tall, good-looking woman from an assimilated Jewish family has dark eyes and a mind of her own. She is close friends with the playwright Bertolt Brecht, the Hungarian-born Bauhaus professor László Moholy-Nagy, the writer and cultural critic Siegfried Kracauer, the composer Kurt Weill and the singer-actress Lotte Lenya. Her heart is torn between three brilliant philosophers – Adorno, with whom she maintains their long-term, long-distance relationship, but also Ernst Bloch and Walter Benjamin in Berlin. Her involvement with Bloch is sexual too, but as is often the case, it is the platonic relationship with Benjamin that sounds more like love in their correspondence.

On 27 March 1929, Cole Porter first asks the big question: 'What is this thing called love?'

Initially Dietrich Bonhoeffer loves only God ... and himself. Before this restless young theology student from a good family in Grunewald takes up his first overseas post with Barcelona's Protestant community, he writes to the pastor there, Fritz Olbricht, a tough old Bavarian, to ask how best to prepare. He has heard that the weather in Barcelona is hot but changeable, and is wondering what kind of suit and fabric Olbricht would recommend. Does he need special sports clothes for the clubs? What suits and ties do men wear to dinner? It is four whole weeks before Pastor Olbricht's anger at the vain young theologist in distant Berlin abates. He replies that, regrettably, he is unable to resolve the younger man's clothing dilemmas, but, being a vicar, he would certainly be advised to pack a cassock.

It has been some spring for Bertolt Brecht. Easter Saturday saw the premiere at the Theater am Schiffbauerdamm of his former lover Marieluise Fleisser's play *Pioneers in Ingolstadt*. In the programme he writes: 'This play allows us to examine specific atavistic and prehistoric emotions' – Brecht's own prehistoric emotions, for example. In the play, Bertha, the maid, discovers that her lover, Korl, not only has other women besides her but is married and even has children. This was precisely the shocking discovery that Marieluise Fleisser had once made regarding Brecht, and so she has Bertha lament: 'We missed out on something important. We missed out on love.' Yet shortly after the premiere, the atavistic and prehistoric Brecht moves on to his next act – he doesn't intend to miss out on anything in life, other than love.

On 10 April 1929, he weds Helene Weigel, with whom he already has a young son. He describes her as 'kind, gruff, brave and unpopular', to which we might add: 'the polar opposite of her husband in every respect'. What does he do straight after saying yes at the registry office in Charlottenburg? He races to the station to pick up his mistress. The only problem? He's still clutching the wedding bouquet – a bunch of tired daffodils. When he confesses to Carola Neher at Zoo station that he married Helene Weigel half an hour before, an 'unavoidable' but 'insignificant' act, she hurls the wilted flowers to the ground and turns furiously on her heel. She has travelled the whole way to Berlin from Davos, where she had been nursing her dying husband, the poet Klabund,* to find that Brecht has gone and got married again – and, not for the first time, to someone other than her. The events of that spring come as an even greater shock to Elisabeth Hauptmann, Brecht's closest colleague and lover. When she hears about the whirlwind wedding, she attempts to kill herself in her flat. However, six days later, as soon as she has recovered her health and her wits, she starts writing a new play and calls it – this is no joke – *Happy End*.

She asks Brecht to write the songs for it in return for a third of the fee. He eventually has to call in Kurt Weill for the music, leaving him free to make tweaks to the play itself during a working holiday in Bavaria with Hauptmann. When rehearsals begin in July, Brecht provides his personal take on happy endings. The leading role in one lover's play is taken by another, Carola Neher, since she happens to be in Berlin, while Brecht's wife acts the secondary role of 'The Lady in Grey' – a casting that speaks volumes. The male lead is played by Theo Lingen, new partner of Brecht's ex-wife Marianne Zoff and stepfather to Brecht's daughter Hanne (I realise it's hard to keep track). Brecht's sadistic desire to see all his women suffer simultaneously makes for good drama. It is now, of all times, that *Uhu* magazine chooses to ask him what he thinks about jealousy. A swaggering Brecht answers: 'The bourgeois are now the last representatives of what was once a tragic virtue.' He writes this while smugly contemplating a plaster cast of his own face that sits on his desk. If your whole world revolves around yourself, there's every chance you'll get whiplash. With Brecht,

---

*The pen name of Alfred Henschke (1890–1928).

however, this only ever happens to the many people who dare to disturb his orbit.

The nights Walter Benjamin has shared with Asja Lācis, the charmless Latvian Communist he met on Capri, come to a most unsatisfactory ending. As they lie there, eyes half-open, still half-asleep, he tries to tell her about his dreams. Asja 'didn't want to hear them and interrupted him, but he told her anyway'. She tells him that her only dream is that he will finally divorce Dora, his wife. This is followed by breakfast, where the mood is like a limp slice of rye bread.

On 14 March 1929, Christopher Isherwood, a twenty-four year old who has recently dropped out of his medical studies and joined the literary scene, boards the afternoon train from London to Dover. Outside it is raining, with thunder and scudding clouds. He is wearing his Cambridge tie, and he hangs his wet Burberry coat on a peg to dry. In dark, foggy Dover he takes the steamer to Ostend, and the third-class bar is full of loud soldiers posted to Wiesbaden. Two of them recognise his tie and raise their glasses. In Ostend he catches the train to Cologne, where a station official solemnly holds up a wooden sign announcing the train to Berlin like an imminent revelation. Once aboard, he dozes and watches the dreary winter landscape flash past, his mind empty yet conscious that his future begins here. Though his luggage is light, his desire weighs heavy. He's thinking of Berlin because Berlin, he knows, 'meant boys'.

Isherwood lives next door to Magnus Hirschfeld's famous Institute for Sexual Science. He goes there almost every day for five o'clock tea with Karl Giese, the partner of Hirschfeld, the notorious 'Einstein of Sex'. When Giese talks about Hirschfeld, an imposing scholar decades his senior who boasts a big bushy beard, he refers to him reverently as 'Daddy'. Isherwood respectfully calls Giese a 'sturdy peasant youth with a girl's heart'.

Daddy Hirschfeld had acknowledged in his 1928 essay 'My

Relationship with Great Literature' that poetry had been his 'first love' before he dedicated himself to sexual research – it is no wonder that he repeatedly invokes Schiller and Goethe as primary witnesses in his writings on homosexuality. Hirschfeld takes particular pleasure in having an author as a neighbour. Many times, Isherwood shows English friends around the institute's museum – a 'must' for friends of homosexuality, because Hirschfeld spent decades collecting the finest artefacts, aphrodisiacs and curios from sexuality's grey zones. In 1929, Hirschfeld is writing a new book about sexual stimulants that is four hundred pages long and contains one hundred detailed and instructive illustrations.

An admiring hum runs around the bar whenever wise old Hirschfeld enters Eldorado, Berlin's most famous temple of homosexuality, in order to trade theory for practice at the end of the working day. Here, Isherwood tells us, he is known not as 'Daddy' but as 'Auntie Magnesia'.

Even Albert Einstein, the inventor of the theory of relativity, knows that time and space play a significant role in love and are not easily overcome. 'Writing is stupid,' he writes in a telegram to his wife on the lakeshore at Caputh. 'This Sunday I will kiss you on the lips.' So Sunday = kiss × time squared.

Billy Wilder is also busy writing in the early summer of 1929. He's working on the script for his film *People on Sunday*, one of the last silent films and, more importantly, a true Berlin film – meaning low-budget but sexy – written in the Romanisches Café over umpteen cups of coffee. They have acquired some cast-off Agfa film from UFA studios, but after filming starts in July, it is interrupted again and again because money has run out. Four of the five main actors have never acted on camera before. The scriptwriter is a dancer, a reporter and a rogue, the assistants bail on the project, and the actors have to make it up as they go along. The film is initially shot at Zoo station amid the deafening din of arriving trains, and then in a small clearing out in Wannsee. They eat sausages and potato salad, and there is much flirting under tall pine trees, lingering shots of sudden sunlight on skimpy summer dresses, and men puffing on cigarettes when they forget their lines. This suits the two leading actors to a tee – they tend to forget their lines in real life as well, and Wilder and his business partner Curt Siodmak have told them just to play themselves. And so the cab driver and the wine merchant, the female model and the female record seller are entirely themselves in a film that is as ephemeral and illogical as life itself. Or as life in Berlin, at any rate.

Lust, quickly satisfied under tall pines on a Sunday, still causes some pain and much melancholy in the light of a bedside lamp that evening. There is no mention of love – and not because this is a silent film.

Around the same time, the satirist Kurt Tucholsky and journalist Lisa Matthias are lounging on a lawn beside a large Swedish lake like two of the lead actors in *People on Sunday*. This isn't a silent film, so they can chatter on and on – which is what they've been doing from the moment they met at a fancy-dress party. Tucholsky, who has just returned from Paris without his wife to succeed the late Siegfried Jacobsohn as head of *Die Weltbühne* magazine, has told the thrill-hungry young woman about his marital problems in those first intoxicated hours – 'as middle-aged men are inclined to do at dawn', the seemingly seasoned Matthias later records.

Lisa Matthias: twice married, twice a mother, with her tomboy looks, her cabriolet, her extravagant love life and her witty texts about driving and Hemingway's trips to Berlin, in 1929 and 1931, when he roamed the streets in a charming drunken haze and bought avant-garde art at Alfred Flechtheim's gallery. She was the model Berliner woman of her time, courted not just by Tucholsky but by the publisher Peter Suhrkamp and the writer Lion Feuchtwanger too.

To start with, they see little of each other aside from short trysts at Tucholsky's pied-à-terre, but 'Lottchen', as he calls Lisa, immediately stars in his features as a typical chattersome Berliner.

However, as Lisa Matthias becomes more of a fixture in Tucholsky's articles than in his life, her pout also becomes more fixed. When he does see her, all he wants to do is jump into bed with her. As she complains to a friend: 'There's a bit too much lovemaking with no real love. Neither of us can really stomach it.' No matter though: 'It's still an interesting affair.' Her intellectual needs are attended to, and one should not be too greedy emotionally: 'Love is always a little bitter, Daddy says. It's true.'

He was her 'Daddy' – and she? *I Was Tucholsky's Lottchen* is the title she gives her memoirs. There we learn that the sofa is their 'meadow of sin' and that Tucholsky snores so loudly that she always stomps off to the guest bedroom at around two in the morning. Yet this is still somehow not enough for Matthias: she wants her poet to herself, without his journalist colleagues, without all the other coffee-house patrons, without the hum and whirr and aggravations of Berlin. She wants to go away with him. Then again, she has yet to experience what it means for a woman to go on holiday with Kurt Tucholsky: it means love as material for his next book. His romantic holiday in Rheinsberg with his lover Else Weil resulted in *Rheinsberg*, the enchanting 'Storybook for Lovers', and his journey across the Pyrenees with his current wife, Mary Gerold, formed the core of *Among Other Things in the Pyrenees*.

As he and Lisa Matthias set out for Gripsholm in Sweden in April 1929, he already has the speech marks in mind. They hurtle northwards in Lisa's Chevrolet, which bears the registration plate IA 47-407. And when Tucholsky has crafted their Swedish escapade, with the occasional whimsical embellishment, into *Castle Gripsholm: A Summer Story*, he will dedicate it to 'IA 47-407' in the book's preface. His wife, Mary, may not recognise the reference in far-away Paris, but the drinkers on the café terraces along the Kurfürstendamm and in Schöneberg certainly will – Lisa used to casually park the car on the pavement at all hours of the day and night. To be so easily identified as the partner of the great Tucholsky will fill her with silent pride.

Anyway, they're in Sweden, lying alongside each other on an

extremely green lawn in Läggesta, across Lake Mälar from Gripsholm Castle and squinting at the camera. Their eyes say, 'Let's see where this takes us.' They soon find a cosy little summer house built of the finest red wood and try living as lovers, even if Lisa keeps reporting that she 'has no great erotic interest'. He is funny though, this Tucholsky, and so she is seduced again and again and leaves their shared bed only when his snoring becomes unbearable at around 2 a.m., as she so precisely consigns to posterity. And the next morning, when the birds are chirping outside, the sun has tickled the cats awake and motes of dust are floating around the room, when the kitchen smells of coffee and high spirits, they occasionally even consider themselves happy. They go outside, down to the lake, swim, splash each other and laugh. They eat semolina with hot mixed berries; Lisa stands in the kitchen cooking custard for 'Daddy' to eat with his. She is his 'mother, cradle, comrade', Tucholsky tells her – and it's meant to sound romantic. After they have made love in the afternoon and Lisa has gone off to swim in the lake again, so wonderfully cool at that hour, Tucholsky sits down at his desk and writes to Mary in Paris: 'Otherwise, it's all very so-so – I live like a hermit here.'

Picasso still occasionally paints his wife, Olga. In previous years he used to paint her almost constantly, with her graceful ballerina's body, but Marie-Thérèse Walter is his main model nowadays. 'How terrible that a woman can tell so clearly from my pictures when she was replaced,' Picasso says. This sense of having been replaced almost drives Olga mad. She screams, rages and storms around before sliding into depression for weeks on end and checking herself into clinics on the shores of quiet, distant lakes. In Picasso, her anger kindles the forces of rebellious creativity inspired by guilt and defiance.

And so, on 5 May 1929, Picasso agrees to paint Olga again. Whereas posing for a portrait was once a game between the two of them, a wrestling match, an erotic trial of strength, now it is a cold war. Neither of them says a word. Picasso stares at her and paints. In her nakedness she no longer feels admired but exposed. She sits on her chair, freezing. Self-hatred is festering away inside her, as well as hatred for the man she once loved so much but who constantly cheats on her now. Picasso paints stoically on. At some point he cuts short his work and adds his signature to the bottom of the still-damp oil painting. Olga wraps herself in a kimono and comes round behind her husband to look at the painting. Her legs give way from the shock. The picture shows not a woman but a monster, its face twisted in horror, its limbs deformed. She dresses and leaves without another word.

Picasso stands by the window, smoking and thinking of Marie-Thérèse, who is due to come and see him later. Picasso's paintings of Olga in 1929 are not portraits but exorcisms. Picasso wants to paint her out of his heart; he doesn't care what effect this has on her. He calls the picture *Woman in a Red Armchair*. It is the first nude in a long-running feud.

Erich Mühsam often forgets that he's married. It isn't that he doesn't love his Zenzl; no, that's not it. He does love her – and, above all, her character.

There are just so many other things to do. Mühsam, the thick-bearded, ever-restless social revolutionary, the Communist voice of warning and proponent of 'wild living' and a more humane Germany is still vaunting anarchism and persuading young workers to join the liberation struggle, even after spending five years in jail for his efforts during the Bavarian Soviet Republic. He likes going to the theatre too, loves drinking in the bohemian pubs of Berlin and Munich, plays chess, flirts, writes for the German Communist Party's *Red Flag* newspaper and travels around the country, rushing from one lecture to the next. Whenever he gets particularly excited about some young revolutionaries, he brings five or six of them home to the Bruno Taut-designed revolutionary horseshoe-shaped Hufeisensiedlung estate in the Britz district of Berlin. He tells Zenzl that all these people are moving in with them for the foreseeable future. Anarchism doesn't stop at the front door, he tells her. And she goes to the stove and cooks sullenly for seven or eight rather than two. She knows that he has generally been to bed with at least one of the young female revolutionaries. If she cries about it, he looks at her in astonishment and says he always told her he could only tolerate a 'free marriage'. Does she remember agreeing to that? She did, Zenzl replies, but she doesn't agree anymore. Then she gets angry and sobs and shouts, and Mühsam stays away for a few days, sometimes a few weeks. It's not much fun being married to an anarchist.

On 1 May 1929, International Workers' Day, he's out in the streets without Zenzl, who has warned him to be careful. He marches through the streets of Treptow with the Communists, delivering fiery speeches; there are some small skirmishes with the police, and then the next day he moves on to Neukölln where the workers have erected barricades and are fighting ferocious running battles with the police. It ends in slaughter, Berlin's 'Bloody May', after which the German Communist Party's combat wing, the Alliance of Red Front Fighters, is banned.* However, on 6 May, while everyone is still up in arms about the thirty-three dead and two hundred and fifty injured, Erich Mühsam, this eternal romantic, joins the Anarchist Youth in Weinmeisterstrasse close to Alexanderplatz and gives a speech about 'freedom in love'. It is not known whether he returned home to Zenzl after this or went about his free-loving ways elsewhere.

The only letter Vladimir Nabokov – later such a major author but for now a relatively minor one – writes to his wife in 1929 contains two words and an exclamation mark: 'Caught *thais*!' Perhaps he leaves it on the bed while she is still asleep in the sun-filled room in the small hotel in Le Boulou in the Pyrenees where they are on their first proper holiday together. His catch is a butterfly, a rare

---

*Watching the street fighting from his friend Fritz Sternberg's window, the sight makes Bertolt Brecht turn white as a sheet and he becomes an even more fanatical Communist.

Spanish specimen from the *Papilio* genus. Véra smiles when she sees the note because she knows her husband loves nothing better than to stride across meadows, his feet damp with the night-time dew, catching butterflies in his white net.

Vladimir snared Véra a few years earlier using nothing more than words. A poem called 'The Encounter' that he published in the Russian émigré newspaper *Rul* contained verses no one but she could decipher:

> I wander and strain to hear
> the movement of the stars above our encounter
> And what if you are to be my fate ...

Very soon afterwards, Vladimir realised that Véra was his fate, and so he wrote:

> I must tell you one thing ... Maybe I have already told you this, but, just in case, I will tell you again. Pussycat, this is very important – please – pay attention. There are many important things in life, for ex.: tennis, the sun, literature – but this thing is simply incomparable with all of them – it's so much more important, deeper, broader, and more divine. This thing – there's no need for such a long foreword; I'll tell you directly what the matter is. Here: I love you.

That was the moment when Véra, this beautiful, glittering, noble butterfly, knew that she need fly no more. The couple were married and somehow scraped by in the strange world of 1920s Berlin. Most of the Russians who had fled to Germany before the October Revolution had long since packed up and moved on to Paris. But Véra worked for a law firm and translated, and Vladimir gave tennis lessons, acted as an extra in films produced by UFA studios, and taught bright boys chess and old ladies Russian. Mainly, of course, he wrote, and they owed their wonderful southern springtime holidays in 1929 to Ullstein Verlag, who had printed advance copies of his new novel, *King, Queen, Knave*, paying him the enormous sum – by his standards – of 7,500 marks. Nabokov had smuggled a reference to his bliss with Véra into the book, giving them a waltz-on part as a couple to whom all eyes are drawn:

> Franz had long since noticed this couple; they had appeared to him in fleeting glimpses, like a recurrent dream image or a subtle leitmotiv – now at the beach, now in a cafe, now on the promenade. Sometimes the man carried a butterfly net. The girl had a delicately painted mouth and tender grey-blue eyes, and her fiancé or husband, slender, elegantly balding, contemptuous of everything on earth but her, was looking at her with pride; and Franz felt envious of that unusual pair ...

Véra and Vladimir Nabokov are a very unusual couple: they are happy together.

On 8 July 1929, Jean-Paul Sartre finally meets the popular Simone de Beauvoir for the first time outside the walls of the Sorbonne. He is joined in his small room in halls by his fellow student René Maheu. Only seventy-six students from the whole of France have been entered for the École Normale's *agrégation* exams, and successful candidates will get a lifelong job as a philosophy teacher at a French high school. Following the written test, everyone is revising for the oral examination, which is regarded as horrendously difficult. The pressure is almost unbearable – candidates must read the entire history of European philosophy. Entering Sartre's room on a social visit, de Beauvoir is shocked by the dirt, mess and smell, but she tries not to let this put her off; when they are all seated, she delivers a forty-minute interpretation of Leibniz's metaphysics. Sartre and Maheu find little to add; they had imagined a more relaxed get-together. Maheu, who is attracted to de Beauvoir, is especially disappointed by the formality of her visit. She's knocked off her stride only once during her presentation – by the sight of the bedside lampshade, which is a patchwork of red underwear. She's unaware that it was given to Sartre by Simone Jollivet, his lover from Toulouse, a high-class prostitute with literary ambitions – and it's better that way. When de Beauvoir has left, the two men try to come up with a nickname for her. Sartre is keen on 'Valkyrie' because she strikes him as being like a Nordic virgin goddess of war. No, Maheu retorts, she's like a beaver that gnaws away at the trees of knowledge and assembles them into a new building, so she's *le castor*. This meets with Sartre's approval. The next time they all meet up, they call Simone de Beauvoir 'Castor', a name she'll keep for the rest of her life.

When the results of the written examination are announced on 17 July, Sartre and de Beauvoir discover that they have both passed and are therefore eligible to take the oral exam. Their matchmaker, Maheu, has failed, however, and leaves Paris without further ado. That same evening Sartre invites de Beauvoir to dinner for the first time, orders a bottle of fine wine and declares, 'From now on *I'm* going to look after you, Castor.' The next morning, they continue revising their philosophy – and they go on to spend the next fortnight together, with Kant, Rousseau, Leibniz and Plato for company. Now and then they go for a cup of coffee or a glass of wine in the evenings, followed by an outing to the cinema to watch a Western. The next morning at eight o'clock, she sits down to study again. There are no signs of affection for now, but they're already entwined in thought.

The results of the oral examination are posted on 30 July. Sartre comes first, with de Beauvoir second. The happy runner-up departs the next day with her family for her aunt's house in the countryside and spends a long summer in the fields and vales of Limousin. As she roams the meadows, she thinks of Sartre but more often of his good-looking friend Maheu, noting in her diary: 'I need Sartre and love Maheu. I love Sartre for what he gives me and Maheu for what he is.' Yet it is not Maheu but Sartre that she invites to see her in rural Saint-Germain-les-Belles. He jumps on a train and takes a room at a small hotel nearby, and they meet up every day to laze in a small clearing in a chestnut coppice, drinking cider, eating baguette and cheese, and philosophising. It's warm, it's August and a light breeze is coming from the mountains. They exchange tender kisses, and as night falls, they dream of a future together. These are the most wonderful days of their lives.

When the erotic dancer Josephine Baker and the Italian count Giuseppe 'Pepito' Abatino decide to get married in Paris, they hold a press conference at the Ritz hotel. The world's newspapers report on the event, printing photos of the happy, giggling couple, and from that moment on they are considered man and wife. It is the Cinderella story of a girl from the slums of St Louis who has won the heart of a dashing European nobleman. However, the bridegroom would rather not tie the knot at a registry office because it would blow his cover. He isn't actually an Italian count from a lineage stretching back centuries nor a gallant cavalry lieutenant, but a simple Sicilian stonemason.

Josephine Baker, on the other hand, really is an exuberant twenty-one-year-old African-American girl with no education, no false modesty and no sense of timekeeping. What she does have is an unerring sense of rhythm and a unique gift for dancing. Pepito the stonemason moulds her body into the perfect modern sculpture, and even in the twenties that means making her into a brand. He celebrates her talent, cultivates her foibles and annihilates her opponents. Josephine Baker becomes 'Josephine Baker', and soon she is capable not just of dancing her name but also of adding the quotation marks that jiggle around the two words like the skirt made of bananas that becomes her trademark.

When Georges Simenon, the great crime writer, was Josephine's manager and lover, he merely kept her papers in order and made sure the bills for her silk underwear were paid once in a while and that she was on time for her revue at least twice a week. Pepito has bigger ideas. He wants to clean up, and Josephine Baker goes along with this. It's the first time a white man has been eager not just to bed her but to marry her (or at least to claim to intend to) and that's the kind of emotional support she's been missing all her life. It isn't just stability Pepito is offering her, but a career plan. The posters advertising her revue at the Folies Bergère now read: 'Starring Joséphine Baker, Countess Pepito Abatino.' Along with his title he has bestowed an acute accent on her name.

Pepito has seen to it that women can buy their daughters Barbie-like Josephine Baker dolls as well as Josephine Baker skincare products for themselves. He launches a tanning oil, a body lotion and the famous Bakerfix pomade with which the woman whose name it bears and her manager love to gel back their hair. As for the men, they can carry on dreaming of the Black dancer's beauty and abandon, long after seeing her perform. Pepito calls Josephine Baker's show *Un vent de folie – A Breath of Folly*. He knows what he's doing. This is the breath of fresh air that all of Paris has been yearning for in the late 1920s, but he can also see that the effect is gradually wearing off. So first he has Baker publish an autobiography, although she is only in her early twenties. In this guileless and eccentric book, she talks about cosmetics and her pets, about her pink dressing gown and Paris. Next, they make plans to have the great Viennese Modernist architect Adolf Loos build them a house in the centre of the city. It would have been spectacular: an iconic building with a striped black-and-white marble façade and the whole interior designed as a stage for Baker, Europe's first African-American superstar, with a pool in the middle for her to be a swimming Venus. Sadly, though, the plans are never realised – by now her star is on the wane in Paris. Pepito's response is to organise a grand European tour that veers between triumph and racism.

Before setting out, Josephine has to bid farewell to her pets. With a heavy heart, she leaves her budgerigars, rabbits, cats and piglet behind. The only animals allowed on the train are her Pekinese lapdogs, Fifi and Baby Girl. They are joined by fifteen trunks containing 196 pairs of shoes and 137 costumes and furs. It's not hard to see why Pepito's mother would write in a letter to a friend that Josephine could easily send a few more clothes and shoes her way. Another item on the customs list: sixty-four kilos of face powder. This is one product the savvy Pepito has cannily declined to market. After all, if everyone knew that Josephine Baker powdered her face before performances to make her look whiter, she could kiss her large Black following goodbye. For the white people of Eastern Europe, on the other hand, sixty-four kilos of powder are nowhere near enough. While the Parisian dance sensation reaps acclaim on stage in Vienna and Budapest by night, by day her detractors bring out the big guns. Everywhere she goes, conservative and religious groups close ranks against her. As her train rolls into Vienna to the sound of cheering from the crowded platform, the bells of the Paulanerkirche ring out to denounce this spectacle of carnal desire and sinful cavorting, with the populace instructed to foreswear the 'Black devil'. At Sunday Mass, priests describe the dangers of the nefarious dances Josephine Baker will perform that evening in such lurid detail that many in the congregation hurry away to secure a ticket as soon as the Lord's Prayer has left their lips. The result is that Baker plays to full houses at the Johann Strauss Theatre for weeks.

On she travels through Europe, with her fifteen trunks, two dogs and one husband – to Budapest, Prague, Zagreb and Amsterdam. She is even granted permission to perform in Basel despite Switzerland's stringent regulations on nudity on stage. The sole exception is Munich, due to Bavaria's 1929 clampdown on public morals. The most violent protests occur in Berlin, although as recently as 1926 it had been the scene of her greatest triumphs. Berlin was where she was seduced by the German-American actress Ruth Landshoff and revered by diplomat, writer and patron of the arts Harry Graf Kessler, who wrote a ballet for her. So dear are her memories of the city, its buzz, its breakneck lifestyle and its tolerance that she actually planned to stay for six months and perhaps even establish an offshoot of her French club, Chez Joséphine. But the breath of folly is gone. The day after her appearance on stage alongside a blonde German dancer, one critic fulminates: 'How dare you allow our gorgeous blonde Lea Seidl to perform with a Negro?' The far-right *Völkischer Beobachter* brands her a 'half-ape', and when the newspaper reports aren't racist, they're antisemitic. The revue organisers are Jewish, and the combination of a naked Black dancer and Jewish promoters is too much for the Nazi press. When a gang of Nazi paramilitary troublemakers hurl stink bombs during a performance, Baker packs up her things in the middle of her routine and leaves. The show is cancelled, and she and Pepito flee back to Paris in the early summer of 1929.

When Anaïs Nin and her banker husband, Hugh Parker Guiler, aka Hugo, relocate to Paris in the twenties and move into a flat at 11 Rue Schoelcher, right next to Montparnasse cemetery, it's impossible to guess that thirty years later Simone de Beauvoir will move into the very same apartment. In any case, in Nin's disillusionment at finding herself newlywed and in Paris, she notes in her diary: 'I wish I'd never come. One must be in a romantic mood in Paris or it's a complete let-down.' Hugo keeps giving her new editions of *The Kama Sutra* that he buys from booksellers on the banks of the Seine, but in her diary Nin writes: 'I love purity.' Other than that, the only thing she loves are her diaries, the true elixir of her life. She fits each one with a small lock and wears the key on a gold chain around her neck. She only ever removes it while she's learning to belly dance, but her teacher deplores her lack of talent. She'll have to come up with something else. She often doesn't get out of bed for days on end, and she fills diary after diary with musings about her lethargy. She doesn't really know how to love, so she tries to learn by devouring D. H. Lawrence's *Women in Love*. She writes in her diary that she is entranced by the way Lawrence hurls himself into chaos, 'in the sense that delving into chaos is a characteristic of our epoch'. It would soon be a characteristic of her life too.

At around the same time, Henry Miller is also reading *Women in Love* on his bed in his small apartment on Clinton Avenue in Brooklyn. Right now, though, he finds himself deeply unloved by that sector of humanity. He can't get over the fact that his wife, June, has invited her lover, Mara Andrews, into their flat, while he has to sleep on the sofa. Night after night, the two women drink their way around town. One evening Miller feels so desperate that he hangs their marriage certificate on the mirror in the hall, so it will be the first thing they see after staggering up the stairs. But they walk straight past it on their way to the conjugal bed.

Ruth Landshoff always kisses with her eyes open; she likes to know whose lips are glued to hers. In the late twenties she flits around Berlin like an agitated bird, twittering and hopping between Josephine Baker, the set designer Mopsa Sternheim, Klaus Mann and the playwright Karl Vollmoeller, between cafés, salons and cabarets, between high and low culture, and between the sexes. People are almost shocked when she manages to sit still for once and even more so if she stops talking. As soon as she smiles, the whole world is bathed in gold. But when she doesn't smile, she looks as if she's crying.

Today she's picking Charlie Chaplin up from the airport. She is supposed to show him Berlin, but mainly she will show him herself.

On 6 July 1929, forty-nine-year-old Alma Mahler – Gustav Mahler's widow – finally marries the writer Franz Werfel, eleven years her junior, and becomes Alma Mahler-Werfel. They've been living in sin for ten years, and Franz is most relieved to be able to return to Alma's house in Breitenstein am Semmering as soon as the wedding is over. At the time of their marriage they are, in fact, on the brink of splitting up. Alma's plan is for Franz to produce 'great literature'. She's usually away travelling, and he is glad to be left alone as much as possible. Not only does Alma love to gossip all day, chattering endlessly about who's having an affair with whom, but also Franz has become terrified of her antisemitic tirades. Four weeks before the wedding, she ordered him to renounce Judaism, and she categorically refused to let his Jewish parents attend the reception. When her blood is up and she begins to drain glass after glass of her favourite Bénédictine liqueur in her quest for 'powerful sensations', frail Franz packs his suitcases, dons his hat and heads for the peace and quiet of the mountains. No sooner has she raced off to Venice after their wedding than he secretly re-joins the Jewish community. She writes drunkenly in her diary: 'I drink to be happy.' Meanwhile, he writes one book after another so as not to become unhappy.

The poet Hugo von Hofmannsthal was exhausted when he came into the world in 1874.

> The weariness of peoples quite forgotten
> I cannot banish from my eyelids

he wrote as an eighteen-year-old prodigy. Yet Vienna was actually just rousing from its slumbers, and the world spirit was awakening wild, creative forces in Egon Schiele and Georg Trakl, Ludwig Wittgenstein and Sigmund Freud, Arthur Schnitzler and Karl Kraus and many others. Hofmannsthal stood on the sidelines, buffeted by the modernisation that was accelerating all around him. He was a legend at twenty-five but at fifty-five he is a well-dressed fossil, an intellectual aristocrat, an unbearable snob who occasionally furnishes Richard Strauss with librettos. Now and then he produces a piece of prose as exquisitely spun as the tips of his moustache. He had declared that the 'conservative revolution' should be the great vision of the twenties, which for him includes an unflagging defence of marriage. It's true: every one of his comedies and librettos is a strident glorification of marriage. All his views on the institution, he writes to his friend Carl Burckhardt, are hidden in his plays. So well hidden, apparently, that his wife, Gerty, has to search long and hard for them. For the great theorist of marriage is not a particularly active practitioner. His primary virtue as a husband appears to be his tolerance. He thinks it completely normal, for example, that his wife shows no interest in the issues he discusses with his friends and that she leaves the room when he proposes to read something aloud. 'Marriage', he says, 'is not about sharing everything.'

He expresses this opinion in his books, though in a slightly more convoluted form. Marriage, he writes in *Ad me ipsum*, resolves the 'two antinomies of life – that of passing time and permanence, and that of loneliness and community'. Life without attachment would result in a life without purpose, while a person who did not marry would vegetate in a sort of 'pre-existence'. It is fairly obvious why Hugo von Hofmannsthal's theories gained little traction in Berlin and Paris during the Roaring Twenties. In Rodaun, however, the well-to-do Vienna suburb to which he has withdrawn, and at the Salzburg Festival, married couples welcome his sung theories with a grateful smile and briefly clasp each other's hands.

How often does Hugo hold Gerty's hand? It's hard to say, for there are two people who never feature in his prose or letters – Gerty and himself. He is considered even by his friends as the most private of men regarding both his inner life and his Jewish heritage, and he doesn't intend to change that. As early as the 1920s he warns everyone against writing his biography – it would be 'silly', and he was planning to leave instructions to 'prevent such twaddle'.

He keeps the most private and vulnerable parts of himself under lock and key; his oversensitive soul has outlawed any physical or erotic impulses. For him marriage is an intellectual affair. But does he realise that this, like so many other good concepts, contains a practical flaw? His wife has three children by him – Christiane in 1902, Franz in 1903 and Raimund in 1906 – but Hofmannsthal makes sure he is away on an extended international lecture tour around the expected time of each birth. Nor is he in any hurry to come back. He has an incredible gift for elusion. Friends, obligations, children, work. And women? We don't know. Although as a young man he rejected advances from the poet Stefan George, he does cultivate close friendships with a number of homosexuals, including the dramatist and diplomat Leopold Andrian, the poet Rudolf Alexander Schröder and the writer Harry Graf Kessler. Early on, Kessler perceptively notes that when Hofmannsthal talks to women he acts 'a bit like a diplomat, like an eighty-year-old'. In reality, he has just turned thirty.

After his first encounter with Gerty Schlesinger, his future wife, he writes to her brother to inform him why he has chosen her as his spouse: 'She faces life with assurance and without longing.' This appears to relax him. Gerty is 'thankfully devoid of gravity' or, expressed in far less pleasant terms, she has a wonderful way of 'warding off anything that is intellectually beyond her by serenely accepting her intellectual limitations as a fact of life'. She is very happy in this state, he writes, and hence there is no point in 'educating her with books or conversation or anything else'. This, then, is Hofmannsthal's image of the ideal wife.

The certainty with which he proclaims he cannot 'imagine life without marriage' always seems like an amulet to ward off an evil spell. For him, marriage appears to be the epitome of perfect solitude; a lifelong attempt to undercut his attraction to men with a torrent of words. It is as if the author of the libretto for *Der Rosenkavalier* wished to create a particularly brilliant specimen of 'the husband' to protect him from himself. It almost seems as if he managed to conceal his true inclinations from himself by permanently burnishing the veneer and lyric armour of art. There is no Aschenbach casting longing gazes at young men on the Lido as there is in Thomas Mann's *Death in Venice*; no smart waiter strutting through his diaries as there is in Mann's. Hugo von Hofmannsthal's stance on marriage bears similarities to his attitude to heroism. During the First World War he loudly extolled the soldier's virile appetite for sacrifice but moved heaven and earth to get himself transferred at the earliest opportunity from the murderous frontline to the comfort of his study.

There's no escaping his fiercest battle, though. Scarred by life at the age of only twenty-six, Hugo and Gerty's son Franz moves back in with his parents in Rodaun. He is battling to step out of Hugo von Hofmannthal's shadow by writing poetry, falling unhappily in love and ranting against an all-powerful father who favours his sister over him. Again and again, though, words fail him and he is left to rage in silence, as if he can't really express the agonies tormenting his soul. Then suddenly one night, on 13 July, there is the crack of a gunshot from Franz's room. In their separate bedrooms, Hugo and Gerty wake with a start. Franz has killed himself. Hugo is reduced to sitting apathetically in his armchair. While attempting to rise to go to his son's funeral two days later, he dies of a cardiac arrest – a broken heart. 'He who has the Son has life; he who does not have the Son [of God] does not have life'.* He is buried two days later in Kalksburg cemetery alongside Franz. Hugo was very attached to the Franciscan Order and, in accordance with his last wish, is buried in a Franciscan robe. This great theorist of marriage thus ends his life as a chaste monk.

Klaus Mann's obituary for Hugo von Hofmannsthal reads more like an obituary for Franz, full of sympathy for an insufficiently loved son's need to depart a life where he is suffocated by his father's fame. 'He died as one of us, as our brother. He failed where we too might have failed; we were certainly not much stronger than him. Since we live on, we are now partly responsible for his death and therefore also for his father's which followed.' What monstrous words for one son to write for another, including the revelation that he has long known that his open homosexuality is a constant embarrassment to his father. There are virtually no photos of Thomas and Klaus Mann together, and in the few that do exist, Klaus, who usually loves to strike dandyish poses, is tense, his smile insecure. Life only gets more oppressive for Klaus Mann soon afterwards, when his father is awarded the 1929 Nobel Prize in Literature. Within days of the announcement, Klaus begins to take morphine to numb his pain, in addition to his customary cocaine. He doesn't attend the Nobel Prize ceremony in Stockholm: his father didn't invite him.

A cult of coolness is in the air in 1929. Should someone's eyes well up with tears, people will argue that the heart is just a muscle and romanticism a nineteenth-century style. 'We were all very normal

---

*1 John 5:12.

children of the cold peace. We were all callously cold, and most of us knew that it would all go wrong again soon enough,' recalls Lisa Matthias, Kurt Tucholsky's long-suffering 'Lottchen'. The traumatic effects of the First World War and the terrors of ice and darkness ensure that men in particular gird themselves against any display of emotion. Walter Gropius with his starched suits and fixed stare at the Bauhaus in Weimar and Dessau; Max Beckmann in *Self-Portrait in Tuxedo*; the author picture of fur-collared Ernst Jünger in *Storm of Steel* – the New Objectivity artists take a cold snobbery towards themselves and others to the extreme. This imperative of artificiality is a departure from the Expressionists' ideal of 'authenticity'. Now painters look at their models as doctors would: please undress, but don't reveal anything to me.

Otto Dix, a passionate reader of Nietzsche, paints himself as a North Pole explorer, and Georg Grosz boasts about his 'pack-ice personality'. In his stiff leather jacket, Bertolt Brecht declares 'Praise the cold!' in *The Reader for City-Dwellers* – and Ernst Jünger demands 'below-zero literature'. How best to go about this? In his *Guide to 'Licentious' Berlin*, Curt Moreck recommends that 'amid the glistening spotlessness of glass and nickel' in the new bars lining the Kurfürstendamm, 'one can cool one's insides with fantastically mixed American iced drinks'.

Is being cool an exclusively male pursuit? Of course not. Tamara de Lempicka practises it her whole life in her painting, experimenting with materials and effects until she has found her style. Cold skin, as smooth as enamel, reminiscent of billboard messages, the bodies thin and contorted in the style of the Italian Mannerists. Later, when people notice how precisely what Lempicka paints complements the classic elegance of the French furniture of the period, it will become known as Art Deco. Later still, when Andy Warhol expresses his admiration, it becomes clear that Pop Art Deco would be an even more accurate description. Everyone whose portrait Lempicka paints has the sense that they are becoming an icon. Lempicka, a Polish émigré in Paris, holds her head proudly, like a trophy, her body as smooth as a negligee. She is the female dandy who embodies the new age and people pay absurd amounts to sit for her, especially since modelling often isn't the only form of collaboration. 'I need lovers to inspire me,' Lempicka says – and men and women inspire her equally.

The only person to get nowhere with her is the Italian poet Gabriele D'Annunzio, a sex maniac. He has summoned Lempicka to his country estate to have his portrait painted, but first he wants to go to bed with her. On the evening she arrives, the sixty-three year old comes into her bedroom and undresses. She asks him to put his clothes back on. He hasn't realised that, for her, work comes first and pleasure later, and she hasn't realised that he can only be painted by someone of whose boundless admiration he is assured. After being kicked out of her room, he has sex outside her door with a maid, whose duty it is to be ready to satisfy him at any moment. Lempicka departs the next day. She paints herself instead: *Tamara in a Green Bugatti* is a commission for the German magazine *Die Dame*. The original is small, the same size as the magazine cover, just thirty-five by twenty-seven centimetres, but it is a great picture. The lady is holding the black steering wheel in one brown leather glove; you can almost feel her foot on the accelerator. Red lips, eyeliner, a look that is both novel and unstoppable because, as the writer William Boyd will later say, 'the steady gaze ahead gives nothing away'.

Lempicka owns a Renault, but she knows that this is all about *mise en scène*, so she paints a gorgeous Bugatti parked in the street outside the Café de Flore and then, back at her studio, inserts herself in it. The moment they spot this painting on the cover of *Die Dame*, Ruth Landshoff, Annemarie Schwarzenbach, Erika Mann, Maud von Thyssen and the racing-car driver Clärenore Stinnes – the first to drive a mass-produced car around the world – feel as if they're looking in a mirror. The seat next to Lempicka in the picture is empty – the 'new woman' needs no passenger. She knows where she's heading, and she knows how to brake.

When the filthy-rich Baron Raoul Kuffner, owner of the largest contiguous estate in the whole of the late Austro-Hungarian Empire, comes to Lempicka's studio in 1929, she agrees to paint his Parisian mistress, the Andalusian dancer Nana de Herrera. First, Lempicka is horrified by how badly the dancer is dressed and asks her to remove her clothes. Then she is horrified by how little erotic charge the woman exudes. For the first time, Lempicka paints her model exactly as she is – no larger, no sleeker and no grander. In a near-demonic burst of passion and for an unprecedented fee, she paints the billionaire a picture in which his lover looks ugly, inhibited and much older than she is. When the baron sees in the studio how unattractive his mistress looks and how much more attractive her portraitist is, he embarks on an affair with Lempicka. She has turned the painting commission into a contract killing, and from now on she knows that you can achieve anything with pictures – and destroy everything too. Including love.

In 1929, Gustaf Gründgens and Erika Mann get divorced. Given the state of their affairs, this appears a far more sensible decision than the one to get married a few years earlier.

Here's what happened. Author and actress Erika, Thomas Mann's openly lesbian daughter, met the homosexual actor Gustaf Gründgens during rehearsals in Hamburg for the four-part play *Anja and Esther*. The other two actors were Klaus Mann and Pamela Wedekind. Initially Gustaf was as unsure as Erika whether each of them might not be better off opting for Pamela, but then they got together and soon announced their engagement, whether out of frustration, boredom or overconfidence – as did Klaus and Pamela.

Gründgens was actually living quite happily with the artist Jan Kurzke at the time. 'Jan really is my alter ego,' Gründgens wrote to his concerned parents shortly before the wedding. 'I need to live in harmony with him to create.' Then, however, he greeted Klaus Mann from the stage in Hamburg with the following words:

The younger generation has found its poetic voice in Klaus

Mann ... With unsparing love he shows his generation in all its knowing ignorance, its inhibited lack of inhibition, its pure depravity. One has to love them – these people who love so abundantly – and their tribulations, however painful we know them to be. And above all one must love these people's poet.

For some reason, though, Gründgens ignored his own injunction and fell in love with the poet's sister instead of the poet. There was a certain piquancy to this wedding in the Mann family. The best man was Klaus Pringsheim, Katia Mann's brother and Erika's uncle, who flirted quite overtly with the groom during the wedding reception. For their honeymoon, the bride suggested that they take the same room at the Kurgartenhotel in Friedrichshafen in which she and Pamela Wedekind had stayed four weeks earlier. From there she wrote a pining letter to 'beloved Pamela whom I love beyond measure'. Klaus Mann and Pamela swiftly rode to the rescue of this couple who had no idea what to do with themselves. They invited along another guest, a good-looking athlete called Hermann Kleinhuber who was running lonely laps in front of the hotel. The very next year, in 1930, Gründgens will spend the holidays on Lake Maggiore with this jogger. (By then Pamela will be with Carl Sternheim, and Klaus and Erika entirely obsessed with one another.)

Katia Mann's mother, Hedwig Pringsheim, summed up the situation in her wise and stoical way: 'It is a strange modern marriage that would take the efforts of the Holy Ghost to bring me the joy of being a great-grandmother.' After the foursome's reunion in Friedrichshafen, Erika Mann and Gründgens moved into a flat at Oberstrasse 125 in Hamburg and named their cats after Anja and Esther in the play, so as not to forget the other couple.

Appropriately enough, Klaus Mann soon joined them in their new apartment to write the play *Review for Four*. Their best man, Klaus Pringsheim, was invited to compose the musical score, and his friend Mopsa Sternheim became set designer. The leading roles were once more taken by Gründgens, Erika Mann, Klaus Mann and Pamela Wedekind – 'repetition compulsion', Sigmund Freud would have called it. The play was a total flop. Gründgens handed over his role to another actor soon after the premiere, the planned tour of Germany was a disaster, and the end of Erika and Gustaf's joint stage career simultaneously spelled the end of the marriage performance they were trying to keep up.

Gründgens has moved to Berlin to act, living first in his Hamburg friend Jan Kurzke's studio flat before succumbing to the charms of Francesco von Mendelssohn, perhaps the most garish bird of paradise in the well-stocked aviary of 1920s Berlin. Mendelssohn is a descendant of the great philosopher and the son of the rich banker, as well as a gifted cellist and an outrageous eccentric. The seats of his cabriolet are upholstered in ermine, and at society balls he likes to slide out of his fur coat and expose his naked body to the excited throng. Desperate for the next kick after his latest standing ovation, Gründgens goes out with him on nightly bar crawls through Schöneberg. He is increasingly cast as soulless schemers, roles he plays with elegant depravity.

Once he has freshened up at the theatre, Gründgens dives into Berlin's homosexual subculture with Francesco von Mendelssohn, for the first time giving free rein to his narcissism and lust. As Christopher Isherwood notes with delectation, late-twenties Berlin has a place for every taste. Eldorado, with its muscle-bound male dancers in chastity belts, is still the main draw – and also a spot popular among heterosexual Berlin bohemians for an early or late cocktail. There is also the Schnurrbarttempel ('Moustache Temple') for older married men, the ongoing sailors' balls at Florida, and transvestite performers dancing to tango music at Mikado. Since Frederick the Great's time, Prussia's moral motto has been 'each must live as he sees fit'. Gründgens and Mendelssohn tend to go to the already legendary Jockey-Bar in Lutherstrasse and to Silhouette in Geisbergstrasse, a cramped, smoky dancehall where young men sit at the bar in women's clothing, strings of fake pearls dangling over their flat chests.

The more success Gründgens has on stage, the more eccentric his lifestyle becomes. He buys a riding jacket, a Burberry coat and a tuxedo at the Hermann Hoffmann fashion boutique, a tailcoat, a silk suit and a dressing gown from the Viennese tailor Knize, and from the Dello & Co. car dealership, a brand-new Opel cabriolet in a shrill shade of red, with red-leather upholstery. He collects what he has ordered but rarely pays for it, leading to regular complaints from vendors and the bills being exhibited in court and – much to our delight – in the history books.

Anyway, Erika Mann's marriage to the driver of the only red Opel in Berlin is legally dissolved for very sound reasons. Since life always writes the best punchlines, that spring Gustaf Gründgens signs his first film deal with UFA studios to play the lead role in the musical *Never Trust a Woman*. When the divorce papers finally come through from the district court shortly after the premiere, Gründgens and Mendelssohn crack open a bottle of champagne and spruce themselves up for a night out in Schöneberg's transvestite bars.

Most people have a one-way ticket out of the womb, but the writer Erich Kästner keeps trying to return. One woman after another shares his bed, but his 'dear Mummy' Ida in Dresden is always the first to hear about them, soon followed by his readers. He likes to go on holiday with Ida to Lake Maggiore or the Baltic now and then, to rest and recover from Berlin. In truth, though, he thoroughly enjoys the big-city, bohemian lifestyle. He sits in Café Josty in Schöneberg, chewing his pencil and drinking one milky coffee after another. One day, a young woman in a striking hat cycles past. The next day, he's in Café Josty again, and on his third cup of coffee – again, the woman in the hat on her bike. He grabs his pencil and starts scribbling. Before he has even got to know her, he transforms her in his notebook into a fictional character – Pony the Hat, the legendary cousin of the legendary hero of his *Emil and the Detectives*. (Ever the good son, he doesn't leave his mummy out of this book either, immortalising her as the devoted Mrs Tabletoe.)

One day, Kästner catches the cyclist's attention as she's passing Café Josty and winks at her. Her name is Margot Schönlank and she's on her way to the college where she studies advertising. Shortly afterwards, he announces his conquest in one of his letters to his mother in Dresden: 'My new girlfriend is an awfully nice chap. Too much in love again, though. It makes no sense in the long run.' In the long run, Mummy is always best. But, writes Kästner, pouring his heart out, he feels a bit superfluous around Berlin's modern women: they've grown so independent, with all this working in offices and masturbation and standing on their own two feet, that 'they simply don't need men anymore'.

Women don't need men anymore: this is the unsettling news for men in the late twenties. They no longer need them to finance their lifestyles because they can take care of that themselves – in Berlin and other cities, at least – by working in an office. As the poet Mascha Kaléko puts it: 'From nine to five they are referred to as "Miss". After work they have a first name too.' Nor do they need men to get from A to B, because they drive their own cars, pose on the bonnet and enjoy the wind in their hair with a little lapdog by their side. Women don't need men for sex now either: they have the option of obtaining gratification with their girlfriends or by themselves. If they do get involved with a man, however, he knows that the woman chose him as much as he chose her – and that she can end it just as speedily as he can. 'Sleep with him, yes, but no intimacies,' observes Kurt Tucholsky, a connoisseur of such women. He generally gives his lovers male pet names, as do Erich Maria Remarque and Erich Kästner. Men seem to be trying to blur the boundaries between the sexes, but of course they don't stand a chance. The female dandies sit in the bars along Berlin's Kurfürstendamm, at Schwannecke and Schlichter, smoking and dancing. They love to dress up in a man's suit and tie like Marlene Dietrich. They write, too – stinging, gossamer-light articles and reviews for *Uhu*, *Die Dame*, *Querschnitt* and the other newspapers of the Weimar Republic. More than anything, though, this new generation of women writes books that shimmer just out of reach, no longer portraying morals or utopias but a hunger for new experiences.

Female authors' heroines are only interested in men as a side dish. Charlotte Wolff describes going to the Verona Diele bar in Schöneberg with Dora Benjamin, Walter Benjamin's first wife: 'It was normal for men to escort lesbian women to their playground. As soon as they entered the club, however, they faded into the shadows and became wallflowers who followed the action from their seats at small tables.' Following the action from small tables: this was modern man's new and unfamiliar supporting role. The same is happening in literature, as a new generation of female authors creates a new generation of heroines, in Irmgard Keun's *The Artificial Silk Girl*, Mascha Kaléko's *The Lyrical Shorthand Pad*, Vicki Baum's *Grand Hotel*, Ruth Landshoff's *The Many and the One* and Gabriele Tergit's *Käsebier Takes Berlin*. Ditto in photography studios near the Kurfürstendamm, as a new visual language takes hold. Women liberated from the grip of male desire, as exemplified in the black-and-white photos of Marianne Breslauer, Annemarie Schwarzenbach, Frieda Riess and Lotte Jacobi. This is also true of the paintings of Lotte Laserstein, who explores her girlfriend Traute Rose's body from ever-changing angles and a constantly shifting perspective. Women described and observed by women. This aesthetic revolution is driven by audacity and femininity. All superfluous detail is stripped away on the march towards equality, so Ruth Landshoff casts off the letter 'h' and slims her pen name down to Rut. The figureheads of this new way of thinking are Marlene Dietrich and Margo Lion, who extol the salutary virtues of lesbian love in their revue *It's in the Air*. In it, the two women go shopping for underwear together, singing: 'When the best friend's with her best friend'. When the best friend's with her best friend, they no longer need a man.

It all gets off to such a good start. A truck is about to run over the young Lee Miller as she crosses a New York street, when at the very last second a dapper young man pulls her out of harm's way. The man's name is Condé Montrose Nast. He's the publisher of *Vogue* and the most powerful man in the fashion world. Within a few weeks, Miller is his lover. Within a few months, her portrait by the great Edward Steichen is on the cover of *Vogue*. She doesn't want to be photographed all day, though. Her father has been taking pictures of her since the day she was born, mostly in the nude, and he didn't stop when she became a grown woman. Now, in this warm New York summer, Miller no longer wishes to be an object; she wants to be a subject, meaning a photographer. Edward Steichen writes her a reference to give to the star photographer Man Ray in Paris. Two days later, she boards a transatlantic liner.

Arriving in Paris by train from Le Havre, she immediately takes a cab to Montparnasse and rings the doorbell of Man Ray's studio at 31 Rue Campagne Première. The concierge tells her she can ring all she likes – Man Ray has gone away for the summer. Depressed, Miller picks up her suitcase, crosses the Boulevard Raspail and goes into a small café on the other side. It's too loud and full downstairs so she climbs the narrow steps to the first floor, orders a coffee and looks out in disillusionment at the busy summer street. All of a sudden, Man Ray comes up the stairs and sits down at another table. Miller can hardly believe her eyes. He too has a suitcase and is clearly having a final coffee before heading off on his summer holidays. Miller goes over to his table. 'I'm your new pupil,' she tells him. He glares up from under bushy eyebrows at the tall, bold beauty before him. He stares at her red lips, which look as if they've been painted with a fine brush. Pulling himself together, he says, 'You can't be, because I don't have any pupils. And anyway, I'm just about to go off on my summer holiday to Biarritz.' Without batting an eyelid, Miller shoots back, 'Yes, I know, and I'm coming with you.'

When they board the train in Paris she is his pupil, as they sit in their compartment she becomes his model, and by the time they reach Biarritz she's his lover.

*

Only one of the great German Expressionist painters survived the war. Franz Marc and August Macke were both killed in action, but Ernst Ludwig Kirchner, though permanently scarred by the experience, lives on, far from the Moritzburg lakes and Potsdamer Platz where he painted his famous female figures. He has holed up in the Swiss Alps with Erna Schilling, having previously lived with her in an airless apartment full of wood carvings, thick rugs and heavy curtains in Berlin-Wilmersdorf. After all the exploding grenades in the trenches, he cannot stand any noise but the sound of cowbells, the mountain winds whistling around the house and the distant cries of the eagles circling over the peaks. Here, slightly below the Stafelalp and above Davos, he has moved into an unfurnished farmhouse where the dark rooms are encased by heavy beams. His paintings here are very different from his earlier works, more elegiac in tone, stranger in their colouring. Women and goats bizarrely painted pink, bright green and garish purple. The daily chores of the farmers around him – the mowing and hammering, milking time – have a calming effect on him. Sometimes he takes the bus down to Davos and sits in a café as he used to do in Berlin, but it isn't the same now, and so he drinks his coffee, flicks through the newspaper and hurries back to his alpine meadow. He's a survivor. A catalogue of his printed graphic works is in production and his Expressionist paintings have been included in major exhibitions. However, no one is interested in his new work apart from Erna. On their travels she sometimes gives her name as 'Mrs Kirchner' with a silent smile. She's often sick and in pain, and in vain the doctors try to help her. She goes on spa holidays and comes back no healthier than when she went away.

In every phase of his life, Ernst Ludwig Kirchner feels compelled to paint his immediate surroundings – and so now he paints mountains, farmers and the ubiquitous fir trees. He sometimes paints Erna and himself too, closely entwined. His withdrawal from the world has driven him to resignation, or vice versa. His views on men and women are fairly traditional. 'A woman's soul', he says, 'is shaped by every man who has possessed her sexually. Each one leaves his shadow on her.'

He calls Erna, who has been overwhelmingly shaped by the shadow he casts on her, his 'faithful companion'. He finds a description of their form of cohabitation in the American judge Ben B. Lindsey's book *The Companionate Marriage*, which was published in German in 1929. In it, Lindsey makes the case for childless marriages and for spending an amicable life together without too many duties apart from taking responsibility for each other. This is more or less what Ernst Ludwig Kirchner sees as still possible up here in the mountains, his nerves shot to pieces by the war and his soul mortified by too many years under the influence of morphine. He has underlined two sentences in Lindsey's book several times: 'The fact is that the use of *imagination* in connection with the sex impulse is one thing that has served to raise the human race above the brute level. Such *creative arts* as Music, Painting, Sculpture, Poetry, the Dance, Love and Religion itself have sprung from this union of sex and imagination.' When Kirchner has finished reading the book, he passes it to a young married couple in Davos.

In autumn 1929, the Cologne-based photographer August Sander, whose cold and meticulous eye produced the black-and-white portraits of people in the late twenties that are etched in our memories, wishes to photograph the Dadaist Raoul Hausmann in his present romantic circumstances. That means: with his wife *and* his lover. So Hausmann takes off his shirt and shoes, shows off his suntanned torso and puts his right arm around his prim spouse Hedwig in her knee-length skirt. She looks into the camera as if delighted to have been relieved of her marital duties. Her husband's left arm is draped languidly around his lover, Vera Broido, whose skirt is a decisive four inches shorter. Her gaze is also a decisive ten per cent more relaxed. Sander calls his photograph *The Artistic Marriage*. Trios seem to enjoy a longer half-life than classic duets in this period. This one lasts until 1934, after all.

Franz Hessel works as an editor and translator for Rowohlt publishing house in Berlin and has translated Casanova and Balzac and also, in tandem with Walter Benjamin, Proust's *In Search of Lost Time*. He has found a woman as transitory as his thoughts: Doris von Schönthan, a flickering central star in Berlin's bohemian firmament, known only as 'Jorinde' in bars and the Café des Westens. Believe it or not, her birth name was Frau Ehemann ('Mrs Husband'); she took her present name from her adoptive father, the writer Franz von Schönthan. This alone might be enough to scare her off marriage, but Franz Hessel finds it reassuring because he already happens to be her husband. A journalist, 'Jorinde' presents the newest fashion trends in *Die Dame*, takes photographs and flits through life. Hessel runs around after her and gives his first piece about her the title 'A Light Springtime Fever in Berlin'. The next is called 'Doris in the Rain'. He writes about Doris in her bedroom, Doris on the lake shore, Doris in the street. These may well be his finest texts. Through his adored character, Berlin suddenly becomes tangible, and Doris is elevated to a magical figure of the kind that has inspired the German Romantic imagination since Caspar David Friedrich. He usually only sees her from behind and has to write at the same speed as she walks. Our flâneur Franz Hessel gets into the swing of things, and his most important book, *Walking in Berlin*, is infused with enormous energy.

On 2 August, it is announced in *Le Journal de Dinard* that Monsieur and Madame Picasso have again taken up quarters in Brittany, first at Hôtel Le Gallic and then in the stately Villa Bel-Event. What passes unmentioned is that Picasso has once more brought along his lover Marie-Thérèse Walter, who is staying at the small Albion guesthouse.

Every afternoon Picasso moves from the beach chair he shares with Olga and his son Paulo to Marie-Thérèse's towel. While Olga hides under a parasol to preserve her noble pallor, Marie-Thérèse roasts in the sun all day. She knows Picasso loves her tanned skin and her blond hair, which is turning still more golden with the effects of salt and sunlight. Picasso and Marie-Thérèse take pleasure in their secret games of hide and seek. She doesn't ever want to be Madame Picasso; she wants to remain his muse.

In August 1929, Erich Kästner is holidaying on the Baltic coast with his mother. Afterwards he asks his girlfriend Margot – Pony the Hat – to look for a new flat for him. To his 'dear Mummy' he writes: 'Pony will have a bit of running around to do, but she loves it, the tiny tot.' Pony finds a pretty three-room apartment at Roscherstrasse 16 in Berlin, on the fourth floor overlooking the garden and a chestnut tree with plump fruit stretching out their bright-green prickles to the sky. Kästner's mother arrives in Berlin from Dresden on 1 October, bringing with her pillows and spoons for her darling son. Pony supplies him with some items from her parents' flat as well as a waste bin and a serving tray. Kästner writes to his mother: 'She felt useful, and that made her happy.' Pony regularly prepares dinner for him and cooks for his first guests. Sometimes she is even allowed to spend the night at his apartment. One morning, while still half-asleep, she tells him about a dream she has had. A few days later she recognises it in a poem called 'A Nice Girl Dreams', published in *Die Welt-bühne*. Kästner doesn't love women; he uses them. He writes: 'She walked as if through eternity. She wept. And he laughed.' Kurt Tucholsky, whose attitude to feelings is very similar, counts 'A Nice Girl Dreams' among his favourite poems, yet he also sees exactly what is behind it: 'So characteristic of Kästner that not one syllable is in the dreaming girl's defence. I think Kästner is scared of feelings. He isn't unfeeling; he is scared of feelings because he has so often seen them expressed in the slushiest sentimental terms.'

Time to take a quick breather before we travel to the Mediterranean, to Spain, where things will soon become very unclear – and very hot. The northerly *tramuntana* wind is blowing down from the mountains in brutal gusts, though it brings not cool relief but only confusion. The people to whom it brings confusion are Paul

Éluard and his wife Gala, René Magritte and his wife Georgette, Luis Buñuel and Salvador Dalí.

Éluard should really have had sufficient warning that taking his wife with him on visits to ambitious Surrealists abroad wouldn't be beneficial to his marriage. After all, when they met Max Ernst for the first time in Cologne in the early twenties, Ernst soon afterwards painted Gala with her breasts bared, and there began an open *ménage à trois* that first wore down Max Ernst's fainthearted wife and then the more big-hearted Éluard. Paul fled to Asia, but Max and Gala, exhausted by now from several years of wild loving, followed him there and brought him home. Gala is a constant source of provocation among Surrealists in Paris: André Breton refers to her as the woman 'on whose breasts the hail of a certain dream of damnation melts'. Paul repeatedly extols his wife's erotic attributes to the Surrealist artists, elevating her to the status of an eccentric icon, but when he returns from a year-long stay in Arosa to cure a lung ailment, they each carry on so many affairs that the charm wears a bit thin. Yet still he plays the troubadour to Gala: 'There is no life, only love. Without love all is for ever lost, lost, lost.'

They have a daughter together by the way – Cécile – but Gala deposited the girl with her grandparents at an early age. Raising children is not her thing, she tells her astonished husband, and he goes along with her decision. Now, in the summer of 1929, after Paul's recovery, they are eager to give their relationship another try. Paul even buys a new Parisian flat for the two of them and fixes it up with expensive furniture and carpets. Then they set off with countless suitcases and in high spirits on the day-long journey to godforsaken Cadaqués, where legend has it that oddball Salvador Dalí gets up to his artistic mischief. Now that he has made *Un Chien Andalou* with Luis Buñuel and exhibited the self-portrait *The Great Masturbator*, everyone wants to meet him. The gallery owner Camille Goemans wishes to talk to him about a major autumn show in Paris. For the time being, though, it is still summer. The sun blazes down, and the wind sends waves crashing against the coast and the surf flying into the air. The fishermen glower at the urbane travellers from Paris and continue mending their nets. They hear and see nothing, their magnificent unknowingness like seaweed at the bottom of the sea.

That first evening over dinner with the Éluards, the Magrittes and Buñuel, Dalí keeps bursting into hysterical bouts of uncontrolled, high-pitched laughter. He stands up unsteadily, goes outside and comes back a few minutes later as if nothing has happened; he has shaved his armpits and stuck a geranium in his hair. The Parisian Surrealists and Dalí's potential future gallerist, though partial to outlandish behaviour, prefer to concentrate on dismembering lobsters while shooting one another furtive glances. Might the young artist at the head of the table not be quite right in the head?

Only Gala doesn't share this view. She immediately falls for the strange man with the suntanned body and black moustache. She recognises his nature and obsessions at first sight; sensing his fear of the lust that controls him like a monster, she takes him by the hand. There's a slightly blurred photo from this time in which Dalí and Gala are lying side by side on the stony beach, their hands tightly intertwined on his chest. Their eyes are closed, but she has a blissful smile on her face. The man taking the photograph is Gala's husband, Éluard. He sees the smile, takes the picture and packs his bags.

Luis Buñuel also senses this new energy. Only yesterday he was shooting his new film with Dalí, *L'Âge d'or*, but all of sudden he can no longer get through to the artist as he sits beside Gala, raptly clutching her hand. After a while Buñuel snaps and hurls himself at Gala, throttling her until Dalí begs him to stop. The next day Buñuel too leaves Cadaqués.

The only people left are Gala and Dalí. 'Gala became the salt of my life, the crucible of my personality, my beacon, my double – MYSELF,' Dalí later rejoiced. They will sleep with each other only once, because he is terrified of the female sex. When Gala gets to know him, he is a twenty-five-year-old virgin. Gala understands all of this and runs a sympathetic hand over his black hair. With his mania safely in her care, he no longer finds himself laughing hysterically for no reason. When everyone else, including Gala's husband, has left for Paris, they quickly move into a tiny hut on the shoreline in the next bay, away from everything, with no one but a few fishermen for company. When her sexual needs become too pressing, she sometimes goes out to sea with the most handsome of them. Dalí is always relieved when she sets sail with a fisherman. He wants her to have a good time, and he sits down at his easel to enter his imaginary world and paint her backside. The sight of buttocks does not arouse his monstrous lust and does not threaten him. The sun is high in the sky and time melts. When Gala returns, they eat freshly caught lobster. 'Beauty should be edible, or not at all,' Dalí says.

The artists in the Bauhaus want to create a new human being with an idealised body and mind. One aspect of their thinking remains utterly traditional: the 'masters' are all men – Wassily Kandinsky, Marcel Breuer, Lyonel Feininger, Oskar Schlemmer and Josef Albers. Enthroned above them is the patriarch of the movement, Walter Gropius. The only role foreseen for women is as students, the exception being Gunta Stölzl. Seven years after she started out in Weimar as a student, she is permitted to call herself a 'mistress' in the weaving workshop in Dessau, but this doesn't change much – the masters dismiss weaving as a typical female household activity.

Stölzl is in on the action from the first second, initially under the spell of the painter and theorist of colour Johannes Itten, then under the tutelage of Paul Klee, and finally as Oskar Schlemmer's senior student. In Schlemmer's most famous picture, *The Bauhaus Stairway*, which now hangs in MoMA in New York, she and her pupils are the abstract figures walking up the stairs. All the knowledge she has gleaned from the great painters flows into her tapestries – abstract artworks of soft and fluid poetry. But this is too steeped in clichés about feminine aesthetics for Gunta Stölzl's liking. She pulls off a far more daring plan. Under her leadership, the Bauhaus textile department in Dessau becomes a laboratory for industrial design. She weaves with cellophane and in her work-shop she develops the *Eisengarn* fabric made from strong waxed cotton that is used to cover tubular-steel furniture. She regards the workshop as a think tank: 'Weaving is building, making orderly structures out of disorderly threads'. Stölzl discovers that this also applies to love. She braids the disorderly threads of her life into an orderly structure when she marries the Palestinian architecture student Arieh Sharon in 1929, just before the birth of their daughter Yael on 8 October. She had asked her brother Erwin whether he had any legal objections to the Palestinian citizenship she was acquiring by marriage, and he said it was not a problem.

Suddenly, however, Gunta Stölzl, a new mother and a new Palestinian, comes up against the limits of the progressive Bauhaus movement. There is room for free love, apparently, but not for children. In a magnificent display of defiance, she tries to combine her professional role with her role as a mother by breastfeeding her baby at the Bauhaus, but this prompts much loud tutting, from men and women alike: Is this really necessary? Arieh, an early Zionist whose kibbutz has sent him to the Bauhaus, supports her in her desire to transform the role of working mothers there. However, Sharon's life is getting increasingly uncomfortable. He has taken charge of construction of the Trade Union School in Bernau, where, as in Dessau, he repeatedly faces questions about his nationality.

The year 1929 marks the definitive end of the twenties, and the end of the Fitzgeralds' marriage. When they arrived in Europe from the United States on the *Aquitania* in May 1921, they embodied a new American flair, the shimmering Jazz Age, a lust for life instead of meaning. This was global conquest dressed in a summer suit and a cocktail dress – the ravishingly wild Southern belle Zelda and her husband, Scott, the polite, blond prophet of doom who wrote love stories of a timelessness and elegance no one had ever read before. First *The Beautiful and the Damned*, then *The Great Gatsby*: these were the Grimms' fairy tales of the twenties, their truth as melancholy as it was brutal. The Fitzgeralds quickly became bright lights in the sky of English-speaking Paris, which revolved around Gertrude Stein and James Joyce, Sylvia Beach and her Shakespeare and Company bookshop, Cole Porter and Josephine Baker, John Dos Passos and, of course, Ernest Hemingway. Every year, things had become more complicated for the Fitzgeralds. Zelda had begun to giggle to herself for minutes on end, and Scott got abusive when he has drank too much, which he always did.

When they return to Paris from America in the spring of 1929, hoping to reconnect with the hope and glamour of those early days, they lose touch with each other. They are like two trapeze artists, one of them dangling from the other, with a gaping void below. In her first love letter to Scott, Zelda had written that she could never live without him and would always love him, even if he should one day start to hate her. Now, as spring settles over Paris like a warm woollen blanket, that time has finally come. Zelda practises ballet while Scott practises self-destruction. She dances all day; he drinks all night. When *The New Yorker* asks him for a short autobiographical text, he sends them the list of the alcoholic drinks he has consumed in recent years. He drinks to experience his depravity and to be as abject as he feels when he's sober. When the taxi drivers bring him home in the early morning from his tours of Rive Gauche bars and he stumbles up the stairs, Zelda is usually getting up to do some stretching exercises before her ballet lessons. She has finally been accepted by the famous Madame Egorova, who used to dance in the Ballets Russes with Nijinsky and now runs Paris's best ballet school at the Mansarde de l'Olympia on Boulevard des Capucines. Zelda worships the Russian lady, taking her a fresh bunch of white gardenias every day and a new perfume every week, and when the teacher touches her ankle to correct her posture, Zelda gets goose bumps all over her body. She thinks it's love, but it's probably just obsession. All she cares about is pleasing Madame Egorova and she keeps training, drinking nothing but water at home, tying her feet to the bedposts at night and sleeping with her toes turned outwards to increase their flexibility. But her toes are already twenty-nine years old and can no longer be bent like young willow switches. Even when she is rowing with Scott in the brief moments when he is sober and the two of them are at home together, she turns her feet outwards and smiles like a ballerina. They tear each other to pieces and torment each other in the most ingenious ways imaginable. Zelda is writing short stories too now, but when *College Humor* magazine adds the by-line 'By F. Scott and Zelda Fitzgerald' in a bid to boost sales, she blows her lid. Spurred on by the competition from Zelda, Scott suddenly starts writing new stories for a few hundred dollars a pop. The invariable subject for both is a married couple's inability to talk.

Scott's favourite activity this summer is escaping with Hemingway, who makes for a wonderful partner to ponder the meaning of life while getting smashed. One evening in June 1929 at Michaud's, Scott tells Hemingway in a choked voice that Zelda has told him his penis is too small. Hemingway suggests that they go to the toilets right away – he wants to take a closer look. And in his expert opinion, everything is perfectly fine. But Fitzgerald can't be consoled, and Hemingway realises his friend is clinging to his inadequacy as an excuse for his defeat. Hemingway suggests that they go to the Louvre the next morning so Fitzgerald can compare his genitals to the Greek and Roman sculptures, but Fitzgerald is wallowing in his supposed deficiency and declines. Zelda said it, so he takes it as truth. One more reason to drink.

The ballet school goes on holiday for the summer, and the Fitzgeralds realise that they need a holiday themselves if they are not to rip each other apart in their apartment on Rue Palatin. They travel to the Riviera, where they dip into the proceeds from Scott's short stories to rent a villa called Fleur de Bois. They are going to 'swim and get tanned and young', Scott writes. Most of all, they need distracting from themselves. Help is once more at hand in the form of Sara and Gerald Murphy, the fabulously rich American socialites who own the Villa America in Antibes. There's no better place to forget the outside world: cocktail parties on a lush, close-cropped lawn under palm fronds, with beautiful, suntanned,

white-clothed people from New York and Paris, chilled champagne, quiet jazz, the sparkling Mediterranean down below and
the warmth of the setting sun on their backs – but this time none
of it works. Zelda spends entire evenings with a mindless smile
on her face, as if she were at the barre in the Paris ballet studio
rather than by a fence high above the surf. 'My latest tendency',
Scott writes to Hemingway from the Riviera, 'is to collapse about
11.00 and, with the tears flowing from my eyes or the gin rising to
their level and leaking over, tell interested friends or acquaintances
that I haven't a friend in the world.'

'You came into my room only once the whole summer', Zelda
will later say. 'I scarcely remember you that summer', he will later
reply.

On the last day of summer, they travel back to Paris, back to
their misery, with a few new open wounds. As Scott drives along
the corniche, high above the thundering waves, Zelda suddenly
grabs the steering wheel with a mad laugh and wrenches it around
to face the drop. She wants to send them and the car plunging into
the surf. Scott is somehow able to wrest the wheel back in the other
direction, as a few stones from the side of the road fall into the sea.

Ruth Landshoff races through the twenties as if she is permanently
high, in a series of ever-changing relationships, ever-changing
automobiles and with ever-changing lapdogs, but with unchang-
ing charm. As a niece of the publisher Samuel Fischer,* she plays
croquet with Thomas Mann and acts in Murnau's *Nosferatu* while
still at school; as an adult she fools around with Charlie Chaplin
and Arturo Toscanini, Oskar Kokoschka and Greta Garbo, Josephine Baker and Mopsa Sternheim. Oh, and she has also recently
modelled a collection of bathing wear with Marlene Dietrich. That
is why, on this splendid summer's day in 1929 at the Palazzo Vendr-
amine in Venice, holding an ice-cold martini and looking out over

---

*Samuel Fischer (1859–1934) founded the leading publishing house S. Fischer
Verlag, which still exists to this day.

the Canale Grande, she tells Karl Vollmoeller, her current dalliance, 'Go for Dietrich. She has legs you'll want to run your fingers along all day.'

Vollmoeller has been sitting in his palazzo for days with Carl Zuckmayer and Ruth Landshoff, ruminating over the screenplay and cast list for *The Blue Angel*. It has taken him years to persuade Heinrich Mann to sell the film rights to his novel *Man of Straw*. Now he needs a lead actress – the blue angel, Lola Lola. 'Dietrich?' Vollmoeller asks, with scepticism. How is he supposed to convince the director, Josef von Sternberg, and his lead actor, Emil Jannings, that an unknown cabaret dancer should play the main role in this outrageously expensive UFA movie? 'We'll manage,' Landshoff says with a laugh. And, of course, they do.

When Konrad Adenauer shudders at the sight of the bill for a four-week family holiday on Lake Thun in Switzerland, his wife senses that something's wrong. Later on, when the children have finally fallen asleep in their train compartment after endless games of ludo, Adenauer tells her about his worries – or at least some of them. Adenauer, the mayor of Cologne, was a very prosperous man by virtue of his family background. In the last year, however, he has become embroiled in the stock-market frenzy in the United States, selling all his shares in German blue-chip engineering and crane-building companies, the Elberfelder paint factory and the Rheinisch gasworks, and investing his whole fortune in artificial-fibre manufacturers called American Bemberg and American Glanzstoff. Their prospects were so tempting that when he ran out of funds he kept on buying, on credit. Suddenly, though, both firms went bust, which explains why in the summer of 1929 Adenauer is in debt to Deutsche Bank to the tune of one million marks. His worry is that, thanks to this Swiss hotelier, his problems will now come to light. He doesn't quite put it to his wife in these terms; he merely mentions short-term money problems. Gussie doesn't believe a word of it.

*

On 14 October 1929, Jean-Paul Sartre and Simone de Beauvoir spend their very first night together – in their new Parisian flat at 91 Avenue Denfert-Rochereau, fifth floor. The wallpaper is a startling orange colour; this they will never forget.

When the Fitzgeralds reach Paris in September, it is not their marriage that crashes and burns but the global stock markets. First they buckle, then they try valiantly to hang on, but on 25 October 1929, a day that will be known as Black Friday, they drop like a stone.

He is slightly put off by her chain-smoking – up to three packets per day. Otherwise, Claus Schenk Graf von Stauffenberg can find nothing to criticise about Nina Freifrau von Lerchenfeld. 'I would like you to be the mother of my children,' he says in October 1929 at a ball in Franconia, gazing deep into the nineteen-year-old noblewoman's eyes. She takes a quick breath, sensing that this may be the most heartfelt declaration of love he will ever manage to make.

'Do not forget me, and do not forget how much and how deeply I know that our love has been the blessing of my life. This knowledge cannot be shaken, not even today.' Thus ends one of the most vexing love stories of the twentieth century. It is Martin Heidegger's fortieth birthday, 26 September 1929, and it is on this very day that his Jewish lover, Hannah Arendt, the author of these lines, marries their fellow student Günther Stern. She hopes that marriage and this choice of a wedding date will chase away all thoughts of Heidegger, but it doesn't work.

The wild young baroness Lisa von Dobeneck spends a cosseted and carefree childhood on horseback and in the suites of castles surrounded by the lush meadows of that green and enchanted region of Lower Saxony which shades into dark forest near Hildesheim. There are crayfish in the ponds, automobiles in the garages, strawberry punch on the terraces and grain swaying in the fields. Born in 1912, she has the world at her feet. At fifteen she was on the cover of *Die Elegante Welt,* and aged seventeen, in the summer of 1929, she plays a game of tennis with young Gottfried von Cramm on his courts and plays her way too into his affections with her forehand. When he writes a love letter to her between two tennis tournaments in October 1929, she responds: 'I am glad about your love, and it seems almost as if I returned it.'

When it becomes clear to the singer and cabaret artist Trude Hesterberg that she is going to lose out to Marlene Dietrich for the starring role in *The Blue Angel*, the film adaptation of her boyfriend Heinrich Mann's novel *Man of Straw*, she dumps him.

Occasionally, someone's life is upended in a moment. They spend the next decades running along this slanting plane, trying to work their way up it and yet always sliding back. Alfred Döblin's life was upended at ten when his father walked out on the family, leaving his mother to bring up her five children in absolute poverty. Max fled with his lover to America via Bremerhaven. The day before his disappearance, he got his son to tie his shoelaces for him, as his massive belly prevented him from bending down far enough. Alfred will spend his whole life trying not to follow in his father's footsteps.

Again and again, Alfred is tempted to leave his wife, Erna, who tyrannises him with jealousy and refuses to speak to him for days. Ultimately, he always stays or comes back – one of their four children has just turned ten and he is desperate that the boy shouldn't suffer his own experiences at that age. (His sons will later say that their father's failure to split up with their mother was the worst thing that ever happened to them.)

Before the First World War, Alfred, who had become a neurologist, was in contact with Ernst Ludwig Kirchner, as well as with contributors to the journal *Der Sturm* including Herwarth Walden and the whole of Expressionist Berlin. Now, in the twenties, he has settled at Frankfurter Allee 340 in the east of the city. There, on the gloomy ground floor, he opens his surgery to patients between four and six in the afternoon. There too sits the old type-writer on which Erna types up however much her husband has written of his novel *Berlin Alexanderplatz* during the day, in hand-writing that is illegible to all but him and her. Almost every day he takes a stroll from their flat to the square that exerts such a magical pull on him, closely observing the streets and lives around him, trying, as he puts it, 'to palpate the edges of this mighty creature'. Almost every day he reads what he has written to the photogra-pher Yolla Niclas, twenty years his junior, at the Unter den Linden cake shop. Her real name is Charlotte Niclas, and she is Jewish like him, but he immediately renamed her after they met at a ball, conscious from the first instant that this was the woman he had been waiting for. She acquiesced to the name, just as she acqui-esces to everything that comes from Döblin. That first evening it was as if an angel had taken her by the hand. Riding clandestinely on his back, she flies through the twenties with him. Every time he reads to her from *Berlin Alexanderplatz*, her eyes well up with tears. Afterwards she boards the No. 78 tram and makes the hour-long journey back to Schlüterstrasse in Charlottenburg, where she still lives with her parents. Very soon she even becomes a regular guest in the Döblin household, where she is introduced to the sons as 'Aunt Yolla' under the suspicious eye of Döblin's wife. She begins to take photographs of the writer as he becomes more and more famous – alone, peering mischievously through his thick glasses or playing with his sons. Berlin's magazines are greedy for these photos, and Döblin's lover shapes his public image in the *Frank-furter Zeitung*, *Querschnitt*, *Die Dame*, *Das Magazin* and *Uhu*.

Naturally enough, he got to know Yolla at exactly the age at which his father met his lover. The first thing he did when he met her was remove his glasses. She has all the gentle, elegiac and romantic qualities he so loves. His wife, who has all the hard, prac-tical and pragmatic qualities he so detests, once told people at a dinner party that she had never seen her husband without his glasses on, which came as something of a surprise to those present. From the outset, Yolla has been the free spirit, the body and soul

he has been longing to meet. He repeatedly tries to escape from his
marital hell. He shaves off his goatee and moves into a guesthouse
in Zehlendorf. Erna writes to him there to tell him that she will
kill herself if he doesn't come back. He begs Yolla to force him to
choose between her and his wife, admitting that he cannot do this
of his own free will. This is asking too much of young Yolla: she
loves her idol too much to blackmail him. 'We shall take the path
that heaven has laid out for us, beloved soul.' What about him?
He takes the path that Erna has laid out for him. He buys Yolla
some flowers to emphasise his remorse and moves back in with his
family. He has to sleep on the couch for a week before he's allowed
back into the marital bed. And every evening, when their sons are
asleep, Erna types up all the pages that her husband has read to
his beloved that morning, about how Franz Biberkopf, the hero of
Berlin Alexanderplatz, is torn between staying and going, about
leaving and making sacrifices and the fatigue that drowned hopes
bring.

In his letters Alfred increasingly calls his beloved Yolla 'little
sister', to which she responds with 'little brother'. They take refuge
from reality under the mantle of sibling affection. As for Erna, she
starts manically collecting cacti. Eventually every windowsill is
lined with them, and when Yolla visits Alfred during his surgery
hours, Erna comes into the room to water them.

Berlin Alexanderplatz is published in 1929. It makes Alfred
Döblin world-famous, but he remains desperately unhappy. Soon
afterwards he writes a play he titles *Marriage*. As we have seen, he
knows his way around the subject as well as he does around Alexanderplatz. He takes the express train to Leipzig for the premiere
with Erna and Yolla. When his wife has to nip off to the toilet, he
tells Yolla how disappointed he is that she never rescued him from
his marriage.

Alfred Döblin must have walked from Frankfurter Allee to
Alexanderplatz a hundred or even a thousand times during the
twenties. On this spring day, however, Wolfgang Koeppen is

walking in the opposite direction, from Alexanderplatz to Frankfurter Allee. He is fascinated by Döblin's novel and can't believe that the author is actually a practising doctor. He only believes it when he finds himself staring at a sign that reads *Dr Alfred Döblin. Surgery hours 4–6*. He wants to express his admiration but doesn't have the courage, which is why he is considering going to see Döblin as a patient. However, he doesn't have the courage for that, either. He stands outside for a long time until the last patients have left, and then walks slowly back to Alexanderplatz, lost in admiration. Finally, he retreats to Charlottenburg in the west of the city. Koeppen and Döblin never meet. A pity, and yet entirely in keeping with a man whose life and work will remain a largely unfulfilled promise.

In the autumn of 1929, Düsseldorfer Strasse 43 in Berlin is the stage for romantic drama on an epic scale. Thea Sternheim has rented two apartments there. She lives in one of them with her beautiful but untameable daughter Mopsa, who is hopelessly addicted to two drugs: a painkiller called Eukodal that she was first given after a motorbike accident at the AVUS motor-racing circuit, and cocaine, which she was introduced to by Klaus Mann and her lover, Annemarie Schwarzenbach.

There have been men, too. Only this summer she had a difficult abortion. The father was probably René Crevel, a homosexual poet with whom Klaus Mann was head over heels in love and who saw Mopsa as his soulmate. Before that, she twice went to bed with the doctor-poet Gottfried Benn; in her heart of hearts, Thea can forgive neither her daughter nor Benn – she has never felt closer to anyone since he amused the Sternheim house in Brussels with his excessive bowing and his poems in the aftermath of the First World War.

Now, though, Thea is trying to save her daughter by taking her into her home and weathering her constant torrent of insults. In the flat next door, she is trying to save her ex-husband, Carl Sternheim, having rescued him from a psychiatric clinic in Kreuzlingen near Berlin. He has stage-three syphilis with brain paralysis. He's uncontrollable, delirious and out of his mind. Nevertheless, his fiancée, Pamela Wedekind – Erika Mann's former girlfriend and Klaus Mann's ex-fiancée – suddenly moves into the flat where Carl lives with his carer, Oskar. Thea is now subjected to unceasing invectives from her daughter, her ex-husband and his bride, despite the fact that she is paying for their lodgings. She persuades Oskar to give her opiate injections to cope with the madness.

Carl goes completely mad when a barber accidentally shaves off his moustache. When the author Annette Kolb comes round to comfort Thea, she mistakenly rings the doorbell labelled 'Stern-heim'. Pamela Wedekind opens the door with a gasp. Behind her, the beardless Carl barks out curses from his bed. Annette Kolb stammers a quick apology before going to her friend's flat. They sit down at the coffee table in a fluster. Annette Kolb voices her disbelief, to which Thea responds, 'Well, my dear, this is the New Objectivity.'

As the two ladies leave the house that evening to take a walk and escape from the various daughters, brides and ex-husbands, they run into Dr Gottfried Benn in the stairwell. He bows, doffs his hat and says, 'My respects.' Carl has summoned him in the hope that this specialist in sexually transmitted diseases will be able to cure him of his delirium. They return his greetings politely but curtly – the stairwell is dark and cold – and Thea requests that he not ring at the wrong door so as not to rekindle the flame her daughter carried for him. Benn gives her a quick, sympathetic smile. Mopsa, however, has recently been inflamed with a new passion – and it is far from certain whether it is any better for her. Rudolph von Ripper, a peculiar Austrian author with a disconcerting jaw and distorted features, is known to all as 'Jack the Ripper'. Having converted Klaus Mann to morphine, he has got Mopsa hooked on it too. Inspired by how nice it is to get high together, they decide to get married.

Thea is dismayed when her daughter announces their impending wedding. Then Oskar quits. He can't go on, he confesses; her husband's melancholy has 'corrupted' him. She accepts his resignation. Once, when Pamela is out, Thea tries to evangelise her husband, folding his hands in prayer and talking about Jesus' love. This sends him into a fit of rage, during which he jumps off the balcony and breaks a rib. This time it is Thea who calls the doctor.

The next day Thea takes all Mopsa's share certificates and letters of hypothecation to a lawyer to ensure that her daughter cannot sell them for drug money. When she makes her way home through a wild autumn storm that threatens to tear the leaves from the grand old oak trees, the doorbell rings. Carl solemnly informs her that he is going to marry Pamela Wedekind. When he has left, Thea decides she needs a sedative and a glass of brandy to go with it. Berlin's evening newspaper is sufficiently informed to comment: 'Now Mopsa Sternheim will have to call her friend Pamela "Mum".'

Lisa Matthias knows that Kurt Tucholsky has other women in Berlin, as well as his wife, Mary, in Paris, whom he no longer wishes to divorce. Ever since he moved in with her in October 1929, after their return from Gripsholm Castle, she has tried to take up so much of his life that there's no room in his bed for anyone else. Tucholsky is constantly telling her that he has 'important meetings'. Unfortunately, though, when he leaves his notebook lying around open one day, Matthias learns that his 'important meeting' on 6 November was with Musch, on 7 November with Hedi, on 8 November with Grete, on 10 November with Emmy, with Musch again on 11 November and on 12 November with Charlottchen.

When she exposes his impressive record of infidelity, Tucholsky goes down on his knees to beg forgiveness and presents her with one hundred roses. Matthias writes to a friend that Tucholsky is 'a poor madman whose sex life is turning into sex mania'. She realises that there's no point in dreaming of marriage. When she has gone to bed, Tucholsky writes an affectionate letter to Mary in Paris, enclosing a nice fat cheque. Then he sits down at his typewriter and composes his 'Ideal and Reality', which is published in *Die Weltbühne* on 19 November:

Before

In the still of night, in monogamous beds,
You picture all the things you lack in life.
Nerves crackle. Oh, if only our hearts and heads
held that which, absent, causes this quiet strife.

*

As the public backlash to Josephine Baker's European tour shows no sign of abating, Pepito suggests they try their luck in South America. There too, however, Catholic forces are raging against declining moral values. The racist animosity reminds Baker of the humiliations of her childhood, yet still she goes out on stage every night and dances for a better world, trying to block out the one around her. Things with Pepito are deteriorating. The better he is as a manager, the worse their relationship becomes. In Rio de Janeiro she meets the French architect Le Corbusier and is bowled over by his drive to make the world a more rational place. She seduces him with a fleetness of foot that redefines space, just as his architecture does. They decide to catch the same steamer, the *Lutetia*, back to Europe. During the day they take long walks around the deck, which Pepito avoids as he is usually feeling seasick.

On 9 December 1929, as the ship crosses the Equator, there is an evening celebration in the ballroom. Baker has dressed up as Le Corbusier for this event and he has dressed up as her. For an instant, as they float into the Northern Hemisphere under a starry sky, they each feel as if they are in freefall. The orchestra is taking a break, and their table has fallen completely silent. They glance at each other, and when the trumpet player strikes up again with a Charleston, they get up to dance, slightly uncertain in their inverted roles. A little laughter is a big help. Pepito takes his leave and returns to their cabin, complaining that he's not feeling well. Baker and Le Corbusier dance on and on until everything's spinning before their eyes. Afterwards they shower together, and Baker washes the black make-up off the architect's white skin. The world is back to how it should be. He draws her in the nude as she poses on the bed in her cabin. She could perhaps show me a little more

59

respect, Le Corbusier thinks to himself. Then she picks up her guitar and sings to him in her wonderfully childish voice: 'I'm a little blackbird looking for a white bird ...'

One verse that Gottfried Benn writes in the twenties will outlive him – and the decade, too: 'Life is the building of bridges over rivers that seep away.' He may have first written these words on the back of a beer mat on 17 December 1929, the day that Mopsa Sternheim marries the morphine addict Rudolph von Ripper. Present along with Benn at the registry office are her parents, syphilitic Carl Sternheim, lashing out in all directions, and Thea. Mopsa is still madly in love with Benn, who three years earlier had pumped her stomach of the Veronal sedative she had taken to commit suicide. Now he is her best man. He twitches slightly as Mopsa, high on drugs, says yes to Rudolph. Thea has tears in her eyes. Only ten days later Mopsa, totally out of her mind by now, is admitted to a rehab clinic. What people in the twenties desperately needed was love (or therapy at least); what they got were narcotics.

Some marriages, Thomas Mann says, arise from circumstances beyond even the most experienced author's imagination.

Ernst Jünger is sitting in his flat at Stralauer Allee 36 on the rough eastern side of Berlin, where he argues almost every evening with his revolutionary nationalist friends and where he has chopped up the furniture for firewood at least once that cold winter. He's writing his meandering, almost surrealistic novel *The Adventurous Heart* and recounts a dream in which his greengrocer suggests that well-aged human flesh goes well with purple chicory. Ernst keeps his own heart cool, barely above zero. His wife, Gretha, knows a thing or two in this regard. He remains untrue to her his whole life, hoping when he tells her about his affairs late at night she will understand that a creative man like him cannot help but seek thrills elsewhere from time to time. When Gretha isn't sufficiently sympathetic, Ernst secludes himself with Carl Schmitt, the brilliant

professor of public law in Berlin, who has got remarried to Duška
Todorović, a 'tolerant' Serb with whom he practises a strict division of marriage and eroticism: Duška has to comfort him when he
returns in low spirits from his sexual escapades with female students
and prostitutes. Unlike Gretha, she is willing to do so. Like the
equally war-scarred Ernst Jünger, Schmitt is perpetually looking for
a state of emergency on the battlefield of love, so terrified is he of
becoming stranded in a comfortable home. He uses sex as a physical stimulant and goes out looking for it before public appearances
or major essays. He needs the 'feeling of power after a sexual orgy',
he tells his wife; she ought to understand that he cannot find this in
the conjugal bed amid the medicine on the bedside table, the slip-
pers on the rug and the worries of everyday life. In Carl Schmitt's
view, a wife's primary duty is to keep him on an even keel before
and after his extramarital excursions. In his presence she sheds no
tears, but she does weep with Gretha Jünger on many dark Berlin
evenings when their spouses are out chasing heartless adventures.

During the shooting of *The Blue Angel* at the UFA studios in
Babelsberg, Friedrich Hollaender composes the song 'Ich bin
von Kopf bis Fuss auf Liebe eingestellt', later adapted as 'Falling
in Love Again (Can't Help It)'. His line 'For I can only love and
nothing else' perfectly encapsulates Lola Lola, the lead character.
Hollaender composed it in F major, but Marlene Dietrich's voice
is so low that in the film he has to play it in D major. Throughout Marlene Dietrich's life, men are ready to adapt their ideals to
reality – and their key signatures, too.

The engagement of Lisa and Gottfried von Cramm is announced
on Christmas Eve 1929 at Burgdorf Castle, in the presence of both
families. Lisa is seventeen, with a predatory demeanour; Gottfried
is twenty and already possesses the timeless elegance of a gentleman. He is on the verge of becoming one of the best tennis players
of all time. The couple's early engagement causes less of a shock to
their families than to those who have tried to win one or the other's

heart. One man who is very much in love with Lisa is Bernhard zur Lippe-Biesterfeld, who will go on to marry the Dutch crown princess Juliana instead. Dismayed as he is at the news, he appears to keep his composure. 'I had a very sensible letter from Bernilo in which he wrote that he would certainly not do any harm to himself and that we should stay friends, etc.,' Lisa tells her fiancé. The main mourner for the newly spoken-for Gottfried is a man called Jürgen Ernst von Wedel, whose brother married Lisa's sister and who is a member of the young couple's inner circle. Lisa relates to Gottfried while he is away at a tennis tournament in Venice: 'J.E.W. is no longer cross with you. In a moment of weakness, he confessed to me that he is still very, very fond of you. Your picture at the Lido almost gave him a heart attack. He came round again this evening especially to see it.' And so at Burgdorf Castle the bride and the groom's best friend reverently study the photo of the fantastic-looking, suntanned Gottfried von Cramm, his hair combed back and his body clad in white linen.

This certainly wasn't the plan. Walter Gropius, the former Bauhaus director in Dessau, is always in control of events and his love affairs. After his marriage to Alma Mahler, whom he pinched from Oscar Kokoschka, he was getting on rather well with his second wife, Ise. She helped him organise the Bauhaus, and the rest of his life too. When she was close to persuading Konrad Adenauer to bring the Bauhaus to the Rhineland, Walter wrote her a gleeful letter: 'My sweet Mrs Bauhaus, you are a real all-rounder and you're entitled to swell with pride. All of us here feel the utmost respect for your achievements. I am deeply touched by you, my lucky star, and I love you more and more.'

But a few years and a few rows later, this lucky star has suddenly changed orbit, despite the considerable comforts of the director's new villa in Dessau, where there is a toaster, an iron, a hairdryer, a vacuum cleaner and an electric goose-plucking machine – the Modernist manifesto in practice.

Gropius quits the Bauhaus. You might call it a midlife crisis, or personal fulfilment – he longs to go back to being an architect. So Ise and Walter move into a large apartment at Potsdamer Strasse 121a in Berlin. A profile of Ise appears in *Sie und Er* magazine under the headline 'The artistic marriages of our architects'. Ise, it reads, is 'the ideal new sporty wife with self-confidence and youth'. The writer Harry Graf Kessler calls her 'a very pretty young woman'. In June 1930, they go on holiday to Ascona, in the shadow of Monte Verità on the Swiss shore of Lake Maggiore. Together with their old Bauhaus comrades Marcel Breuer and Herbert Bayer, they rent the Casa Hauser, sit in the sun on the terrace for hours and play boccia, Gropius in a stiff suit and Bayer with his tanned torso and white linen trousers.

In July, Gropius's enforced return to Berlin marks the beginning of an affair between Ise and the Bauhaus master Herbert Bayer. This too could be termed a midlife crisis, or personal fulfilment. In September, sensing Ise's growing detachment, Walter writes to her: 'Love me, even if I am now so grey and tattered.' She doesn't reply. He writes that he is determined to pay more attention to her in future; he has neglected her. But still she doesn't answer. He rings up and then writes again: 'What is wrong with you? You were so cold and stiff on the phone. Why is your mood so gloomy?' By this time it is October. Ise is enjoying her passionate fling in Ascona and keeps extending the lease on the Lake Maggiore house. She guesses that her lover will soon be engulfed again by the clouds of everyday life, which already occasionally darken his brow. After all, he is married too. In truth, he tells her, he's finding it tough that of all the people he could have fallen in love with, it had to be the wife of his mentor, and his father's friend.

When Leni Riefenstahl performed as a dancer in 1920s Berlin, Fred Hildenbrandt wrote in the *Berliner Tageblatt* that she unfortunately lacked a dancer's most elementary skill: 'The ability to express emotions.' She was merely a 'dummy with no blood flowing through her arms'. He's right: they contain only adrenaline, not to mention a good deal of morphine. She keeps breaking down and having to go into rehab. Her lover and fiancé, the film director Harry R. Sokal, says she's hooked on 'the exhilaration of success'. She also seems to have been hooked on the power of fiction: it is still unclear which stories in her memoirs are true and which ones she made up. In either case, there were plenty of men.

She has lost the love of her life, Hans Schneeberger. With his love of cinematography, mountains and skiing, he was her ideal partner. When he left her for another woman, she went crazy. She screamed for several minutes in her room, then wandered around her flat in tears and stabbed herself repeatedly with a paper knife – she had to kill her love. Soon, however, she began a new life that led her from the world of dance into the dream factory of film. Sokal introduces her to Luis Trenker, and he in turn to the director Arnold Fanck. Sokal ends their engagement when he realises that Riefenstahl has embarked on relationships with both Trenker and Fanck to secure a lucrative role in *The Holy Mountain*. Later, it will often be cameramen who become her lovers, for example Hans Ertl, who films *S.O.S. Eisberg* with her, and Walter Riml, who worked on *The Blue Light*. Riml warns Ertl: 'Don't get caught up with this vamp or the same will happen to you as to me. I want to warn you about this woman because we're just candy to her, there to be eaten for as long as it's fun.' The director Sokal, her former lover and now her neighbour at Hindenburgstrasse 97 in Berlin-Wilmersdorf, once put it thus: 'Her partners were always the best in their field. There was a streak of elitism to her nymphomania.' There is one man Leni Riefenstahl worships entirely platonically; in her flat she has erected a small shrine to Adolf Hitler, with countless gold-framed photographs of him. When she meets him for the first time at a secret location by the North Sea,* she employs an orgiastic image: 'It seemed as if the surface of the earth were spread out before me, like a hemisphere that suddenly splits in two

---

*All we know from Riefenstahl's heavily fictionalised memoirs is that this meeting took place somewhere on the coast near Wilhelmshaven, where Hitler was speaking at a campaign rally.

and a gigantic jet of water came spurting out, so enormous that it touched the sky and shook the earth.'

There he goes on his lonely way, slightly hunched as he trudges across the gravel in the small gardens of Huis Doorn. Last year his wife erected a marble bust in front of a box hedge. No doubt she meant well, but he cannot stand the sight of it. It is a bust of him when he was in power, looking proud, moustache tips twirled and chest weighed down with medals. The sight of this bust is a daily humiliation for Kaiser Wilhelm II because now he wears civilian clothes and takes his afternoon constitutional in a light-coloured summer suit. In the distance he can hear a siren, a horse and cart, a few cars, then nothing. At least there's the crunch of the gravel, he thinks, as he continues his laps of the grounds in his Dutch exile. Today, as every afternoon, he wonders if running away back in those murky November days of 1918 was the right thing to do. He wasn't toppled, and to this day it isn't just his political opponents who regret the lack of a proper coup d'état; he does too. He feels as if he's merely away travelling, as if the throne in Berlin were still waiting for him. Now he chops wood all day with his good right arm, his left tucked away in his jacket pocket. Chopping wood helps him to feel a bit manly. He enjoys the moment the axe sinks into a log and splits it apart. Bang! Bang! And another bang! Then, at long last, teatime comes.

He started growing a beard the day he arrived in Holland, stubble at first, but by Christmas 1918 it had become a full white goatee. He carries this beard defiantly before him now, those legendary moustache tips as white as snow, but on this late summer's day in Holland they hang down limply. He doesn't notice the curtain from Schloss Bellevue in the chambers on the first floor of Huis Doorn that mask furniture from the city palace in Berlin that has been pushed gently aside. His second wife, Hermine, peers out at him on his lonely walk. She comes from the Principality of Reuss Elder Line and, standing there amid the effects of the abandoned Prussian castles, she still dreams of his triumphant return to the diehard monarchists in Berlin. Back when she was still married to the Prince of Schönaich-Carolath, she used to have a large photo of him standing on her piano. The images proliferated after her husband died until the entire apartment was crammed with pictures of the object of her devotion. Then, when Empress August Viktoria died in Doorn, she wrote such a heart-rending condolence letter to her idol that he couldn't help but get engaged to her, a woman thirty years his junior.

Hermine made sure from the very first day that the servants addressed her husband as 'Your Majesty', just as she did. She makes regular trips to Germany to forge alliances so that one day, somehow, she may become empress. She asks Göring, she asks Papen and she asks Hitler. Wilhelm leaves her to it and thoroughly enjoys the idolisation. She does occasionally wear him out, though; for example, when she organises one of those group visits from Berlin and hundreds of unknown tourists acclaim him with cries of 'Your Majesty'. Wilhelm knows he is emperor no more. He chops wood for hour after hour, goes for walks and smokes cigarettes. He's in a never-ending lockdown: according to the terms of his agreement with the Dutch government, he must stay within a ten-mile radius of Huis Doorn.

Annemarie Schwarzenbach falls head over heels in love with Erika Mann, who in return only wants to hug her. Erika is enchanted by the gentle disposition of this androgynous daughter of a Swiss silk manufacturer, but she also glimpses the abyss in Annemarie's dark eyes. She is familiar with this look of profound disorientation from her brother Klaus. As with him, she puts her muscular arms around Annemarie, encourages her and shields her from the stresses of the world. Annemarie doesn't discover the lover she has longed for in Erika, but at least she gains a mother. 'Your child A' is how Annemarie signs her enraptured letters to her peer, or 'Your little brother'. They do indeed look like sisters – the same regular face, boyish physique and bob, both toying with gender in the way they dress, one a writer, the other a photographer inspired by the independence that comes from having her own car. They love to race through Schwabing or along the Kurfürstendamm and then get out, order an absinthe on a café terrace, peel off their leather cabrio gloves and catch the looks from the back tables out of the corners of their eyes.

The whole of Europe is reeling from the impact of the financial crisis. Or not quite the whole of Europe, for day after day, thousands of new Reichsmarks flow into Erich Maria Remarque's bank account. His anti-war novel *All Quiet on the Western Front* is a best-seller during the late Weimar Republic and has sold a million copies by June 1930. It took Remarque a decade to put what he suffered during the First World War into words. It is this long silence, this search for a mode of expression and his unhealed psychological and physical wounds that allow him to voice the anguish of an entire generation. His childhood in the nice city of Osnabrück wasn't nice. The family moved house twelve times, his elder brother died, he lost his mother to an excruciating battle with cancer, and home was a place of fear and sorrow: the kitchen was never filled with the aroma of coffee and high spirits. Then, on his eighteenth birthday in June 1916, his call-up papers arrived. Two years of war, sustaining wounds, living in constant fear for his life, in constant despair. It took him ten years to digest this while he worked as editor of the tyre manufacturer Continental's corporate magazine and then as a journalist for a sports newspaper in Berlin. At last, in this thrusting, fast-paced city, in his free time between the Six Days of Berlin track-cycling race, tennis tournaments and boxing fights, car races on the AVUS circuit and in the slipstream of this speeding miracle called life, Remarque can finally write about the paralysing forces of war: 'We are superfluous even to ourselves.' He describes what a whole generation is incapable of feeling. Born Erich Remark, his decision to take 'Maria' as his middle name is a sign of his veneration of Rainer Maria Rilke, who died in 1926, the hero of all those whose terrible ordeals lead them to conclude that silence is the only appropriate form of communication with the rest of the world.

*

Did any painters profit from the First World War? No. The refined Franz Marc was shot on the back of a horse – the very animal his paintings elevated to a symbol of a higher spiritual life. August Macke, the merriest of the German Expressionists, also died a horrible death on the endless battlefields of Flanders. Ernst Ludwig Kirchner did survive but withdrew, profoundly traumatised, to the mountains, where he relies on morphine to face the daily dread that any minute another bomb will go off next to him. Only Otto Dix manages to process the terrors of the war into pictures that rival anything he did before. With the same wide-eyed gaze with which he absorbed the sight of shredded corpses, he now observes the sexual battlefields of Berlin, the whores and the big shots, the empty poses and the flailing attempts of dead bodies to keep on dancing, death-mask smiles already visible in their faces, as in his *Metropolis* triptych. In painting, too, the boundaries between beautiful and ugly are now a purely theoretical question. Instead, as professor at the academy of fine art in Dresden, his teaching pays unwavering attention to real life, the permanent collision of violence, death and eros. This is New Objectivity. 'You need to have seen humans in the unfettered state of war to know anything about humans.' The root cause of every war, Dix says, is a vulva. And when the war is over, it is with this same cold gaze – more head-hunter than portrait artist – that he looks at the human body.

He trains his great, staring eyes on the dancer Anita Berber, the queen of Berlin's nightlife whom he and his wife, Martha, really did carry to her grave in 1928, in her red dress, painting her as a twenties icon with a deathwish. All his other portraits are also painted as if he had to prepare a wanted poster. More disturbingly, he looks at his own children the same way, painting the new-born Ursus and Nelly as no one has ever painted babies before: creased and shrivelled, crumpled from the process of being born, their eyes wide in horror at being cast out into the world.

*

Josef von Sternberg simply cannot make up his mind during the shooting of *The Blue Angel*. Filming with Marlene Dietrich in the daytime, he falls for her airy gravity, her vulgar nobility, her sensual detachment. Then he shows the rushes to the ice-cold, mysterious Leni Riefenstahl, who cannot forgive him for casting Dietrich rather than her as Lola Lola. Dietrich is just as allergic to Riefenstahl, hissing like a cat whenever she appears on set at UFA's Babelsberg studios. Sternberg falls more and more in love with his leading actress with every day of shooting. She is no longer directing her charms at the pompous Emil Jannings, who is playing the eponymous straw man, but at the director behind the camera. Dietrich senses the 'divine and demonic powers' of this austere man so obsessed with detail and so full of imagination that, under his wing, she is on the way to becoming the woman she wants to be. She says later that he and his camera created her – 'a combination of technical and psychological skills and pure love'.

Sternberg visits Dietrich in her Berlin flat on Kaiserallee. In front of her husband and her curious daughter, Maria, she makes tea for the famous director. What they don't know is that Leni Riefenstahl can see into the back rooms of Marlene Dietrich's apartment from her rooftop terrace. And what we don't know is whether what Riefenstahl writes in January 1930 – it 'wasn't sure whether Marlene or I would be the one to follow Sternberg to Hollywood' – is true.

Erika Mann falls in love with the actress Therese Giehse, and the basis for this love is laughter. They first meet at a cabaret performance by Karl Valentin and Liesl Karlstadt in Munich, where they sit next to each other, giddily intoxicated by each other's company. Unlike Erika's marriage to Gustaf Gründgens, however, this relationship is not a joke. No, Therese is her second great love after Pamela Wedekind. This time, however, rather than two women supporting each other as the suffering daughters of suffocating fathers, these are two spiky young loners who admire each other for their otherness. On the one hand there is Therese – introverted, serious, carving words out of silence, still living with her mother and sister and only really coming out of her shell on stage; on the other, Erika – criss-crossing Europe in her car, always quick-witted and high-spirited, whether at home where Thomas Mann held court or at artists' haunts in Berlin, Munich, Paris and New York. It is precisely their differences that will lend them such stability, partly because each can make fun of the other's foibles.

When Margarete Karplus has finished her doctorate in chemistry in Berlin, she goes to Frankfurt to complete her training with the chemical conglomerate IG Farben. The following year she starts to help running her father's leatherware factory. Living together in Frankfurt, she and her fiancé, Theodor Wiesengrund Adorno, realise that this might, in fact, be true love. She scales back her contact with Walter Benjamin to an intimate correspondence, sending him the occasional cheque by way of support. Actually, this suits Benjamin, for he loves playing the medieval troubadour, languishing in longing to the point of nostalgia. Adorno suspends his constant stream of minor flings. Sometimes love is like a good cup of tea – you just need to let it brew for a while.

Josef von Sternberg leaves his wife, Riza, for Marlene Dietrich. By late January 1930, *The Blue Angel* is in the can, and in mid-February he takes the *Bremen* back to Hollywood on his own and finds a food basket from Marlene Dietrich in his cabin. Two days after Sternberg's departure, Berlin newspapers report that Dietrich will soon follow him to Hollywood.

This was not a golden age of true love. It was the age of 'Reasonable Romance', to quote the title of an Eric Kästner poem of the time. First they share a bed and 'then they lost love as others might lose a stick or a hat'. Over the winter Kästner has lost his love for Margot Schönlank, aka Pony the Hat. She weeps bitterly and he comforts her. This is his nature, he says; there is nothing to be done about it. He moves on to the next lover. He calls her 'Moritz'

in his letters; she hasn't been identified. He travels to his beloved
Lake Maggiore with her, but, as he confides to his mother, 'Moritz
didn't want to come at first because she loves me and I don't love
her.' She decides to go with him in the end, and on 10 March
1930 he writes to his 'dear Mummy': 'We really should chop off
everything that makes a man. Otherwise this mess will never end.'
Self-castration suggested in a letter to his mother – what a gift
to any Freudian. Kästner doesn't chop anything off, of course.
Indeed, he makes many more women miserable, as he grows ever
colder. In the poem 'A Man Gives Information' he admits with
disturbing honesty:

> You knew me, yet you never got to know me,
> While I was scared your love might be too strong.

That, then, is the state of love in 1930.

The American embassy in Paris organises an afternoon reception on 7 March 1930. Pretty music is tinkling quietly, the low
sun is shining through the windows, glasses are clinking, and the
whole atmosphere is incredibly civilised. The great photographer Jacques-Henri Lartigue is bored, though. After exchanging
a few words of broken English with a peroxide-blonde American woman, he hangs around at the bar for ages, waiting for his
next drink. Then, on the way to the cloakroom, he is struck by
lightning. The bolt comes from two hooded brown eyes brimming with longing. 'Bonsoir, Madame,' he stammers. She is clearly
heading for the dancefloor, so Lartigue adjusts his course and
asks her first for her name and then for a dance. Her name is
Renée Perle, she says. She's from old Romanian aristocracy. This is
poetry to Lartigue's ears. When he feels her lips almost touching
his during a slow dance and lays his hand on the cut-out back of
her dress without meeting any resistance, he is hers. They leave the
reception after that dance and spend the next two years together
virtually without a break.

There are many uncrowned queens in the early 1930s, most of them screen actresses, but if there's one woman whose aura and sensuality jump out of every Lartigue photograph, it's Renée Perle – whether in Biarritz, in Juan-les-Pins, Cap d'Antibes or Saint-Tropez. Flowing white trousers, olive skin, white blouses, a gold chain or an understated bracelet. Pure elegance, suffused with quiet nobility and simmering passion. And always that utterly unbelievable mouth, the short, slightly wavy hair and, of course, those dark eyes saturated with unfathomable Eastern European melancholy. Only in the occasional photograph where she opens her mouth, exposing her small teeth, does the icon suddenly become human. But Lartigue wants her to be an icon, which is why he asks her merely to sketch a smile on her face. He wants to photograph her closed, painted lips, wants to capture her feminine body in the white summer clothing in front of the sea, the palms, the promises of paradise. During their two-year symbiosis, not a day passes without Lartigue taking her picture. They're obsessed with one another. Nowhere do the early thirties look more sensual and noble than in these black-and-white photographs. This is deification.

It doesn't take long for Renée Perle to begin worshipping herself. She rents a studio in Paris to paint her own image daily. The paintings are incredibly kitsch – always the same closed lips resting on her pale face, like two canoes on a moonlit lake. Then Lartigue joins her and photographs her painting portraits of herself in her studio. Initially he revolved around her, but now she revolves entirely around herself. This cannot end well.

It's obvious to Heinrich Mann that there is something desperate about his affair with Trude Hesterberg. He has to find a way out of his marriage to his wife, Mimi, who spends the late twenties fighting to save it – fighting too against her own weight issues at spas in Marienbad and Franzensbad. Harry Graf Kessler takes a far more benevolent, artistic view: Mimi Mann is 'pretty attractive, a somewhat more corpulent Renoir'. Yet Heinrich's affair with

Trude spells the end of his marriage, which is legally dissolved in the spring of 1930. Heinrich moves to Berlin, while Mimi stays in Munich with their daughter, Leonie, and writes to her ex-husband after the dust from the divorce wars has settled: 'You are the only man I am willing to suffer for.' By this time, however, the fifty-nine-year-old Heinrich has already sought solace with Nelly Kröger, a thirty-two-year-old hostess at the Bajadere bar in Berlin's Kleiststrasse, travelling to southern France with her in spring 1930. (He has, in fact, repeatedly taken his women on spring trips to Nice, always to the Hôtel de Nice and always to the same room. Call it 'repetition compulsion'.)

Heinrich has always felt an almost sentimental attraction to the oldest profession, leading to constant disapproval from his morally upright brother Thomas. He met Nelly at the Bajadere one evening during the winter when he was feeling especially sad about his divorce, and the tips of his dark-blond moustache were especially droopy. When the two other ladies bowed out of his life, he 'intensified' the relationship with Nelly, meaning that he bought her underwear and drew her in the nude, a pastime he has always loved. Something is different now, though. Nelly is the first good-time girl with whom he actually wants to settle down.

Anyway, he goes with Nelly to a cinema on the Promenade des Anglais on 23 March 1930 to see *The Blue Angel*. A week before the official premiere, UFA producer Erich Pommer has travelled to Nice specifically to meet the famous author and offer him a private screening under the palm trees. Heinrich Mann enjoys this personal attention. He also enjoys the film's razzle-dazzle because now he has found his own disreputable Lola Lola – not one who drives him mad, but one who holds his hand in admiration – and it's doing him a power of good.

The Blue Angel premieres on the evening of 31 March 1930 at the Gloria-Palast in Berlin. It shows decadence triumphing over the last remnants of male dignity. As lascivious Lola, Marlene Dietrich demolishes the illusion of the true gentleman, leaving the audience in a frenzy. She also triumphs over the last remnants of the silent movie. The future starts here, and she is its herald. That same night, at Zoo Station, a couple of hundred yards down the road, Marlene Dietrich boards the night train for the coast. She plans to set sail for America in Bremerhaven and head to Hollywood. She is accompanied to the railway station by her dumped lover Willi Forst – her husband is in Munich on business and has taken their daughter and her nanny with him. She rings him one last time from the station restaurant to say goodbye, but the screeching of the arriving trains is so loud that she can barely hear what he's saying. She whispers 'Adieu' and hurries off to catch her train. Willi carries her suitcases while she carries herself like a victorious woman. Her Berlin housekeeper is waiting on the platform, ready to undertake the long journey with her. Marlene waves timidly from the train window, still clutching the roses presented to her that evening on the stage of the Gloria-Palast. The next morning, she enters her name on the passenger list in Bremerhaven: 'Marie (Marlene) Sieber-Dietrich, married, actress from Berlin'. As she closes her eyes in her cabin and the waves slap against the ship's bow, she can still hear the roar of acclaim for *The Blue Angel*. In her dreams, she is already on her way to being reunited with Sternberg.

Victor Klemperer is bowled over when he sees *The Blue Angel*. 'It goes without saying that the contents are melodramatic kitsch. But it's effective. Marlene Dietrich is almost better than Jannings. Her unaffected demeanour, not vulgar, not nasty, not sentimental – unconsciously human and depraved: "It's a long time since anyone fought over me" – that one line, devoid of pathos and yet a little grateful. I could write pages and pages about it.' Klemperer appears to sense that in this single line of dialogue Dietrich is expressing something that will apply to the rest of her life. Men will fight over her. For Klemperer, on the other hand, outings to the cinema with his wife offer a rare escape. From outside they are threatened by antisemitic agitators, from inside by Eva's bouts of depression. 'The days drag past, sometimes miserable, always gloomy. I'm scared.' Klemperer's diaries are a unique chronicle of his life as a Jewish Protestant whose position as a Romance philologist at Dresden University is coming under increasing pressure. In them, however, he also testifies, day after day and week after week, to his great love for Eva and to the demons besetting her. To his own help-lessness too: 'The short walks are the worst. Utterly dark, every conversation faltering or veering into desolation. I can no longer get through to Eva, and all my attempts to comfort her she meets with bitterness, and picks their logic apart.'

After their first few nights together, twenty-three-year-old Jean-Paul Sartre asks twenty-one-year-old Simone de Beauvoir to enter into a completely new form of unofficial marriage. It must be based on freedom – on both sides. Does she agree to this? If not, for all his love for her, he will unfortunately have to leave her. Simone gives a little gulp. It isn't so easy for her to kiss her girlish dreams goodbye, and their relationship didn't seem quite so modern two months earlier in the meadows near Limoges, but very well ... She loves this man, and he is clearly only to be had on these terms. He explains to her calmly that if his genius is to come to full fruition, he needs to be able to live out his sexuality freely – to stimulate his creativ-ity. At twenty-three, he says, he doesn't want to deprive himself of affairs for the rest of his life. He also says, 'I'm offering you a life-time of freedom, Simone. That's the most wonderful present I can give you.' It is too soon after her first night of love for de Beauvoir to envision what her own freedom might look like. But faced with such an honour, she decides not to look a gift horse in the mouth and accepts Sartre's other conditions too: complete transparency and honest conversations about everything – feelings, affairs, desires. No children, as they are nothing but a distraction and monopolise one's time and attention. Otherwise, though, Simone need not worry about anything. Of course he will love only her: their love is 'the top priority', the bedrock of their pact. But will she please accept that he doesn't wish to apologise if he has an affair, an 'incidental' fling? Simone gives a quick nod, and Sartre rushes off to catch the train. He's doing his two-year military service at the weather station in Saint-Cyr-sur-Mer barracks. His head is still spinning from de Beauvoir's acceptance of his conditions, and it plunges him, as he later admits, 'into a certain melancholy'.

Walter Benjamin is pushing for a divorce from his wife, Dora, in order to marry his girlfriend, Asja Lācis. He confesses to his friend Gershom Scholem that he has never felt the transformative power of love so strongly as with her, 'and so I have discovered many things inside myself for the first time'. When their divorce finally comes through on 27 March 1930 after a torturous war of attrition, Benjamin has to come to terms with the fact that Asja Lācis has already headed back to Moscow. She obviously wasn't really very serious about him, dumping a man shorn of assets by divorce; everything his wife brought into the marriage has reverted to her. And so Walter is forced to discover another new man inside himself: the jilted lover.

In the spring of 1930, Zelda Fitzgerald has a total breakdown. On the morning of 23 April, Scott takes her to the sadly named Paris psychiatric clinic Malmaison and hands her over to the doctors, a wailing, flailing bundle of nerves who claims she cannot go into the clinic because she'll miss her ballet lessons. Then he drives back into the city, both distraught and relieved. When he gets to their flat at 10 Rue Pergolèse, he continues reading Oswald Spengler's *The Decline of the West*.* To Hemingway he writes: 'Nothing comes close to this book.' Then he scours the kitchen for a bottle of gin. With every drink his face changes, the skin relaxes. After the second shot it's like a death mask; after the second bottle, like a mummy.

---

* *The Decline of the West*, whose two volumes were published in 1918 and 1922 respectively, reclassified history into epochs and contended that the Western world was ending. It was widely read after its publication.

*

Lisa Matthias travels to Sweden with Kurt Tucholsky again, but this time there is none of the magic that impelled them north the previous year. She is deflated by his constant affairs and drained by his marriage to Mary, which drags on and on. She has still promised to arrange a house for him again, though, and she finds one to rent in Hindås. It's blue, it's pretty and nine pine trees cluster cosily around it like a shield. They buy furniture in Gothenburg and she fixes it up a bit for him, but she has no intention of making it as homely as she might. The atmosphere between the two of them is as chilly as Sweden in March, with only occasional bright spells. Then Kurt lays a new Erich Kästner poem called 'Familiar Stanzas' on the new table:

> When loving couples one another shun,
> Their hatred's of a very special kind.
> Nay, even in the things they leave undone
> Their hate is always deeply intertwined.
>
> ...
>
> Like duellists they circle and they spar.
> Well they know their hearts' anatomy
> And keenly where the other's weak spots are.
>
> ...
>
> But suddenly all hate and loathing's gone.
> They just swap looks of weariness and strife.
>
> ...
>
> And they go back to acting man and wife.
> For when at last these times are through and done,
> Love will revert to being something fun.

But Lisa Matthias won't be cajoled into seeing love as something pleasant after such times. She travels back south to her beloved Lugano, from where she writes to a friend: 'Things look grim with Tucho. I can't go on. Being a sailor's wife doesn't suit me.' When she has left, Tucholsky begins to learn Swedish with Gertrude Meyer, the daughter of a Swedish woman living in the next village. In May, it is with her rather than Lisa Matthias that he travels to England.

The only thing Ludwig Wittgenstein finds complicated is love; everything else he understands. However, Marguerite Respinger, a fun-loving young student at the Academy of Fine Arts in Vienna and a friend of his sister Margarethe's, completely turns his head. He wants to kiss her, yet he is terrified by the idea that his incipient arousal will pollute his thoughts. He models a clay bust of her and presents it to his parents. He writes to her almost every day. After receiving her birthday gift of handkerchiefs, Wittgenstein notes in his diary in Cambridge on 26 April 1930: 'Of all the people now alive, the loss of her would hit me hardest. I don't want to say that frivolously, because I love her – or hope that I love her.' Unfortunately, Wittgenstein is obsessed with upholding an ideal of purity. He explains to her that because marriage is sacred, he imagines it without sex or at any rate without children. Marguerite stares at him in disbelief. Even he wrangles with his great ideal. On 2 May, he writes, 'Were I more decent, my love for her would be more decent too.' On 9 May, he writes that he is quite clearly in love, even though unfortunately the situation 'is in all probability hopeless'. He is torn between his longing for her kiss and his fear of being seized by a dangerous sexual desire beyond his control. He considers how to have a marriage in accordance with the rule of chastity, but this is one logical problem that even Wittgenstein cannot solve.

Love, like any utopia, gets bigger and bigger the longer you wait for it.

Ninon Dolbin, née Ausländer (and therefore known as 'the Foreigner'), is still waiting for her entry permit into Hermann Hesse's heart. There are two problems. First, she still gets on well with her estranged husband, the set designer and artist Benedikt Fred Dolbin, from whom she is, to be entirely accurate, not yet divorced

and with whom she quite enjoys spending time in Berlin and south-
ern France (partly to recover from Hesse's mood swings). Second,
Hesse is unwilling to let her get close to him. Ninon, this nostalgic
Jewish woman from Czernowitz, in the most remote corner of the
Habsburg Empire, has adulated him for the past twenty years and
has been writing to him since 1914 when she was just fourteen.
She worships him, sometimes as Zeus, sometimes as St Francis of
Assisi, and at all times as her lord and master. After their first night
together she solemnly declares: 'I cannot call you by your name,
just as the Jews are not permitted to say the word Jehovah.' And
after their second: 'When your head was resting on my lap, it was
as if I were holding the crucified Christ.' She does not indulge in
understatement.

This idolisation is all a bit much for Hesse, however much he
enjoys her putting her sheltering arms around him in his suffering.
His love for Ninon is as confusing as the sentences in his book
Narcissus and Goldmund; its prose is generally a little too solemn
and overwrought, but when Narcissus speaks about love, Hesse
comes up with phrases so pure in their ambiguity that they are
like arrows to the heart. Out of this kind of honest vagueness, he
finally lets Ninon move into Casa Camuzzi, his stone house in
Montagnola in Ticino, the Italian-speaking part of Switzerland –
but only downstairs in the dark flat on the ground floor, where the
walls are rife with mould. Hesse lives upstairs in the sunlit western
wing with its magnificent view of Lake Lugano and the mountains,
waiting in constant hope for that cold surge of creativity. He has
just published *Steppenwolf*, his pitiless confessional novel. Such a
disturbing effect has it had on him and his body, in fact, that he
is constantly ill and whining. Feeling his age for the first time, he
stays holed up in Montagnola, and only occasionally does he let
poor Ninon come up from the damp flat downstairs.

Whenever he wants something from her (and he wants quite
a lot), he leaves a 'house letter' on the small table between the
floors. In the main these are contemptuous instructions, requests
for distance, and meal orders. When he regards her behaviour as

invasive, she learns by letter that her status is that of a 'guest' and no more. Communication in this household is similar to that in a Trappist monastery. This seemingly peace-loving, mild-mannered author with his straw boater and suntanned skin is actually quite neurotic when he feels besieged (and he always does). Very occasionally when he is in a good mood (and he hardly ever is), he will paint a bird on one of his house letters or a watercolour of a tree in the warm style that resembles an illustration from a children's book. Even more occasionally, he will invite the beautiful, gentle Ninon into his bedchamber. He is terrified by the idea of fathering another child. He knows how she longs to have one, which is why he had himself sterilised in Berlin before she moved in with him. He has never told her this, nor about his second precautionary step: he has asked his best friend, the psychoanalyst Josef Lang, to draw up her horoscope.

On 11 May 1930, Zelda Fitzgerald is discharged from Malmaison psychiatric clinic, having managed to convince the doctors there that her ballet teacher cannot live without her. She goes straight to Madame Egorova, talking nonsense and embracing her in front of all the other dancers, upon which the teacher immediately packs her off home. Zelda is so distressed by this that she makes her first suicide attempt. Scott casts around in panic for a solution for his deranged wife. He finds it in French-speaking Switzerland at a clinic called Les Rives de Prangins in Nyon on Lake Geneva – a luxury clinic with box trees pruned in the same style as the ones at Versailles. When Zelda moves into her room, it is not a photo of her husband or her daughter that she places on her bedside table but a picture of her dance teacher. Her attending physician, Dr Oscar Forel, comes to a swift diagnosis: schizophrenia.

It will take time, he tells Scott. Maybe he would also like to undergo withdrawal treatment for his alcohol problem? I have no idea what you're talking about, Scott says indignantly before going to his hotel room and knocking back a double whiskey.

Initially, Scott is only allowed to see his wife once every

fortnight, which prompts him to make the rounds of the luxury hotels in Glion, Vevey, Caux, Lausanne and Geneva. From her sickbed Zelda writes: 'But our divergence is too great as you must realize for us to ever be anything except a hash together ... You might as well start whatever you start for a divorce immediately.' It is still spring. Then summer comes and the swallows fly low; autumn follows and the plane trees discard their yellow leaves; winter arrives and the wind comes whistling off the mountains. Scott doesn't start divorce proceedings but instead sends his wife a bunch of roses every day. Here, in this baleful state, in stolid hotels whose carpets absorb guests' footsteps and tears; here, with very expensive and very bad gin, ruined financially by the cost of the room and the clinic, ruined physically by the enormous quantities of alcohol he consumes every afternoon; here, in the summer and autumn of 1930, drowning in fear, trapped on the shore of Lake Geneva, Fitzgerald writes some of his greatest short stories: 'Two Wrongs', 'The Rough Crossing', 'Babylon Revisited'. Right here he finds the unique tone of his thirties, a blend of sweet and sore. Zelda is administered every then-conceivable medicinal drug – morphine, belladonna, barbiturates – and wrapped in bandages to treat her eczema. She surrenders to it all and smiles like someone from a different planet. When she does resist and goes crazy, she is injected with substances for several days to keep her quiet.

Zelda writes to her husband: 'I'm so afraid that when you come and find that there is nothing left but disorder and vacuum that you will be horror-struck.' She does not yet know that Fitzgerald is about to transform this disorder and vacuum into great literature.

And how does Paul Éluard, Gala's cuckolded husband, react to her obsession with Salvador Dalí? Extremely unusually. He even allows his wife and her companion to live in the Montmartre flat that he bought and furnished for himself and Gala. Sometimes Gala goes to bed with Paul so she is not completely starved by Dalí's weird sexuality. Éluard writes to her in their small house by the water's edge in Cadaqués: 'Love me if you feel like it, exploit your freedom to the full.' And when he slowly realises that he has truly lost the woman he worships to Dalí, he tells her that when he is alone at night he gazes at nude photos of her with great desire. Now, though, he says, he must live the 'life of a vanquished man'.

On 17 April, Pamela Wedekind marries Carl Sternheim. He is in good cheer because his moustache is now restored to its rightful dark-brown resplendence. His eyes dart about, but he manages to say 'I do' at the right moment. In accordance with Pamela's wishes, the wedding is held at the registry office in Berlin-Moabit, where her beloved father and mother got married in 1906. After the ceremony the guests are invited to the restaurant of the Hotel Eden where Billy Wilder once busied himself as a gigolo, Marlene Dietrich played golf on the rooftop terrace and Josephine Baker ate potato salad before going on stage. It is a small party that has gathered for this strange wedding reception for a psychologically unwell dramatist and his young wife. Gottfried Benn has recently stepped down from his role as Carl's physician, commenting that neither he nor Pamela Wedekind was 'fully sane'. He went on, 'There is, unfortunately, nothing to be done but to leave the two to their fate.' That is also essentially the view of Klaus Mann, who doesn't attend the wedding and sends instead, via the *Literarische Welt*, his 'Undelivered Speech at the Wedding Reception of a Female Friend'. He still hasn't come to terms with Pamela's rejection. His undelivered speech is a very unusual attempt to capture the state of love in 1930:

Getting married is like an epidemic among us. Marriage is our pathetic attempt to overcome what we realise is permanent loneliness. What you are letting yourself in for is serious and beautiful – I can come up with no better congratulations than that. I dare not predict that it will turn out well for you. I would speak no other words at your next wedding than today – even if it were *our* wedding.

Klaus Mann and Pamela Wedekind will never marry; indeed, they will never see each other again.

During her agonising over her daughter's marriage plans, the bride's mother, Tilly Wedekind, began talking on the telephone with Gottfried Benn because she knew that he'd treated her future son-in-law. The first time she heard his voice she felt as if she were being 'caressed and hypnotised', and this comes to pass a few days after the wedding. When Wedekind and Benn, both of them born in the warm spring of 1886, meet for the first time, it is just the two of them. Tilly Wedekind is wearing a black afternoon gown under a coat – she is highly amused that the style is called 'Merry Widow'. At 8 p.m. on the dot she hears the doorbell ring, accompanied by a rustling of paper. There he is in the doorway, brandishing a bunch of carnations he has just wrapped up. Having relinquished the medical care of her son-in-law, he wishes to see to the physical well-being of the bride's mother.

She opens the door and sees 'a fairly soft mouth and sad eyes. He has a strange gaze. So far away, so deep, so sad.' She welcomes him inside and they take a seat. Benn tells her about his girlfriend Lili Breda killing herself – what an elegant opening gambit on your first date with a lady who desires you. A counter-spell. But Tilly Wedekind did in fact know Lili Breda. And in intimate detail, for it was Lili who emerged naked from a well during the Munich premiere of her late husband's play *Franziska*. The dots have been joined. At that moment Pamela rings up and asks her mother if she can stay the night because Carl is behaving a bit madly. 'Of course, my dear,' Tilly says, upon which Gottfried Benn quickly packs up and leaves.

Benn invites Tilly Wedekind – the widow of the playwright Frank Wedekind – to the theatre on 24 April and then home to his surgery-cum-apartment in Belle-Alliance-Strasse. But instead of getting undressed, he gets dressed up. She surely has nothing against his donning his doctor's coat, Benn remarks. It's a habit of his and he feels more comfortable this way. As Tilly Wedekind later recalled: 'I thought, right, now he's going to butcher me.'

He has of course celebrated his experiences as a pathologist in his *Morgue* poems, which she read back before the Great War with a pleasant shudder. Now, though, he is hungry for live flesh. Decked out in his white coat, Benn brings in a plate of sandwiches and two glasses of sparkling wine. He asks whether the hair on the back of her neck is shaved – and then runs his fingers gently over her nape.

The cast of Benn's strangest play is now complete, as he stages a feisty *ménage à trois*: in parallel to his dalliance with Tilly Wedekind, he maintains an intense relationship with Elinor Büller, who was Lili Breda's best friend. Thus begins a nine-year-long double life during which neither woman ever gets wind of the other's existence. They are his 'heavenly' (Elinor) and his 'earthly' love (Tilly) – two former actresses, almost the same age, both always immaculately turned out, their souls always ready to catch fire with some touching new verses of his creation. And should the two women perchance wish to visit him simultaneously, he can always tell one of them that as a poet he sometimes needs to be alone or else his creative powers will dry up; she is bound to understand.

'Sexuality', an ageing Freud writes around this time, 'is one of the most dangerous pursuits in which an individual can engage.'

Henry Miller has arrived in Paris; June has stayed behind in New York. He is penniless and tries to earn a few francs by day, but he has to wangle himself a place to sleep each night and a coffee in the morning. He has resolved to become a great author, here and now, so he punches letter after letter into his typewriter, but they simply refuse to coalesce into a text that satisfies him. His pain is still too raw for him to turn his manuscript about an author whose wife cheats on him with another woman into great literature. He finds everything stifling – the city, the heat, his own expectations. 'Montparnasse', he writes, 'is a sad place. In spite of the lustfulness and the drunkenness, these people are unhappy.' He roams the streets, spends every franc he comes by on whores and hangs around at Le Select and La Rotonde, waiting for some American he knows to pay for his drinks. He takes any woman, any bottle, any bed he can get. Henry Miller is forty years old and has reached the end of the line, but then, on 24 August 1931, his novel is finished. June has come over from New York and is outraged when she reads the manuscript: 'You see things only in your narrow, masculine way; you make everything a matter of sex,' she tells him. 'And it isn't that at all ... it's something rare and beautiful.'

June is also struck by the author's unattractiveness after months of neglect – gaunt, almost bald, lacking any spark. She wants him to get 'younger, more pep, more romanticism', she says.

And so, on 25 August 1931, Henry Miller begins a younger, peppier, more romantic book. He inserts the first sheet of paper into his typewriter, takes a drag on his cigarette and types: 'Tropic of Cancer. By Henry Miller.' What on earth is this one about? June asks, to which Miller replies: '*The* Paris book: first person, uncensored, formless – fuck everything!'

Below the soft sand, up above the high canopies of the pine trees, the smell of ripe blueberries in their noses and, in their ears, the sound of the waves pounding on the beach, again and again, again and again. The warm wind is blowing from the west. At some later date, the whole great, odd Mann clan will say that they were so happy that summer of 1930 in Nida on the Curonian Spit in what is now Lithuania, where Thomas Mann had built himself a house by the bright sand with the Nobel Prize money. It stands on a high dune between the Prussian-blue waters of the Curonian Lagoon and the sparkling green of the Baltic Sea, with a magnificent sky full of towering cloud formations arcing overhead. On this flowing transition between the mainland and the breakers, between civilisation and the natural world, light runs riot.

In the evenings the whole family trots up onto the dune's highest point to watch the sun go down. 'All one can do is shout hallelujah,' Katia notes. As a typical member of the clan, she has learned to mask her feelings with irony.

This is a 'holiday'. Thomas informs his wife early on that he is 'bad at unemployed recreation', and she accepts this. He cannot work outside, he says; he needs a roof over his head 'so that thoughts do not evaporate into dreams'. Yes, he really does talk like this – even when it's thirty degrees in the shade. Regarding the location, he says that this is where 'the summer holidays of our school-age children' will be spent from now on, as 'a form of counterweight to our south German residence'. Not even a gale can purge Thomas's head of noun-heavy diction.

The Manns had come here for the first time the previous year, which was when they spotted this plot of land on a rise under tall northern pines with a view of the lagoon. One year of construction work and it was ready to receive them – 'Thomas Mann's summer house', as it is called on the plans. Of course, Nida is far from practical for someone with a south German residence. Over six hundred miles and a two-day journey, first a night train to Berlin, then on to Königsberg the next night, then a change of train and finally a steamer across the lagoon to Nida. A crazy enterprise with all the children and the luggage. They arrive on 16 July, having gone to the station as soon as twelve-year-old Elisabeth and eleven-year-old Michael's school holidays started. The whole village has gathered on the quay where the steamship docks to welcome the prominent new residents. Thomas, wearing a light-beige coat over his three-piece suit, finds this all a little tiresome, whereas his wife judges it their due. Excluding the conception of their six children, the Manns' conjugal bed has always been becalmed, which makes Thomas all the more glad for some extracurricular amusement – even if it is only Nida's waving fishwives. Yet Katia barely displays any emotion either as they go ashore. Everyone in the Mann family has tacitly agreed that the most restrained show of emotion is always best.

Way back when Erich Maria Remarque married the dazzlingly beautiful Ilse Jutta Zambona, he had to make some calculations. His findings: she is a quarter German, a quarter Italian, a quarter eccentric and a quarter melancholic. She divorced a tobacco industrialist for him and they are now moving in together, into an apartment on Hohenzollerndamm in Berlin. He doesn't mention love when he tells his sister about his marriage plans. Instead he says, 'I want to try and make someone happy. Someone else, because it'll never work out for me.' As inhabitants of the modern age, well-versed in psychology, by this point we might guess that it will never work out. The couple don't want any children, only dogs. They buy an Irish setter. Unfortunately, Billy is no good either as a guard dog or at keeping the couple together. Very soon Remarque and Zambona do the rounds of the city's cafés and nightclubs separately in search of new conquests – he with a hat and cane, she dressed like a sphinx in a suit and high-heeled shoes. Zambona starts an affair with the scriptwriter Franz Schulz, who is in the middle of writing *Three from the Filling Station*. This literary threesome is significantly more successful than the one involving Zambona, Remarque and Schulz. Erich climbs in through the open bedroom window one night to surprise Jutta and Franz in the latter's flat. He beats up his rival so badly that Franz is forced to go to the UFA studios for a whole week with a black eye and a dislocated shoulder. We owe these details to Billy Wilder's description of events.

Soon afterwards, however, following the humiliation of Jutta's trysts and the incredible success of *All Quiet on the Western Front*, Remarque begins an affair with his agent and manager, Brigitte Neuner. Neuner controls the public's access to her client – and her own access to his bedroom. Her marriage is on its last legs, so their occasional trysts work brilliantly: invigorating for the circulation, easy on the stomach and discreet. On 4 January 1930, Erich and Jutta's marriage is dissolved by mutual consent, although their relations continue quite merrily even afterwards. The first thing they do after the divorce is sealed is go off skiing together in Davos. Remarque then carries on travelling alone through Europe as he flees himself as much as fame, continuing to write the manuscript that will be fittingly titled *The Road Back*. He soon writes to Brigitte from the seaside resort of Heringsdorf, telling her that eighty pages of the new book are complete and: 'I miss you. Funny, eh? A lot, actually.' So unfamiliar with his feelings and so mistrustful of sentimentality is he that he can only put them into words by saying how funny they seem. It isn't long before Brigitte soon finds it a lot less funny. She is replaced as first paramour at Erich Maria Remarque's court by Ruth Albu, the sweetheart he picked up at Betty Stern's salon after returning from his travels. To cap it all, his ex-wife can't leave him alone either, always hoping there's a road back. She has only fully begun to love Remarque since their divorce.

Barely arrived in Hollywood, Marlene Dietrich starts shooting her first picture for Paramount. Sternberg tailors the script of *Morocco* to her while also keeping a jealous eye on her sex life. They are happy together, but Dietrich misses Berlin and her daughter. She travels back to Europe, rekindles her relationship with Willi Forst, goes to the zoo with her husband, the nanny and Maria and, in the evenings, strolls into lesbian bars and the Romanisches Café, dressed in suit and tie. A trip down memory lane. She reacquaints herself with bohemianism, meatballs and the Berlin dialect. She makes the acquaintance of Franz Hessel, who wants to write a profile of her for a major newspaper, and rehearses some songs. Once she has soaked up enough Berlin life, she starts to yearn for Hollywood and Sternberg – and so she boards the train and the ship again and sails back to America. The show must go on.

Long before Tesla built a factory here, pretty Grünheide twenty miles south-east of Berlin was a favourite excursion spot. Gerhart Hauptmann set his short novel *Lineman Thiel* here, and the publisher Ernst Rowohlt would cycle around the lake when his authors got too much for him. This is also where the great composer Kurt Weill and the great singer and actress Lotte Lenya get to know each other in a rowing boat. Following an extremely turbulent youth in Vienna, Lenya fled from her father's drunken assaults and abuse via Zurich to Berlin, where she found refuge with the dramatist Georg Kaiser and his family. One fine day he asks her to go and meet the composer Kurt Weill at the railway station. The sun is shining radiantly, and she takes a rowing boat across the Peetzsee to the tiny station. She recognises Weill without a second's hesitation. He looks like a professor with those metal-rimmed spectacles, his slightly messy, thinning hair, the beginnings of a paunch, and his amiable and slightly disoriented demeanour. Lotte ushers him into the boat and quickly realises that she's going to have to row the boat herself if they're to make it to the other end of the lake before nightfall. Weill simply won't stop talking – about his compositions, the beauty of nature, the delights of silence. Lenya studies him the whole way, and by the time they get to the far shore, their fate is sealed. In fact, it was sealed by that very first gaze on the platform, hanging there in the air for a fraction of a second too long, linking their eyes like a brief, brilliant ray of light. No wonder – any man would fall in love with her. Those fabulous teeth with the cheeky gap between them, her pure sensuality and, above all, that unique gravelly voice, which melts Kurt Weill's heart. 'When I long for you,' he writes to her soon afterwards, 'I think most of all of the sound of your voice, which I love like a force of nature.' He immediately begins to compose songs for her, and they swiftly move in together in Berlin, get married and taste triumph with *The Threepenny Opera*. Whereas for the stage premiere the producers forgot to put Lenya's name on the poster, much to her husband's annoyance, the screen adaptation in 1930 makes her a star, and *The Threepenny Opera* becomes inextricably linked with Lenya's 'Pirate Jenny'. In the evenings she sings her wicked songs on stage, but afterwards she snuggles up next to her composer in their new flat in Bayernallee, purring like a kitten that has finally found a cosy spot by the stove. Soon enough, though, she uncurls and goes out again, floating on the tide of the night. Weill realises early on that if he wants her to come back to him, he must let her go.

Gottfried Benn trudges through the streets. Though the greatest disasters still lie before him, his gait suggests that he is already carrying their weight upon his shoulders. 'Weighed down by grief, certain of doom' runs his description of himself. Benn says that Rilke, whom he calls the 'untouchable German master', wrote the verse his generation will never forget: 'Who speaks of victory? Enduring is everything.'

In early October 1930, Ludwig Wittgenstein and Marguerite Respinger meet in Switzerland. They talk about marriage and kiss, but then she pulls back and looks away with a gloomy expression. Later she weeps and tells him, as he notes in his diary, that 'she does not comprehend her relationship to me at all'. They row across the Rhine near Basel, drift against the bank of a reed-fringed island and sit in the boat, talking. It's idyllic, but after a couple of long kisses Wittgenstein takes fright. He breaks out in a sweat when his hormones get going. They row back to Basel and he holds her hand; she stubbornly refuses to look him in the eye. Ludwig Wittgenstein, one of the smartest men in the world, is completely lost.

Charlotte Wolff learned to swim in the waters of love at an early age. The small river outside the town walls of Riesenburg was cold and the swimming costumes uncomfortable, but whenever the sun came out during the short summers along this edge of the great empire, she and her girlfriends would take a dip. When Wilhelm II came to hunt nearby with Count Finck von Finckenstein, her whole family would climb into the landau and drive through the endless woods, wrapped in warm blankets, breathing in the mouldy forest scents in the misty morning light, to snatch a precious glimpse of the emperor in full regalia. The kaiser would raise his hand and graciously accept the cheers of his subjects through the railings around the hunting lodge. In those days his moustache was still black. Then, at the age of thirteen, Charlotte fell in love in Danzig with Ida, a mysterious sixteen-year-old Russian Jew, and travelled with her family to Zoppot, where, while the adults were sleeping, they made love for the first time, their feet still dusted with sand and the roar of the sea coming in through the open windows. Neither of them had ever heard of homosexuality, and they had no role models; they just got started.

The parents didn't comment, merely smiled over their coffee the next morning – maybe out of wisdom, maybe out of naïvety. Then one day Ida showed Charlotte a photo of Lisa, her best friend from Odessa, who was now living in Berlin; Charlotte fell in love with the photo, believing Lisa to be the real-life incarnation of Dostoyevsky's Nastasya Filippovna. Every afternoon after finishing her homework, her thoughts would escape from her bedroom in Danzig and connect with the heart of a stranger called Lisa in Berlin. At some stage while the First World War was raging, she made the horrendously long train journey to visit her, under the pretext of a doctor's appointment. They fell in love in a Charlottenburg guesthouse: an idea had become reality. Years later, the mysterious Lisa, long since married into the vast expanses of Russia, visited Charlotte in Charlottenburg, where she was a student, the years with Heidegger behind her. Their roles were reversed, but their love had endured. Charlotte held Lisa's hand. A touch of happiness. Many tears.

But there is life after Lisa. After completing her medical studies Charlotte Wolff becomes a doctor in the national health system, overseeing pre-natal care for women in poor areas of northern Berlin. She lives with Katherine, a tall, beautiful, blonde physiotherapist, in a comfortable flat in a recently built block on the Südwestkorso in Wilmersdorf. Here, after she gets off work in the afternoon, Charlotte writes poems with subversive undercurrents, many of them about her longing for the mythical Lisa, while Katherine stands at her easel in the next room and paints. In the evenings they go out on the town together. 'I was aroused by Berlin's exotic climate,' Charlotte writes. 'It made me feel as if every fibre of my body was alive.' Yet the sexualisation of Berlin life in the thirties disturbs her too. She loves the lesbian bars and she loves the women, but she wants to restore physical love 'to its correct position on the scale of sensual feelings'. In the poems of Bertolt Brecht, Georg Trakl or Alfred Lichtenstein, she thinks, one sees 'that sex per se is a death sentence for imagination and emotions, whereas eroticism continually replenishes them'. It is about swamping the brain with erotic images, she says. It stimulates love, desire and longing – the true substances of poetry.

One more word about Charlotte Wolff, a young doctor but a wise old soul. She said something very sweet and true about love and what happens to people to whom it is denied. 'Disappointment', she writes, 'causes a vulnerability that has the same effect as night does on certain plants: they close their flowers.'

Dietrich Bonhoeffer loves St Augustine more than any living person. In his *Confessions*, the fourth-century saint wrote: 'Our heart is restless until it rests in you.' From this quote Bonhoeffer derives a theory of the present. 'Restless is the word for what awaits us,' he declares to his congregation in Barcelona. 'Restlessness is the characteristic that differentiates man from beast. Restlessness – that is the force that creates history and culture. Restlessness is the root of all spirit.' This restlessness comes from the quest 'in the direction of the eternal', yet one senses that it is also in part the restlessness in the direction of the celibate. Bonhoeffer is twenty-three when he gives this sermon. He has never truly loved anyone but God, but he is attracted to a young teacher at the German School called Hermann Thumm. They go to bullfights together and whenever possible to the opera, touring the bars afterwards and crawling into bed at around half past three in the morning, as he feels obliged to confess from the heat of Barcelona to his parents in shady Grunewald. However, when Bonhoeffer returns to Germany and rapidly rises to become a professor, Thumm announces his engagement at astonishing speed.

In April 1930, Bonhoeffer returns to Barcelona for Thumm's wedding, but there is no record of his mood. Once more, he is intoxicated by the scent of the city's lilac trees and the fresh strawberries for sale on every street corner, and he enjoys wearing a new summer suit tailor-made for him in Berlin. When the wedding reception is over, Bonhoeffer escapes for a week on his own at Tossa de Mar on the Catalonian coast. He needs to recover from the 'events of the wedding', he tells his parents in a letter. He makes his melancholy way to the coast in a first-class carriage, swims in the sea, eats oysters, drinks wine and goes for walks even when the clouds overhead are spitting thunder. He becomes ever browner and more restless – which direction should he take? He doesn't yet know. Dietrich Bonhoeffer is *The Monk by the Sea*.*

Those years in Berlin, the legendary tennis player Gottfried von Cramm will later say, were the time of his life. Late in 1930, Gottfried and his young bride move into their first shared flat at Dernburgstrasse 35 in the west of Berlin. By day Gottfried trains relentlessly on the tennis courts of the Rot-Weiss club, then he and Lisa swim in the western lakes; after that they dive into the bars of Schöneberg and Charlottenburg and float through the night with unwavering grace and elegance.

They soon strike up extra-marital affairs – Lisa with Gustav Jaenecke, her husband's doubles partner, and Gottfried with Manasse Herbst and many others. Here in Berlin the racquet-wielding baron can savour his bisexuality far more freely than at his ancestral seat in rural Lower Saxony. Cramm and Manasse Herbst are regulars on the gay scene, especially at Silhouette on Geisbergstrasse, which also draws Christopher Isherwood and Magnus Hirschfeld. In addition to his rendezvous with Manasse, Cramm also meets up with his childhood friend Jürgen Ernst von Wedel, the man who once visited Lisa and drooled over photos of Gottfried's athletic physique. Lisa von Cramm is loving and indulgent about her husband's comings and goings, and she takes the same liberties as he – not just with men but also with women, including Ruth von Morgen and the photographer Marianne Breslauer. And yet the couple's correspondence from that period suggests that

---

*An oil painting by the German Romantic artist Caspar David Friedrich (1774–1840).

theirs was a happy marriage. The Nazis have not yet begun to take an interest in the elegant tennis-playing aristocrat's personal life.

Simone de Beauvoir suffers from Jean-Paul Sartre's extended absence more than he does. As long as he feels loved, he feels fine. He carries out his monotonous daytime duties at the army barracks and looks forward to being able to light his pipe and reflect on lofty philosophical questions afterwards. He often meets de Beauvoir in the evenings: they travel back and forth between Paris and Saint-Cyr-sur-Mer and later the barracks in Tours. Time is usually short, and they continually find themselves saying hello or goodbye on platforms, in perpetual transit. They often eat together but hardly ever share a bed because she is barred from his barracks and too cowardly to rent a hotel room with him during the daytime. She notes to her surprise that this causes her particular suffering: 'I was forced to admit a truth I had sought to conceal since my girl-hood: my desires were stronger than my will.' Of course, their pact requires that she always tell Sartre what is on her mind, but she doesn't mention this unrequited lust. She begins to realise how perilous her predicament is, that she spends all her time thinking of him, that he means the world to her, that she wants only to read what he reads, hate what he hates and love what he loves. She senses that she is gradually losing touch with the person who ought to be dearest to her heart – herself.

On 28 November 1930, after seventeen months of marriage, Alma Mahler-Werfel writes of her husband, Franz: 'Let him take care of his own mess. Why did I get married? Madness.' Then she goes down to the kitchen in Vienna to fetch a second bottle of herbal liqueur – the first is long since empty. She gazes at the lovely picture Oskar Kokoschka painted of her back in 1913 when he was so infatuated with her. She loves it when men are crazy about her: it's her drug. Kokoschka wrote her a card not so long ago. What if she met up with him again?

As she once did with Kokoschka, she now urges Franz to

produce 'masterpieces'. He should be eternally grateful to her, she writes in her diaries, which are starting to overflow with alcoholic fantasies and antisemitism: 'Once again I serve as an incitement for him to work – due to my impudent, healthy Aryan nature. A dark Jewess would have long ago turned him into something abstract. That is the danger that lurks inside him.' It is questionable whether Werfel's soul benefited much from her turning him into something so concrete.

In December 1930, Lisa Matthias pays Kurt Tucholsky one last visit in his Swedish house in Hindås. He has made the most of his time in Sweden, wringing literature from that ecstatic first summer with his 'Lottchen'. He inserts some jocular correspondence with his publisher, Ernst Rowohlt, at the beginning, in which Rowohlt encourages Tucholsky to write another 'little summer love story' like *Rheinsberg*. 'Love, in this day and age?' the author replies. 'Are you in love? Who still loves nowadays?'

Lisa Matthias gasps as she reads this sitting on the red sofa in the blue house in Hindås where, only a year ago, she believed she had found the love of her life. Her mood is bad enough as it is. She has recently brought down the curtain on her infatuation with Peter Suhrkamp in Berlin, because he has married someone else; she has also found hairpins belonging to Tucholsky's language teacher, Gertrude Meyer, all over his house. It is hard for her to concentrate on this novel about her, but she's scandalised by what she reads: 'So this was the book of our love – I felt an icy wind on my skin. There was not a grain of genuine feeling in it, not a trace of tenderness, no love whatsoever. I felt as if I was falling into an abyss.' Two days later she departs. Her love has been given the literary treatment. 'Love, in this day and age? Who still loves nowadays?' are the words that swirl repeatedly around her head on the never-ending drive back to Berlin. Through birch forests and boundless fields, past lakes and small red houses, along the sea and past fir trees, Matthias drives and drives. She catches the ferry across to Travemünde and then speeds on and on, softly weeping, through the rolling hills of Mecklenburg and back to Berlin.

'A perverted bourgeois,' the gimlet-eyed Harry Graf Kessler notes in his diary the first time he claps eyes on Arnolt Bronnen. A croaky-voiced man brimming with pent-up rage, Bronnen was the most popular playwright of the Weimar Republic in the late 1920s. He is a close friend of Bertolt Brecht and Ernst Jünger, dramatic adviser to Berlin's Funk-Stunde radio station, a balding, blond bonehead and a most unpleasant individual. He poses for *Die Dame* in silk pyjamas beside a mastiff in the Blau-Weiss tennis club's car park in western Berlin, and afterwards, on 1 October, Joseph Goebbels introduces him to twenty-one-year-old Olga Schkarina-Förster-Prowe – a Russian who is constantly drunk and clearly as addicted to sex as to turmoil. Thus begins a love triangle: Goebbels the limping fanatic, Bronnen the lumbering giant and Olga the manic-depressive femme fatale get together on an almost daily basis. Bronnen writes about Olga: 'She could only laugh about love. There must have been certain physical advantages that tempted her to indulge in erotic adventures as frequently and as superficially as possible. This wasn't risky for her as she was infertile.'

Arnolt and Olga get engaged. She has only slept with twenty-eight men before him, she says, and he can trust her. The bride does not appear at her own engagement party in Bronnen's flat – Gretha and Ernst Jünger are among the guests – until around midnight, leading Goebbels by the hand and claiming to have been ironing trousers for 'the Doctor' as she calls him because of his PhD. Her announcement is utterly unembarrassed and full of good cheer. On 17 October 1930, Olga, Arnolt and Ernst Jünger, accompanied by his younger brother, the poet Friedrich Georg Jünger, and thirty Nazi thugs, interrupt a speech by Thomas Mann in Berlin in which he is warning the audience about the rise of National Socialism. On 1 December, they let squeaking white mice loose in the Theater am Nollendorfplatz during the premiere of the film adaptation of

Erich Maria Remarque's *All Quiet on the Western Front*. When the police release them from custody, Olga goes home not with her fiancé but with Goebbels. She declares that the intervention was 'an act of love for him'. Olga and Arnolt are due to get married on 17 December. Bronnen has to promise Goebbels in advance that their marriage will not affect Olga's work for the National Socialist German Workers' Party before he will give his blessing.

The wedding reception is held in the Blau-Weiss club restaurant, where Goebbels introduced the couple to one another just ten weeks earlier. The limping fanatic arrives at the party after midnight and presents Olga with a huge bunch of red roses. Just as the newlyweds are about to retire, the phone rings. It is Goebbels summoning Olga in a voice that brooks no argument. She goes to him. What about Bronnen? Stripped of his status as husband, he slips into his dead father's role: 'I devoted myself to my poor old mother and was glad to have her to myself.' Olga comes back sometime the next night.

Bronnen has been taking care of his mother because he owes her an existential debt of gratitude. Two days prior to the wedding, she testified in court that Arnolt's father was not her Jewish husband but the vicar who wedded them. To her son she wrote: 'You have every reason to feel a Christian, my son.' *Patricide* is the title of Bronnen's most famous play.

By the way, neither Goebbels nor Bronnen knows that Olga Förster has been working for the Soviet secret police since 1929, under the codename Agent 229.

'I want to see things naked and clear,' Otto Dix says. He frequently does see his model Käthe König naked in his Dresden studio – and then he starts having an affair with her. At his well-appointed apartment at Bayreuther Strasse 32 in Dresden's southern suburbs, he is used to the delicate things in life. Chopin was the norm in his parents-in-law's household. But Dix, the working-class lad with the butcher's hands, is just as keen on more common fare. He doesn't let his harsh wife, Martha, re-model him into a gentleman, not even when he becomes a tenured professor. And so at an early stage he begins to commute between the two spheres: homely, sexually well-tempered, domestic happiness on the one hand, and a tempestuous affair with Käthe and her broad Saxon dialect at his studio on the other.

When Simone de Beauvoir realises that Jean-Paul Sartre has renewed contact with Simone Jollivet, the courtesan who once gave him a bedside lamp with a shade made from red underwear, she is assailed by jealousy. Sartre tersely points out that they had agreed that their relationship was to be untainted by jealousy. He is convinced that controlling one's emotions is a question of will-power. No one need 'indulge in a spot of sadness' – that stems entirely from intellectual indolence.

After more than an occasional spot of sadness, Walter Benjamin eats a wad of hashish around 9 p.m. on 7 April 1931. He asks his cousin, Dr Egon Wissing, to document his hallucinations, which is how we know what he experienced after taking the drug: 'An image that arises without an identifiable context: fishing nets. Nets spread over the whole earth before the end of the world.' A few weeks after coming down from his high he draws some con-clusions about his life as a man with Jula Cohn, his wife Dora, and his lover Asja Lācis: 'Overall, though, the three great loves of my life define not just its sequence and its periodisation but also its experiences. I've known three different women in my life and three different men inside me. Writing my life story would involve describing the rise and fall of these three men.' His friend Charlotte Wolff once formulated it differently, with kindness and clarity: 'Walter reminded me of Rainer Maria Rilke, for whom the longing for one's beloved was more desirable than her presence.'

On 4 May 1931, Elisabeth von Hennings gets divorced from Bogislav von Schleicher in order to marry his cousin, Kurt von Schleicher, on 28 July. This divorce will have fateful consequences.

President Paul von Hindenburg has long trusted Schleicher, who has warned him insistently against opening the gates of power to the Nazi Party. Then, however, the Nazis break into a lawyers' chambers in Charlottenburg, steal all the documents about the Schleichers' divorce and feed the juiciest details to Hindenburg. The president believes in the sanctity of marriage, and the doubts these documents raise about Elisabeth von Schleicher's honesty cast her new husband in a bad light.

In early 1931, Curzio Malaparte is awaiting the publication of his book *Coup d'État: The Technique of Revolution*. He is actually half-German and was originally named Carl Erich Suckert, but after his lungs were corroded by German poison gas during the First World War, he threw in his lot with his sentimental homeland, Italy, where he was born in 1898, and changed his name. Despite the cataclysm of the war, Malaparte has remained a Futurist, but unlike Napoleon 'Bonaparte', he has always put his faith in the worst-case scenario – the 'Malaparte'. He doesn't stay long as editor-in-chief of the Turin daily *La Stampa*, a position to which he ascended with Giovanni Agnelli's assistance. After spending many nights writing *Coup d'État*, he ends up taking the manuscript to Paris for fear of retaliation by Mussolini and his henchmen.

So, aged thirty-one, he loiters, unemployed and virtually state-less, in the streetside cafés of the Latin Quarter. He sees Josephine Baker dance, James Joyce stay silent and Picasso hold court. He also sees all the Germans arrive – the writers, the journalists, the flâneurs who love Paris because they love themselves more after a glass of wine and a wander along the Seine in the soft light of the consoling street lamps. Malaparte studies them all with merciless exactitude. He is a huge womaniser, and a patient one to boot. He lurks like a lion for hours on the terrace of Le Select, positioning himself at the last outside table on the left, right next to the sturdy trunk of a plane tree. There he cultivates his status as an inscru-table Italian aristocrat, ordering nothing but coffee and absinthe, undressing the other people on the terrace with his probing gaze and listening to their conversations. Here in early 1930s Paris, while the city enjoys a brief respite from world events, and Germans and Americans succumb to its magnetism, this elegant German-Italian man sits and tries to understand fascism on café terraces, in libraries and by reading the papers. Then he writes about the aesthetics of the coup d'état as if it were purely a matter of form, not content. His book comes out in French in the spring of 1931. In it he predicts that Hitler will come to power not via a coup d'état but thanks to parliamentary compromise – an 'accidental dictator' is the phrase he coins. The Germans with whom he discusses this theory think he's mad. They fail to see that his book is about the defence of freedom or that his critical insight is that Hitler's relationship with the German people is a problem of gender trouble: 'Hitler's intelligence is in fact profoundly feminine: his mind, his ambitions, even his will are not in the least virile ... Like all dictators, Hitler loves only those he can despise ... Hitler is the dictator, the woman Germany deserves.' German and French people alike can only shake their heads when they read this. The general feeling is that Germany deserves a different woman to the one this peculiar Italian envisions in his nightmares.

For the opening night of the Pan-Palais gentlemen's bar on Schiffbauerdamm ('Fifty tabletop telephones, a dance band and very robust prices'), Gustaf Gründgens turns up with his new boyfriend, Carl Forcht, Klaus Mann's former lover. Gründgens comes in a tuxedo, Forcht in an evening gown. The two of them are now living together in Gründgens' flat at Bredtschneiderstrasse 12, along with Gründgens' sheepdog and his butler, Willi, who patiently runs through his lines with him when Forcht is in the shower or having a lie-in.

After the Pan-Palais inauguration, Magnus Hirschfeld, the head of the Berlin Institute for Sexual Science, sets out on a world lecture tour. He wants to raise people's awareness about homosexuality and 'sexual intermediaries', as he calls them. He gives talks and does research in Russia, America and Asia. In 1931, he meets a twenty-three-year-old medical student called Li Shiu Tong in Shanghai, an impeccably mannered and gorgeous-looking Chinese man, and falls in love with him. Li Shiu Tong will never leave his side again, and Hirschfeld, a target of Nazi hatred since the twenties, will never return to Germany after this lecture tour.

The target of Erich Maria Remarque's love in 1931 is Ruth Albu, a beautiful and well-read nineteen-year-old actress who is still (only barely) the Austrian writer Arthur Schnitzler's daughter-in-law. She readily swaps sides to be with Remarque, whom, she later says, 'was the love of my life. I thought I would never be able to love anyone again.' The love affair has far-reaching consequences for Remarque because it leads him to art and also to the southern Swiss town of Ascona, the two greatest passions of the next stage of his life. Albu introduces him to the dealer Walter Feilchenfeldt, with whose help he quickly acquires an impressive collection of French art. Paintings by some of France's greatest artists, including Degas, Cézanne, Toulouse-Lautrec and Renoir, are paid for with the proceeds of *All Quiet on the Western Front*. It wasn't easy for Albu to get close to Remarque at first, for his novel's unbelievable success had transformed him into a recluse. He moved out of the flat he shared with Jutta Zambona after their divorce in 1930 and into a suite at the Hotel Majestic, but there, according to Albu, he wrapped himself 'in his solitude as in an elegant cashmere jumper'. Sadly, he increasingly turned to drink, even when he went back to his hometown of Osnabrück to write, accompanied only by his dog, Billy.

Yet, with her carefree nature, and with the help of a trip to Ticino in the warm days of late August 1931, Ruth Albu manages to liberate Remarque from his depression and his snobbery. Scared by the ban on the film adaptation of *All Quiet on the Western Front**
and attacks on cinemas by rampaging mobs from the SA – the

---

*Spurred on by Joseph Goebbels, Nazi Brownshirts disrupted viewings of the film and it was banned on 11 December 1930.

Nazi Party's paramilitary wing led by Ernst Röhm – Remarque is looking for a discreet exit from Germany.

In Porto Ronco, a few miles from Ascona on the shore of Lake Maggiore, at the southernmost tip of Switzerland, Remarque and Albu find their dream villa on the very first attempt: Casa Monte Tabor. One radiant day they turn off the main road to Italy in their Lancia and drive down to the lake. First they see Monte Verità – the fabled hill that was a centre of pacifist and artistic movements in the early twentieth century – and then this lonely rundown house with shuttered windows by the lakeside. A local barber gives them the seller's name; they drive over and that same evening Remarque and the Swiss estate agent shake on the deal. Divine intervention.

The villa used to belong to the artist Arnold Böcklin, and it was the view from here over the two Brissago Islands that inspired his legendary painting *The Isle of the Dead*. It is here that Erich Maria Remarque wishes to enjoy life from now on, for the sum of 80,000 Swiss francs.

He asks the two women in his life – his ex-wife Jutta, and his new lover Ruth – to make the house habitable as quickly as possible, and they buy linen and furniture while he travels to Berlin and goes to the bank. In autumn 1931, it is still relatively simple to transfer your assets from a German bank account to a Swiss one, and he also gets a helping hand from a third ally: his manager and former lover, Brigitte Neuner. How lovely that all these women seem to have remained on good terms with Remarque for so long.

Picasso can now lead his double life in very comfortable circumstances. The stock-market crash has little impact on him – he has stashed away the huge cash proceeds from the sales of his paintings in a back room of his flat. In fact, he benefits from the crash because it allows him to pounce when the owner of a fantastically spacious château in Boisgeloup in Normandy goes bust. Two floors, endless corridors, green shutters and magnificent grounds where he can pursue his newfound passion for sculpture. The greatest advantage is that he no longer needs to haul each year's harvest – all the canvases, paints and sketchpads – back to Paris as he has done every other summer. No, he can keep it all here at the castle, though he still occasionally travels to Paris to visit his wife and child.

During the week, Marie-Thérèse Walter becomes his châtelaine. Once a fortnight, when Olga and Paolo come to see Daddy at the château for a family weekend with guests and punch and campfires, Picasso's muse goes off to Paris to stay with her mother and sisters for a few days. The sculptures he creates in Boisgeloup are almost all modelled on Marie-Thérèse. Picasso transforms her slender, statuesque body and aquiline profile into a profusion of abstract and concrete works dotted around the estate. It was actually her shadow on the beach in Dinard that first inspired him to make these sculptures. He cannot live without this shadow during this period, not even when he visits Olga and his son near Juanles-Pins on the Riviera during the summer holidays of 1930 and 1931. There, Marie-Thérèse stays at a guesthouse a few streets from them and sunbathes until she receives a summons from her lord and master. She is good at waiting: she knows her time will come. Just that morning Picasso wrote to her: 'I can see you before me, my beautiful landscape, and I never tire of looking at you stretched out on your back on the sand. My darling, I love you.'

In 1931, Erich Kästner is writing a new novel with the working title *Going to the Dogs*. It is a portrayal of Berlin morals, but the publishers aren't happy with the title or some of the depictions of moral decay; it ultimately appears as *Fabian,* with the subtitle *The Story of a Moralist.* It is in fact Kästner's own story, containing many elements of his biography. A hero who cannot get over his first love frantically clings to his mother, forgets his father and hops distractedly from one bed to the next as he roams through anonymous, breathless, breakneck Berlin, a modern 'Sodom and Gomorrah'. It is an inventory of the emotions, steeped in deep despair and gallows humour.

The press is unanimous in its praise, with paeans by leading reviewers such as Hermann Kesten, Alfred Kantorowicz, Hans Fallada and Hermann Hesse. (Incidentally, there were precious few critics as incisive as Hesse at the time. It is also worth noting that the quality of the reviews is amazing – as is the Weimar Republic's painful awareness of its own finiteness, evident in stylistically brilliant articles by Jewish authors who, only a few months later, will be driven out of Germany for ever.)

Kästner isn't able to revel in his success, though, because his romantic adventures have landed him a dose of the clap. He has to put his sex life on hold from July to December 1931 and make a weekly visit to Ernst Cohn, the physician who treats him for sexually transmitted diseases. Cohn uses silver compounds and sulphonamides and even experiments with electrical charges. It's not much fun. 'I could hack the chest of drawers to pieces,' he writes to his mother of his frustration. She is the only woman he tells about his disease, describing it in great anatomical detail in his letters. He keeps it a secret from everyone else. A revelation that the book's author had caught gonorrhoea would have clashed somewhat with Fabian the moralist's tirades against moral decline.

In 1931, Erich Remarque publishes the sequel to *All Quiet on the Western Front*, which recounts the bitter experiences of Germans returning home from the war; their homeland seemed intact, and yet everything had changed. Remarque claims that only women could have restored these men's psychological well-being, but they had no desire to do so. They sensed that history had other tasks in store for them, and they were fed up with making sacrifices or idolising men as 'heroes' when in reality they regarded them as narcissists or wimps. They also realised that they were quite capable of getting by on their own. In *The Road Back*, Remarque makes it clear that there is no way back after an event on the scale of this war.

Many veterans tried marriage as an escape route from their derangement, a wedding ring as a safety buoy. In her 1931 novel *Patience Passes*, Margaret Goldsmith writes about men in 1920s

Berlin who have been psychologically destroyed by the war. They are so ravenous and jaded that they propose to women on the dance floor, after the very first waltz and while the music is still playing, having only just learned their names. Disorientation generated an incredible urgency, and the sense that the next war might break out at any moment fuelled a feeling that there was no time to lose. Erich Maria Remarque describes this sensation in *The Road Back*: 'And he wanted to marry because after the war he was lost, because he went always in fear of himself and of his memories and looked for something whereby to steady himself.'

Erich Maria Remarque would have made a perfect partner for Marlene Dietrich even then, but she is still in Hollywood. She also has her own entanglements to sort out. She arrives back in America in May 1931, this time with her daughter in tow. She doesn't give a damn that this slightly tarnishes her image as a femme fatale, which is the role in which the film studios want to cast her. She even has to agree to a clause in her contract with Paramount stipulating that she will never appear with her child in public.

Perhaps Marlene is hoping that her rival Riza von Sternberg, who is still vying for her husband's love, will pipe down if the notorious Lola Lola starts appearing at the studios with her daughter. Meanwhile, Josef von Sternberg has a surprise welcome gift for the object of his affections. He has found the perfect house for her in the best street in Beverly Hills; 882 North Roxbury Drive is dripping with luxury and surrounded by high outside walls to shield her from prying eyes. This is the place Marlene, her housekeeper and six-year-old Maria now call home. Josef is usually there too. Their two Rolls-Royces, his midnight blue, hers grey, stand cosily alongside each other at night in the driveway. Around this time Marlene Dietrich gives Sternberg a photo of herself in *The Blue Angel*, writing on the back in green ink: 'To my creator from his creature.' He responds with a photo of himself in a camel-hair coat and spats with a cane, a twirled moustache and piercing gaze: 'For Marlene. What am I without you?'

May and June 1931 is a joyous period for them both. They film together in the daytime, and in the evenings they cook together.

Marlene's husband moved to Paris with his lover after Marlene left, and Sternberg arranged a job for him there with the European branch of Paramount. Rudi is even inclined to give up their cherished family apartment at Kaiserallee 54 (now Bundesallee) in Berlin, but Marlene voices her dissent – she can't stand it when other people draw conclusions from her life choices. What's more, she needs Rudi in Hollywood – for propaganda purposes. Riza von Sternberg will not tolerate her husband living in a marriage-like relationship with Dietrich. She is taking him to court and also suing Dietrich for defamation. Furthermore, Paramount Pictures can do without the bad press and need both an unblemished star and a director who can concentrate on his work.

Marlene sends panicked telegrams to Rudi in Paris. YOUR PRESENCE HERE WOULD HELP ME A LOT IN PUBLICITY MATTERS LINKED TO FRAU STERNBERG'S COURT CASE. KISSES MUTTI. Rudi doesn't fancy playing happy families in America, but after three further telegrams, he boards a liner in Cherbourg for the four-day voyage across the Atlantic and then makes the 2,500-mile train journey from New York to Hollywood.

Exhausted from his travels, Rudi walks into his wife's new life on 19 July 1931 in a complete daze. A magnificent villa in Beverly Hills, sunny blue skies, palm trees, a chauffeur who holds open the door of the Rolls-Royce for him, as well as his spouse fussing over him like a hen and a daughter who can't get enough of him. The next day, as soon as he has recovered, the family dress up to go out. Marlene wears her trademark suit and tie, at her side is her husband in a light-coloured suit and holding their hands is their delighted daughter; Josef von Sternberg, meanwhile, remains at a respectable distance. Thus arrayed, the family steps outside to meet the press. Dozens and dozens of pictures are taken to tug the American public's hypocritical heartstrings. Rudi repeats the same sentence over and over again into reporters' microphones: 'Marlene and I are both good and sincere friends of Mr von

Sternberg and support him in his battle against this attack by his former wife.'

With that, Rudi has done his bit and travels back to Europe.

The photos of Dietrich's close-knit family have the desired effect. Josef von Sternberg gets off lightly in his divorce proceedings from his wife, and she also drops her case against Marlene. Now that's what you call a PR success.

But what about Rudi Sieber? Back in Paris, he tends not to answer Marlene anymore, not even when she sends him telegrams saying 'MILLIONS OF KISSES'. But then she sends him new shopping lists that include picture books for their daughter and new underwear for herself: YOU KNOW THE UNDERWEAR I ALWAYS USED TO BUY, PRETTY BUT PRACTICAL. A THOUSAND KISSES MUTTI.' Rudi does as he is told and wraps up parcels in Paris for Mummy in Hollywood. His accompanying note reads: 'Think of your poor Papa who is so alone. Billions of kisses, Pops.' Millions of kisses turning into billions of kisses in the space of eight weeks: now that's what you call inflation. And all because he is now rapidly running out of money: 'PLEASE MUTTI SEND MONEY I NEED IT.'

Another man who won't let himself be pinned down is Kurt Wolff, who published Kafka and Trakl before the war and is still living off their sales in 1931. Over the years his business interests have grown less ambitious and his publishing house only really exists on paper now, so he finances his expensive society lifestyle in Munich largely from his wife's inheritance. He's a textbook *bon vivant*, but one who has gone to seed, wedging himself into suits over waistcoats with bursting buttons, a workaholic who has taken to drinking too much now that authors have ceased to seek him out.

But his head was turned when the forthright and rebellious Helene Mosel came to his publishing house to do an internship in 1929. She loves books almost more than he does, which provokes him (but later makes her his equal as a publisher). Helene shares a frugal existence in a small attic flat in Munich with her mother and sisters, but there is something proud and noble about her that prevents her from kowtowing to any man, let alone one who invites her to champagne receptions. Kurt Wolff tries anyway.

Since 1930, he and Helene have been toing and froing between yes and no and between Paris and Munich where, slowly but surely, he has been winding up his publishing house. And his marriage. Elisabeth has fallen in love with her gynaecologist, and they make arrangements for an amicable divorce. Helene, twenty years Wolff's junior, has entered his private life at a favourable moment, first as a secretary and indefatigable translator, later as an all-round assistant at Pantheon Books in Paris, Wolff's pan-European publishing project.

It is also a financially tricky moment. Kurt Wolff Verlag is on the slide, and in the days that follow the stock-market crash he races around trying to drum up funds for new book projects. To Helene in Paris he writes: 'I know you have patience. Don't lose it.' He promises her that he wants to eat and drink less because that might at last allow him 'to love [her] better, more strongly, more properly'.

And the unbelievable comes to pass. Kurt Wolff slims down from the eighty-three kilograms he weighed when they met to the sixty-eight kilograms he will weigh until the end of his life. He drinks less and he writes ever more tender letters to her. Helene is impressed; she begins to feel sure of his love and sees that he is willing to change. To her brother Georg she writes ecstatically: 'We must not wish to possess what we love but love it properly, know the other, be indestructibly linked by the power of feeling.'

Yet when she decides to test the indestructability of this feeling in April 1931 by joining Kurt on the Riviera for two months, she experiences crushing disappointment. He may now be slim and more frequently sober, but he has fallen back into another old habit. He has taken a second lover – the very tall, very elegant and very blonde Manon Neven DuMont – for the summer and for the various parties people throw between Le Lavandou and Juan-les-Pins. Kurt suggests to Helene that she form a *ménage à trois* with him and Manon. She doesn't dare refuse, so he quickly finds a nice villa for the three of them in Saint-Tropez. The cicadas chirp, the waves roar and the figs gradually ripen; it is the south of France we know from postcards, and yet it is hell on earth for Helene. She weeps a lot. Realising that she is cut out for work and even for love but not for bohemian morals, she defiantly starts to write a play. She calls it *Trio*, and the main characters are a forty-four-year-old HE, a thirty-four-year-old SHE and a twenty-four-year-old IT – a tomboy. This is real life, not drama, but Helene can no longer put up with either. One day when Manon and Kurt are out, she writes him a note: 'My love, your world is not mine.' She moves out, leaving luxury and comfort behind, along with the wrong notes of a trio whose instruments are not in tune. The wild mistral nags at the fluttering curtains and her nerves. She settles in her own 'cabanon', a humble hut a few hundred yards away on the edge of a vineyard with a view of the sea.

Here in this hut, with its weathered, red-tiled roof, white-washed walls rampant with climbing roses and green shutters, her new life begins in the summer of 1931. When she moves in, the wind has subsided, the sky is cloudless, it is twenty-four degrees Celsius, lemons are ripening on a large tree outside the window and the church bells of Saint-Tropez chime softly in the distance; the mountains look as if she could touch them. She quickly completes *Trio*. Then, half-healed by the therapeutic act of putting her experiences on paper, she writes to her brother: 'I love Kurt so much that I was able to leave.'

The next thing Helene does is write a shopping list for the market in Saint-Tropez. She has worked all winter, translating every night and every Sunday, saving up franc by franc for this moment. She desperately needs a striped deckchair, she needs a green wooden table for the garden and camping stove, she needs earthenware crockery, she needs curtains, she needs everything for a relatively normal life in one of the world's most beautiful spots. This shopping list is her declaration of independence. And that evening her landlords, a wrinkled old couple of winegrowers, bring her a small cat to keep her company, a warm, grey bundle that makes her so happy she wants to cradle it inside her blouse.

She writes a relaxed letter to her brother telling him not to worry – she knows Kurt will soon come back to her. His relationship with the elegant Manon will founder on 'mutual exhaustion' because 'Manon is one of those women one marries and Kurt one of those men one doesn't marry, and Manon won't stand it for long.' Is she really so sure? In any case, she grows into her independence with every new morning when she joyfully opens the windows of her tiny house and light floods in. Then she starts to write a book she calls *Background to Love*. It turns out to be one of the most enchanting novels ever written about southern France and a guide to how to escape a patriarch and then entice him back again by showing one's independence.

They meet again at the fishermen's ball in Saint-Tropez, and the next morning Kurt packs his bags and leaves the big house to move into Helene's little cabin. She initially finds it hard to have to share her bed with a man again; it was easier with just a cat. But then she realises that she has grown big enough to be able to share. She has become half of a couple; in August 1931, Kurt Wolff and Helene Mosel finally belong together.

Kurt immerses himself completely in Helene's spartan lifestyle. In hindsight, it is as if they were unconsciously rehearsing for the hardships of emigration. In the evenings, as he and Helene sit alone on their terrace with their legs on the green table, quietly listening to nature sink into darkness, she tells him that all of this – the glittering sea in the distance, the fig trees with their biblical scent, the mountains with their cool crowns, the lemon trees with their dazzling fruit, the grasses bending in the gentle evening breeze – is just the 'background'. To what? he asks. 'To love,' she replies.

On 19 September 1931, Zelda and Scott Fitzgerald leave old Europe. In Southampton they board the *Aquitania*, bound for New York. It is the same ship they took in the other direction when they first came to Europe.

In these hopeful September days, Scott writes 'recovered' on a photo of Zelda. They are both hopeful. The therapy at the clinic in Nyon seems to be having the desired effect. She has lost her manic laugh and regained her optimism and her style: 'I loved you most and you 'phoned me just because you 'phoned me tonight – I walked on those telephone wires for two hours after holding your love like a parasol to balance me.' She tightrope-walks her way back into life. In his diary he notes: 'One year of waiting. From darkness to hope.'

They do not linger in New York but push on to her home-town of Montgomery, Alabama. There they rent a house and buy two pets – a Persian cat they name Chopin, and a dachshund they baptise Trouble.

In September 1931, Ludwig Wittgenstein has fled to a remote hut near Skjolden in Norway to find out if he really loves Marguerite Respinger. Receiving his invitation, she travels halfway across Europe to be with him. He arranges accommodation for her in a nearby farmhouse. She wants to talk to him, but he is nowhere to be found. All she finds in her room on the farm is a Bible that he has placed there for her. He has inserted a letter to her in 1 Corinthians 13, a homage to love: 'Love suffers long and is kind ... love bears all things, believes all things, hopes all things, endures all things.' For Marguerite, this heaps too much strain on a relationship that hasn't even begun yet with a partner who is hiding from her. She sets the Bible aside and goes out walking and swimming in the fjord. Through the long, light nights she lies awake in bed, waiting for Wittgenstein to come up to her from his hut. But he doesn't. According to his diary he already regards himself as a 'pig' for merely imagining her naked body. Having achieved nothing, she departs. Even love can wither and die.

Down in Ticino, Ninon Dolbin is still trying to extract a promise of marriage from Hermann Hesse. She sniffs a chance when his benefactor from Zurich, the industrialist Hans Conrad Bodmer, builds him a splendid house on Lake Lugano on a huge plot of land with an endless view towards Italy. It is bathed in sunlight, surrounded by subtropical plants. Ninon decides that she will not enter this new house as his 'secretary' (which she is in all but name) – only as his wife. She wants to save him from his midlife crisis; she doesn't realise that he doesn't want her help because pain whets his creative powers.

Ninon tells him in one of the Casa Camuzzi 'house letters' that she's urgently requesting marriage, but adds: 'It should not mean or change anything between us. It is about our status in public.' Hesse reads it and feels duty-bound to inform his partner of what it means to want to be with him: 'I need a space inside me where I am completely alone, where nothing and nobody is allowed to enter. Your questions threaten this space. Several times recently you have destroyed the tempo at which my soul lives.'

So why does he end up marrying this destroyer of his peace of mind? We don't know. Nevertheless, the marriage is crisscrossed with dividing lines. Ninon and Hermann tell the architects that the new house must have two separate living areas, one for each of them. There are two entrances and only one connecting door between the two halves – upstairs, between the bathrooms. Hesse gets a form of monk's cell containing a bedroom, a study and a warm shower. It is perhaps the task of establishing his independence that has worn him down and perhaps also the fact that everyone has been urging him to get married – not just Ninon but Bodmer, the benefactor who has paid for the house, Katia Mann and Hesse's astrologist Josef Lang. In June 1931, Ninon can finally request a divorce from her husband Benedikt Dolbin, who agrees only too readily (he marries his longstanding lover, Ellen Herz, the following year).

When the divorce papers come through, Hermann publishes the banns of marriage for 14 November 1931 in Castagnola. With the temperature just above freezing, a nasty north-westerly wind and light drizzle, conditions are not exactly rosy, and the day before the wedding Hermann writes to his friend Heinrich Wiegand: 'I am going to the registry office tomorrow afternoon to have a ring put in my nose. This has been Ninon's long-held wish and because she has now had the house built, etc. etc., it is, in short, now happening.' Afterwards, 'Ninon is going on a honeymoon.' Who would have believed that Hermann Hesse, the creator of dream-veiled *Siddhartha* and sun-drenched *Steppenwolf*, would invoke such depressing justifications for getting married? In any case, it's Ninon who has to carry this letter to the post office for him on the eve of their wedding. She reportedly wept. We know nothing about the wedding – only that Hermann Hesse leaves on his own for a spa holiday in Baden straight afterwards, on 15 November, and that Ninon Hesse, née Ausländer, ex-Dolbin, sets out alone on 'honeymoon' on 16 November, travelling by night train to Rome to visit the gods of antiquity.

Not only does Gunta Stölzl run the weaving workshop at the Bauhaus in Dessau, she also spends her breaks pushing a pram around the small park outside it. Her husband, Arieh, is still based at the building site of the new Trade Union School in Bernau. In a letter to her brother in spring 1931, she describes the first clouds on her emotional horizon: 'Sharon is still in Bernau, and we are still leading a weekend marriage, which may not be bad for work but is otherwise so-so.'

The climate inside the workshop is becoming increasingly uncomfortable. There are plots to hound Gunta from her job. The Bauhaus's new director, Mies van der Rohe, is under pressure from Dessau's right-wing city council. A student from the weaving workshop, with whom Gunta is embroiled in a dispute, lodges a complaint with the council and attacks her 'on sexual grounds'. It is unclear whether these involve a lesbian or heterosexual affair, or if this is about her being married to a Jew, but she resigns in rage and leaves the Bauhaus. Her only distraction from her fears and anger is her daughter.

Amid all of this, Arieh departs for Palestine. His passport has expired and he no longer has a visa, so he heads home to renew it. By marrying him, the Bavarian Catholic Gunta has forfeited her German nationality. She senses that this could become a problem as the city council in Dessau is increasingly dominated by the Nazi Party and the Bauhaus is a thorn in their side. In the summer of 1931 she fails in her bid to reclaim her German citizenship and by November she has emigrated to Switzerland with her two-year-old daughter. Her husband writes her a long letter to say that he met someone on the journey to Palestine and doesn't know when he'll be back.

Under Man Ray's guidance in Paris, Lee Miller comes to embody the 'garçonne' or tomboy style. She wears a beret over her short blond hair and plain, figure-hugging clothes over her muscular body. She is a modern woman, and she also happens to be two heads taller than her famous lover. Initially, she really is his docile pupil, but she soon begins to take photographs and emancipate herself. The muse and model morphs into an artist; she's familiar with the old dog's tricks, aware of how he fabricates these unique haloes in his photos and uses light as if it were a paintbrush. Indeed, with some of their photographs taken around 1930 it is impossible to say which one of them released the shutter, the master or his pupil, or to determine whether the latter has become a master herself. In fact, all Man Ray wants to do is to photograph her. Her never-ending neck, her eyes, the languid elegance of her eyelids. Her small breasts that look as if they have been carved from marble. And, over and over again, her lips. Those lips drive him crazy. Even without any lipstick. But when she paints them redder, he is subjugated and so is anyone else who meets her. Man Ray turns Lee Miller into an icon, just as he did with Kiki de Montparnasse. And this time he comes up with a fitting name for her: *La femme surréaliste*, as he titles a 1931 photograph.

When their day's work is done, Man Ray and Lee Miller spend their evenings wandering the streets, dropping in for a drink at the Jockey-Bar where they give James Joyce and Ernest Hemingway a friendly nod before moving on to Jean Cocteau's jazz club near the Rue du Faubourg Saint-Honoré or to Chez Bricktop, a legendary American nightclub where they dance to Cole Porter songs between a couple of glasses of Rémy Martin cognac. Some-times when he is holding her in his arms and dancing in a slightly drunken haze, he can hardly believe his luck. She has helped him to forget Kiki.

However, Miller is gradually escaping from his hold on her. Her father comes to visit her in Paris and Man Ray looks on in astonishment as Theodore photographs his daughter naked, day after day, in the wildest poses. When Theodore returns to America, Miller photographs Charlie Chaplin in her Parisian studio – and starts an affair with him. He has hardly ever met a woman as funny as her, he later says, which he undoubtedly intends as a compli-ment. In December 1931, Chaplin takes her to St Moritz, where she takes pictures of the socialite Nimet Eloui Bey. Bey exudes an irresistible aura because in 1926, in the gardens of Duino Castle near Trieste, Rainer Maria Rilke plucked a rose for her and in the process supposedly pricked himself on the thorns so badly that he died of blood poisoning. And now in St Moritz she poses for Lee Miller, unaware that her greatest rival is peering through the lens. Her husband, the Egyptian businessman Aziz Eloui Bey, has fallen head over heels in love with Miller, whose father complex leaves her susceptible to well-mannered older men in three-piece suits.

The year 1931 sees not only the film of Erich Maria Remarque's anti-war novel *All Quiet on the Western Front* banned but also Alfred Döblin's explicitly unromantic play *Marriage*. Fittingly, Döblin's wife forbids his lover, Yolla Niclas, from setting foot in their new apartment on the Kaiserdamm in Berlin. This precipitates Alfred's nervous breakdown and he heads off to a spa.

In December Richard Osborn takes a friend to lunch at Anaïs Nin's house in Louveciennes just outside Paris. The friend is Henry Miller. Osborn has sent Nin a few chapters from the manuscript of *Tropic of Cancer*, so she's aware of the kind of man her lawyer has in tow. When the two men leave, she confides her first impressions to her diary: 'He is a man who gets high on life. He is the same as me.' This is the forty-second volume of her monumental diary, which will from this day on be entirely devoted to the forty-one-year-old Henry Miller. On 29 December, Miller makes the journey to Louveciennes again, this time for dinner. And this time he has brought his wife, June. Anaïs Nin stands at the upstairs window of her house, and the sight of the young American entering her front garden takes her breath away. An erotic charge runs through her like an electric shock, but of course she cannot show it. Her chow, Ruby, does the job for her by rubbing up against June's legs all evening.

On 6 January 1932, Anaïs Nin meets June Miller alone for the first time. Henry has told her about June's lesbian affairs and she is almost beside herself with lust. She meets June again on 11, 12, 14 and 18 January. They buy clothes in Paris, go to cafés and snatch kisses when no one's looking. Anaïs begs June to tell her what women do in bed together. June is almost as broke as Henry, so she's grateful when her admirer starts buying her lingerie. On 19 January, she leaves Paris in a rush, carrying suitcases full of new underwear. Anaïs's husband, Hugo Guiler, is briefly relieved, having been sure he'd lost his wife to another woman. His world collapses, however, the very next day, when Anaïs invites Henry to spend the night with them. That evening Hugo writes in the diary he keeps because Anaïs forces him to: 'This life seems like hell to me.' For his wife, on the other hand, the gates of paradise have been flung wide open. For the whole spring following June's departure she is fully focused on Henry, and he on her.

In Dresden, the converted Jew Victor Klemperer and his wife find themselves increasingly ostracised from academic and social life. On 5 April 1932, he notes: 'Nothing but fear around Eva and me now. I can no longer feel.' He says that he is living 'in captivity with her'. Their only remaining hope is to get a house, and on one of their walks they come across a plot of land on a slope overlooking Dresden. The address is Kirschberg 19 ... and as they pass, the cherry trees – the *Kirschbäume* – are indeed blossoming. Things perhaps are about to get better.

It's a springtime dream: up above, a chain of snow-capped mountains; down below, the deep blue of the lake; along the promenades, palm trees in whose leaves the wind is singing the eternal song of the south. In April 1932, Erich Maria Remarque has finally moved to Porto Ronco. Spring comes earlier here and autumn ends later; everything is a touch gentler than in Berlin, including the air. And in the narrow streets and on the piazza everyone behaves with a touch more elegance. That partly explains why Erich, the dandy of all the great writers of the Weimar Republic, loves it here. He loves the *grandezza* with which people sit at the bar in Ascona and watch the clouds scudding across the lake. This is the place for him, the first place that feels like a haven. From his desk he looks down on the lake, sees its waters turn from deep turquoise to a strident blue, sees the palm trees, the flourishing rhododendrons whose roots suck up enough water during autumn's long rainy weeks to convert its energy into a sea of pink blooms the following spring. He takes two walks every day: one in the morning to the Gran Caffè Verbano for his first espresso, stopping at the barbershop on the way for a shave, and the second in the evening for a last drink at the Hotel Schiff. After that, he walks back home through the warmth that has gathered in this mountain-ringed hollow.

The phenomenal success of *The Threepenny Opera* and *Rise and Fall of the City of Mahagonny* have made Kurt Weill rich, although he would be even richer if Bertolt Brecht, the fiery anti-capitalist and ice-cold negotiator, hadn't secured the lion's share for himself. Weill's portion of the flood of royalties nevertheless stretches to a beautiful house in Kleinmachnow just outside Berlin. He is, of course, now married to Lotte Lenya, the glittering star of his songs, with her hoarse voice and frivolity that never lapses into vulgarity. But Weill knows that his wife cannot be caged: he can be sure of her admiration but never of her fidelity. There's nothing as hard as earning the love of your own wife.

At the moment, though, if he is absolutely honest, it is less of a strain and much more fulfilling to spend time with Erika Neher, the wife of the set designer Caspar Neher, who has at last come out as homosexual. Erika is making the most of her newfound freedoms, including occasionally on Kurt Weill's couch. Lenya therefore decides not to move out to Kleinmachnow for the time being; she has better things to do. The decisive factor for Weill, however, is that Harras, his darling sheepdog, is happy there.

In April 1932, Lenya accompanies her husband on a work trip to Vienna, where they rehearse for *Mahagonny*'s premiere. The first time she hears the young tenor Otto von Pasetti-Friedenburg sing, her fate is sealed. She completely forgets that her husband is presiding over the orchestra pit below and is struck down by love, right there on stage. Otto is a beau – tall, vain, self-confident and urbane. 'Apart from his good looks,' the play's Viennese director Hans Heinsheimer concludes, 'there is nothing very remarkable to be said about him.' Yet Lotte searches passionately for what is remarkable about him, and within a few days the two of them are an item, spending every spare minute together.

Weill heads back to Berlin with his tail between his legs, and Pasetti-Friedenburg leaves his wife and child for this Pirate Jenny who has come sailing into his arms. They quickly discover that they share a second passion to go with sex: gambling. After six acclaimed performances of *Mahagonny,* they go to the Riviera to try their luck in the local casinos. Lotte Lenya, officially Lotte Weill, enters her name in the Monte Carlo hotel registers as Karoline Pasetti.

The bestselling German self-help book of 1932, published by Mosse Verlag, is called *Is Divorce Really Necessary?* Lenya reads it with great pleasure on the Riviera and recommends it to her husband.

Living together in Hollywood is proving an increasing trial for Josef von Sternberg and Marlene Dietrich as they gradually get to know each other. He thinks her too capricious; she finds him too demanding. After watching her brush her teeth in the evenings too often, he needs to retreat into his imagination to be able to make her shine in front of the camera. It takes him a great deal of effort to help her deliver on the title of her final silent movie, *The Woman One Longs For*.

Nineteen thirty-two is another year that Simone de Beauvoir and Jean-Paul Sartre largely spend apart. He has been given a teaching job in Le Havre while she is posted to Marseilles, six hundred miles away. De Beauvoir experiences some very unhappy months and seeks to vent her frustration by going on frequent hikes in the mountains along the coast. She knows she has entered into a pact with Sartre based on honesty rather than passion, but she finds it hard to swallow. Even Sartre begins to notice that it isn't just de Beauvoir who needs him; he also needs her. As soon as school finishes on Wednesday, he rushes to the cloakroom to fetch his coat and bag and jumps on the early train to Marseilles. When the sun is shining over the Mediterranean and they sit in a quayside bar for the whole evening, drinking wine, eating oysters and talking philosophy, they feel that they might make a go of this peculiar pact. It is only when Sartre starts telling her about his current affairs that de Beauvoir has to keep her composure, largely because she has nothing much of the same to say for herself yet.

The visitors who sign the guestbook at Lion and Marta Feuchtwanger's new home in Mahlerstrasse in the west of Berlin in 1932 are without exception couples whose marital circumstances are troubled. They include Franz and Helen Hessel, Bertolt Brecht and Helene Weigel, Walter and Ise Gropius, Alfred and Erna Döblin. They all feel comfortable around the Feuchtwangers because the couple are passionate practitioners of what is known as 'open marriage'. There is never any question of love in their relationship, but no question of splitting up either. They have two bedrooms – and make abundant use of them.

*

Our problems can travel with us and even come home with us to roost. In Montgomery, close to the house in which she grew up, Zelda Fitzgerald's schizophrenia flares up again, but Scott is in Hollywood, trying to make some money as a screenwriter. Once again she is admitted to a clinic, smiling her mindless smile, shouting, raging and trying to kill herself, and then she starts writing a book to calm her nerves. The poignantly titled *Save Me the Waltz* describes her long period of suffering in Paris and Swiss clinics. However, her husband flies into a rage when he reads the book; he cannot believe that Zelda has dared to fictionalise these memories. Only he is allowed to do that, he writes to her; he is the 'professional novelist'. In a letter to his editor, Maxwell Perkins, Scott writes: 'However, about fifty thousand words exist [of his novel on the same subject] and this Zelda has heard, and literally one whole section of her novel is an imitation of it, of its rhythm, materials, even statements and speeches.'

These are brutal letters, outbursts of madness as Scott Fitzgerald defends his territory and deals a mortal wound to his wife. Certain subjects, he states, must be completely off limits in her writing: her illness, the sanatoriums, the Côte d'Azur, Switzerland and psychiatry. Scott's argument is that 'All this material belongs to me. None of it is your material.' Astonishing: a sick woman deprived of sovereignty over her own sickness. More astonishing still: F. Scott Fitzgerald will conjure a classic by usurping authority over her illness, turning this 'material' into *Tender Is the Night*.

Other models of marriage are available, however. 'You are only loved when you can show your weakness without provoking strength.' This is Theodor Adorno's experience of the profound love shown to him by Gretel Karplus, a beautiful and proud woman. To which all one can say is: congratulations.

In the summer of 1932, Anaïs Nin rents a flat in the working-class Parisian neighbourhood of Clichy for Henry Miller and his friend

Alfred Perlès. She buys him plates, cutlery, furniture and some recordings of music by his much-loved Johann Sebastian Bach. Thus begins a time 'like in paradise' for Miller. His Eve comes to him almost daily bearing apples, and they revel in their sin. *Quiet Days in Clichy* is the title Miller later gives to his book about this time, before he is expelled from paradise.

Where is the most unlikely place imaginable for Walter Benjamin, this urban intellectual, this Jewish man of the mind, author of *The Origin of German Tragic Drama* and the avant-garde metropolitan prose of *One-Way Street*, whose dark eyes glitter behind inch-thick lenses? Also, where is the one place you really shouldn't go if you're trying to shake off a drug habit and to shun the paltriest ray of sunlight by fleeing into the coolness of a study? You got it – Ibiza.

Yet that is precisely where Walter Benjamin heads in April 1932. On the one hand, this is a simple continuation of his German tragic drama and his own personal one-way street. On the other hand, life, as we know, does not conform to a strict logic.

He has already begun work on his great book, *Berlin Childhood around 1900*. When his Berlin friend Felix Noeggerath tells him about his house on Ibiza, Benjamin packs up his stuff, borrows some travel money from his friends and sets off with very little in his luggage apart from the manuscript of his *Berlin Chronicle* and a few Georges Simenon whodunnits, which he reads on deck after boarding the *Catania*, a Valencia-bound freighter, in Hamburg. Twelve days later, when he steps onto the Ibiza quay, he has no idea where he has escaped to, only what he is fleeing – from the inner demons luring him into committing suicide, from his uncertain professional prospects, his disastrous love life and the antisemitism sweeping the streets of Berlin like harbingers of the approaching storm.

With the Noeggeraths' assistance he finds a simple house, Ses Casetes, in San Antonio. His study window offers a magnificent view out over the gleaming blue sea. Benjamin is enchanted by the archaic architecture and the leisurely pace of a rural lifestyle that appears to have endured unchanged for centuries. He admires the island and its inhabitants for 'their tranquillity and their beauty'. After having been bedridden with depression in Berlin and Paris, all of a sudden Benjamin is getting up at seven every day. He walks the short distance down to the beach for a swim and then leans back against a pine tree with a book in his hands. When the temperature rises sharply in late morning, he goes inside to read and write, as he reports to Margarete Karplus, the soulmate who unfortunately chose to marry his friend Adorno. There is no electric light on Ibiza, and no newspapers. Instead there is time and freedom, and Benjamin is initially capable of savouring this. This is in large part down to a young German-Russian woman, Olga Parem, who has arrived in San Antonio; they met the year before at his friend Franz Hessel's.

They meet again on the beach at Ibiza, and they kiss. Olga describes something that seems out of character for Benjamin but is the result of love. He laughs. He laughs all the time when they are together. 'His laughter was magical,' Olga writes. 'When he laughed, the world opened up.'

They persuade a fisherman to take them out to sea, and every evening they clamber aboard his boat and cruise along the coast into the never-ending sunset. Walter falls violently in love. He thinks he has found salvation. Yet the more Olga realises that the man she is embracing is in freefall, the more she withdraws from him, and Benjamin's laughter soon dies. After just four weeks, in a ludicrous attempt to keep her, he asks Olga if she will marry him here on Ibiza. She turns him down, first partially, then entirely.

And the higher the sun rises over the island, the darker Benjamin's soul gets. After his rejection, he looks with growing panic to his fast-approaching fortieth birthday on 15 July. He dreads having to take stock and find so little on the plus side of the ledger. One last time he tries to convince Olga of his undying love, but to no avail.

Benjamin tumbles into despair and writes to his friend Gershom Scholem that he wants to celebrate his fortieth birthday in Nice with an 'odd fellow', by which he means the Grim Reaper. Olga says she will come again for his birthday, but he smokes so much hash with a fleeting acquaintance on the days leading up to it that he spends the big day itself totally stoned.

At around midnight on 17 July he boards the ferry to Mallorca and travels from there to Nice. It's a hot night without a breath of breeze over the water and the sky is overcast, motionless, hopeless. Benjamin has left Ibiza with the intention of killing himself – and he does, in fact, write his will in the Hôtel du Petit Parc in Nice. He sits in his sweltering little room, unable to sleep as night licks at the grimy walls. He knows that intelligence increases at night, but so does stupidity. Everything remains the same, just darker. He sits down at the table again to hone the wording of his will. He bequeaths a silver dagger to Elisabeth Hauptmann, Brecht's colleague and lover. Other than that he has little to give away, apart from the Paul Klee watercolour *Angelus Novus*, which he later reinterprets as the 'Angel of History'; this he leaves to Gershom Scholem. Then he sets about writing farewell letters, including one to his first true love, Jula Cohn: 'You know that I once loved you very much, and even in dying, life has no greater gifts to grant than my moments of suffering over you have given it.'

We do not know how Walter Benjamin managed to muster a renewed desire to live after he'd written this will and these goodbye letters during those moments of suffering in a run-down hotel room in Nice on that oppressively muggy and cloudy 27 July 1932.

What is Hermann Hesse doing during these stormy, hot summer months of 1932? He puts on his linen trousers and light shirt, resembling one of the free-living residents of Monte Verità on the next lake, and weeds the garden for hours and hours. He writes, 'This weeding takes up all my days, though it is absolutely free of any material incentive or speculation because the gardening work yields no more than three or four baskets of vegetables altogether. There is, however, a spiritual dimension to this work. One kneels on the ground and does the plucking as if in worship, purely for the sake of a form of worship in constant regeneration because by the time three or four beds are clean, the first has turned green again.' This is another way for Hesse to escape from the world, by surrendering to the cycle of the seasons.

That summer Kurt Tucholsky publishes the following poem in *Die Weltbühne*:

> If you and she live jointly
> You feel immensely lonely.
> If, however, you're alone
> Life can chill you to the bone.

He has returned to Ticino, the region around Lake Maggiore in the shadow of the Alps that he has grown to love under the influence of his 'Lottchen', Lisa Matthias. His fondness for the lady, though not for the lake, has dimmed. In Switzerland it is Hedwig Müller, a doctor from Zurich, who attends devotedly to his physical and psychological well-being. So devotedly, in fact, that he is almost tempted to relocate to Switzerland – he senses that the air in Berlin is becoming increasingly unbreathable since the Nazi press launched a campaign against him as a defiantly critical Jewish author. Her first name sticks in his throat a bit, so he calls her 'Nuuna'. He is in the habit of giving nicknames to the women he picks, in order to make them his own creations.

Storms of Passion, a romantic drama that goes on general release in German cinemas in early 1932, includes a song by Friedrich Hollaender called 'I Don't Know Who I Belong To'. On their way out of the screening, moviegoers find themselves whistling this anthem of indecision in the face of an ever-growing pressure to make up one's mind. In 1932, Hollaender has finally made up his own mind, choosing Hedi Schoop, a singer and dancer at his Tingel-Tangel theatre in Berlin, to be his wife. The last two cabaret shows Hollaender and Schoop stage at the Tingel-Tangel are tellingly named *High Time* and, just before the theatre closes down, *Once Upon a Time*.

In July 1932, Charlie Chaplin's surprising answer to the question of who he belongs to is Paulette Goddard. After several marriages, several children and untold flings in Hollywood and the rest of the world, he meets the twenty-two-year-old actress on a friend's yacht. She laughs at his jokes, but there's nothing novel about that. What is novel is that she also takes an interest in his heart. The only thing about her that bothers him is her hair. He hates the current trend for platinum-blonde. When Paulette reverts to brunette, he even kisses her in public – on 19 September at Los Angeles airport, before he catches a flight from Hollywood to New York. The next day, photos of this kiss are emblazoned across front pages around the world. Paulette Goddard will one day marry Erich Maria Remarque, but we have not got there yet.

Neither has Erich Maria Remarque. He realises in the summer of 1932 that his inner torments and sense of uncertainty have emigrated to Switzerland with him. Yes, even in one of the most beautiful places in Europe, in Ascona's warm bay along the sun-drenched Maggia River delta, with thousands of francs in his account and a plethora of Van Goghs, Renoirs and Monets on his walls, he still cannot be happy. All is not quiet on the southern front. Of course, he and Jutta Zambona haven't really consummated their separation, despite the two years that have passed since their divorce. Also, he isn't very fond of his new lover, Ruth Albu. She spends an entire winter and an entire spring fighting for his love, furious at his inability to disengage from his ex-wife. She writes to him: 'You have no right to possess two people. I don't even have half a person.'

He responds with a contrite letter from his house in Porto Ronco – the property Ruth found for him. He's aware that his message is not the one she is hoping for. 'I feel as if I am floating on a slowly melting ice floe. I can say, yes perhaps I am incapable of love, but who longs to be capable of it more than I? Yes, I am incapable of loving the way you want and need to be loved.' In August the young relationship between Remarque and Albu collapses. He starts to drink even more, while she starts a new life, writing in her farewell letter to him: 'You would like to love, but you will never know love.'

Night after night, Lotte Lenya and her new lover, the blond tenor Otto von Pasetti-Friedenburg, go to the casino. Every morning, Otto tells her that he has found a new 'dead cert' method for the roulette table. Regrettably, every one of these new methods fails, but her belief in him blossoms anew each day. And where does the money they blow every evening come from? From Kleinmachnow, near Berlin. From Lotte's husband, Kurt Weill.

The Mann family travels to Nida on the Curonian Spit again in the summer of 1932 to enjoy their new holiday home. From his study, Thomas looks far out over the lagoon where the wind furls the waves and the great-crested grebes play their eternal games of peekaboo along the shore. But, he thinks as he watches them, is it possible that something might go under and never reappear? He's working on an essay about the current political situation. Even here, in what used to be the most north-easterly corner of the German Empire, there has been a radical shift in the climate. During the Reichstag elections in Königsberg, SA thugs hunted down political opponents and murdered them. Thomas writes an open letter, 'What We Must Demand', in a mood of new clarity brought on by finding a strange parcel in his letterbox in Nida shortly after he arrived at the seaside. It was a burnt copy of his novel *Buddenbrooks*, sent to him anonymously as 'punishment' for having issued public warnings about the threat of a Nazi regime.

Lion Feuchtwanger and his wife, Marta, have also come to East Prussia this August – to the same boundless dunes of the Spit. The two couples see each other on the beach once, but Lion Feuchtwanger notes resentfully in his diary that Katia Mann deliberately looked the other way. They are not welcome at the Manns' court (a year later, beside a different sea, an encounter will be unavoidable). The Feuchtwangers drive back to Berlin the next day, and the idle Lion praises his wife for racing the whole way home without a break, leaving him free to doze in the passenger seat. It is the kind of feat that impresses him.

At the beginning of September, the Manns also have to head home to Munich as their youngest two children are starting school. One final evening, swathed in scarves against the cold, they admire the sun as it sinks sparkling into the sea, like a frothing golden headache pill. Boarding the ferry to Crantz the next morning, they gaze back one last time at their blue house high on the dune, wave to their assembled staff on the quayside and the villagers who have gathered to say goodbye to their most famous guest and his family. Even a slightly rattled Thomas briefly raises a hand in farewell, as if he senses that he will never again see his house in Nida.

Only one person can force Joseph Stalin to beat a retreat: his wife, Nadezhda. Whenever she flies into a rage because of his affairs and his affectations or because she can't believe he's letting millions of people starve to death in Ukraine, he locks himself in the bathroom of their summerhouse in Sochi. He sits down on the edge of the bathtub as she screams blue murder outside: 'You're torturing your wife, your son and the whole Russian people.' His response is to double lock the door. One of the greatest mass murderers in history barricades himself in his bathroom for fear of his furious wife.

He rescued her when she fell into the Black Sea at the age of three. Later, at sixteen, she fell in love with her rescuer, who had just returned emaciated from banishment to Siberia. A former choir boy, he sang her arias from *Rigoletto*. She was spellbound. Later, he sometimes wrote to her too – 'Dear Tatka, I miss you so terribly. Tatochka, I'm so lonely. Don't stay away so long.' – but gradually this ceased.

Their son, Vasily, was born in 1920, their daughter, Svetlana, in 1926; Nadezhda aborted ten further pregnancies at Stalin's insistence. During the twenties her medical file got fatter and fatter:

continual abdominal pains, head-splitting migraines, bouts of severe depression, panic attacks. Doctors tried to calm her with caffeine tablets, but these had the opposite effect. Remote diagnosis long after the event would define her condition as manic-depressive. A Black Sea inside her.

It probably doesn't help her much that Stalin is as naturally impulsive, thin-skinned and proud as his wife. Yet between fits of rage and drama they repeatedly pledge eternal love to each other. An impossible couple – both of them self-centred, callous and hot-tempered, perhaps too alike to be able to experience lasting happiness together. But when Stalin turns cruel, Nadia plunges into dark depression.

What does he think hell is? Simone de Beauvoir asks him after they've brushed their teeth and before they go to sleep. Sartre sits up in bed again and says, 'Hell is other people before your first cup of coffee.' Noticing her sour expression, he adds, 'I was talking about other people. Not you, Simone. Goodnight.'

Not even Céline, the most cold-hearted and antisemitic of all French authors, can hate all day long. Intermittently, he loves, or at least he pretends to. Louis-Ferdinand Destouches, to give him his full name, is the son of a violent, itinerant financial accountant and an unfeeling, disturbed, cleanliness-obsessed haberdasher, and thus the product of a tragic and merciless childhood, growing up in the most precarious of circumstances. 'You have no heart,' his mother tells him, when it is trauma that has sealed his heart shut. Céline knows that 'real hatred comes from deep down, from a defenceless childhood crushed with work. That's the hatred that kills you.' So all the softness and gentleness inside him were already dead before two stray bullets in the First World War left new wounds in his soul and head, from which blood and bile will gush for the rest of his life. He also has lifelong tinnitus, a result of a grenade exploding next to him in a trench. His eyes, which saw a great deal when he was a child, allowed him to be a doctor and then, during the supposedly Roaring Twenties, to plot *Journey to the End of the Night*, the novel that was to make his fame. It is one long apocalypse, rife with plague, festering wounds and the language of the gutter, a debut novel that pulsates with pounding rage and breath-taking prose, its sentences sometimes threatening to buckle and collapse as if they had walked into a hail of bullets.

Here, heroism is portrayed as naked violence, and cowardice as the last refuge of humanity. While Céline works as a doctor attending to the poor of Clichy and finishes his great anti-war novel in the spring and summer of 1932, he attempts to cleanse himself of the book's dirt by pursuing a number of affairs. He was planning to dedicate his novel to the American dancer Elizabeth Craig, who has been involved with the gaunt fellow for some time, but while correcting the proofs he considers whether to dedicate it to some more recent conquest instead. He's a horny devil, desperate to sleep with any woman he finds 'nice'.

Fear is the subject of his novel. Naked, terrified, heart-bursting fear. In the love letters he writes in parallel to the novel, he acts the unflinching lover – or at least tries to. The tone of the letters never varies: ecstasy about the woman's 'bum', accompanied by disgusting slurs against Jews and Communists; bossy orders and flattering compliments, interspersed with instructions about hygiene. His advice to his lovers is to sink their claws into any man they can find and exploit him 'sensually and financially'. At the end of every letter he writes 'I love you very much', which in his case means no more than 'Yours sincerely'. Writing to his young German girlfriend, Erika Irrgang, with whom he lived in his flat at 92 Rue Lepic for a few weeks in spring 1932 and who now lives in Breslau, he sometimes concludes with 'Heil Hitler' or 'Heil Göring'. He thinks this is funny.

Things get a little complicated in September. Elizabeth Craig is still travelling, the great book that has so tormented him is finished and he's bored. So he invites Erika to visit and even sends her a postal order for 250 francs to pay for the journey. He simply cannot live without her bottom, he writes, 'so we'll try to have a bit of fun in Paris'. As she's poised to depart, she receives a second telegram saying that she can't come after all because he needs to go to Geneva urgently. He doesn't; he just needs to go to bed with a different woman. Five days before, he met the twenty-seven-year-old Viennese gymnastics teacher Cillie Pam at the Café de la Paix. From the café he took her on a walk, and they chatted in a mixture of French, German and English. The next evening, they went out to La Coupole in Montparnasse. They spend every evening and night together for the next two weeks, going for walks, to the cinema, to the Moulin Rouge, to bed. Cillie confesses that she's married and Jewish and that she has a son. Céline is so jubilant to learn that his freedom is not endangered that he cooks her pasta. In 1932, his antisemitism does not yet extend to the bedroom. Cillie soon has to go back to Vienna. As they say goodbye at the station she weeps. He doesn't.

She writes him an ardent letter on the train. He writes back: 'You have a bum as superb as it is unforgettable.' Cillie will later say that Céline always studied everything very closely during a meal in a restaurant and during sex with her, a steak as intently as her thighs. And yet he took barely any pleasure in the actual act of eating or lovemaking.

Lee Miller's fame is growing – as a photographer. Her modelling days are over and so is her time as Man Ray's muse. After she let Charlie Chaplin seduce her she seduced the Egyptian millionaire Aziz Eloui Bey, followed in the summer of 1932 by Julien Levy, her smart New York gallerist whose exhibitions of her work are starting to raise her profile back home. So on 11 October, Miller leaves Paris on the train from Saint-Lazare station to Cherbourg. Above all, though, she is leaving Man Ray, the great photographer, her teacher and now her competitor. She is the love of his life, he writes, and: 'I shall wait for you always.' He takes a self-portrait with a noose around his neck and a gun to his head just as Lee is boarding her New York-bound ship in Cherbourg. The next photo of her is taken with a self-timer: 'Miller family at Thanksgiving.' And so ends a bewildering year with lots of famous lovers for the now quite famous Lee Miller: with a turkey dinner at home, side by side with her darling Pop.

But what about poor abandoned Man Ray? He begins working on his best-known painting, *The Lovers*. His plan is to paint a pair of gigantic lips floating in the sky. To drive away the memory of Lee Miller, he remembers the red lips of her predecessor, Kiki de Montparnasse, who once pressed her freshly painted lips to the collar of his white shirt at a Surrealist party. He noticed their imprint late that night as he removed his shirt, then photographed it. Now that Lee has left him, he takes these photos out of his drawer. 'I was pursued by one of these enlarged photos of a pair of lips, like a lingering dream,' he says. He pins a huge canvas eight feet wide to the wall directly above his bed. Every morning before he leaves for his studio he adds a few touches to Kiki's lips while standing in his pyjamas on the bed in which, until recently, he would lie with Lee. A form of exorcism, but the painting never quite clicks.

The Romanisches Café in Berlin buzzes with energy every afternoon and evening. This is where the spirit of the age lives and breathes in those blazing years before everything goes dark. This is where, every evening, the world is destroyed, saved and created anew. This is the place to see Kurt Tucholsky and Joseph Roth, Erich Kästner and Max Beckmann, Gottfriend Benn and Alfred Döblin, Ruth Landshoff and Claire Waldoff, Vicki Baum and Marlene Dietrich, Lotte Laserstein and Marianne Breslauer, Gustaf Gründgens and Brigitte Helm. The women and men at the other forty-six tables are also well known.

As the clouds of fascism gather and begin to obscure the sky, and the city streets start to feel different at dusk, Mascha Kaléko is staring pensively into space one evening. Her hands fiddle with her small red hat, and her hatless hair is as tangled as her senses. She doesn't know what to do with herself or with all the poetry that's whizzing around her head. It's late and, as so often, her husband, Saul, has gone home early, so she just sits there, eyes peeled and ears pricked, letting the noise and the scraps of conversation and the summer flow through her, waiting for a few words to snag on her inner weirs, thrash about and turn into verse. She loves this rush, although she knows that it comes at the cost of subsequent disillusionment, as in her poem 'The Next Morning':

> I got dressed. You scanned my legs.
> The air smelled of coffee drunk long ago.

She's still working at the Jewish Workers' Welfare Centre and she's still married, but she's obviously starting to cast an eye elsewhere at night; it is this tug of war between the disappointments of her escapades and the longing she feels in the comfort of her home that make her literary voice so popular.

Virtually every newspaper prints her charming poems with titles like 'City Love' or 'Sunday Morning'. So light is their take on the minor miseries of daily life that an entire city is becoming hooked on them. Is it possible, she thinks as she sips her red wine, that longing and disappointment are more closely paired than anything else in this world? All of a sudden, Franz Hessel, the famous flâneur, comes over to her table. He is short and bald and looks like a Buddha. His brown eyes, cheerful face and full lips evoke a mix of Eastern meditation with the epicurean attitude of a French gourmet. He also has a perfect ear for well-composed verse.

Hessel introduces himself as an editor at Rowohlt, the publishing house, and says he has been cutting her poems out of the *Vossische Zeitung*, *Querschnitt* and *Uhu* for months. 'Could you imagine, dear Mrs Kaléko,' Hessel begins in his magnificently antiquated and gauche manner. 'Could you imagine' – here he bows – 'publishing a book of your poems with us?' 'Do sit down,' Kaléko says, stunned, trying to take in her good fortune, and when Hessel turns his kind, warm eyes on her, she says, 'I can imagine nothing better.' They order another Pernod and immediately start brainstorming a title.

By the time she gets home very late that night, Kaléko is certain that her first collection of poetry is going to be published and that it will be called *The Lyrical Shorthand Pad: Verses from Daily Life*. She can't contain her joy. She dances home through the streets, drunk on the future, picks up a small grey feather that a thrush has left on the pavement and sticks it in her red hat.

In autumn 1932, Bertolt Brecht and Helene Weigel's marriage hits its most dangerous crisis. Once again, Brecht has been playing with fire. For the premiere of his new play, *The Mother*, he cast Helene Weigel in the title role, but the maid was played by Margarete Steffin, a twenty-four-year-old Communist from rural Brandenburg who is cut from the kind of cloth Brecht adores. She's a worker's daughter and a fervent class warrior, hard-working, indomitable, devoted and imbued with the ethos of modesty. She has two plaits but only one mission, and this round the clock, even though she has tuberculosis; everything – rehearsals, performances, their trysts, stays in hospital and at spas – has to be arranged around her illness. To enable her to shine in her first stage role against these many odds, the practised sadist Brecht prescribed her elocution lessons with his wife. So the two women were very much on speaking terms when they met, and yet the war that has smouldered between them throughout 1932 has been a largely silent affair.

We mustn't forget Elisabeth Hauptmann, Brecht's closest colleague, secretary and inspiration. She had been a model of self-denial when the master told her he had to look out for his family, but this time she found herself a bystander as a younger rival waltzed right past her and into Brecht's bed. Brecht didn't have time to bother about snags in his elaborate romantic web, and so, as always, she bent to his will. Brecht has forced his family to move home twice because he insisted on housing the constantly coughing Margarete in his apartments, and Helene is adamant about protecting her family from infection. She also knows that Margarete poses a chronic threat to her husband's heart.

The dam of his self-control broke when he seduced the fervent Communist in May during her stay at a Russian sanatorium. The lilac blooms there were spectacular; they always intoxicated his senses and so did young Margarete's wistful gaze. From then on he took Steffin wherever he went, including to Utting by the Ammersee where, for the first time in his life, he bought a house with a garden by the lake and tried to establish a stable web of relationships involving his family and his sick lover. It didn't work out: Helene and their children headed home early. Initially Brecht and Steffin let their passions run wild in the pretty little hut with the gentle lake outside, pears ripening slowly around the house and the clouds high above it all. This relationship, in May in Russia and in August in Bavaria, is probably the most physical Brecht ever had. Full of testosterone and a little tired, he writes: 'To do again what we have done so often is what impels us towards each other.' He also writes a short message to Hanns Eisler, inviting him to visit: 'Don't you want to take a look in Grete's blue eyes?'

Eisler doesn't come, though, and then Margarete Steffin gets pregnant. Brecht tries to force her to have an abortion, citing her illness and her personal circumstances, especially her not having enough money to look after the child. Of course, this is all subterfuge. What terrifies him is that Helene will ask for a divorce and he will lose his 'soldier-like companion' who has devoted her life to him and his desires and political battles. A baby would be a massive complication. Brecht reasons with Steffin for hours. She cries, but he is relentless.

Steffin is traumatised by two previous abortions in 1928 and 1930 (twins the first time) when she had the feeling that the men weren't fit to be fathers. This time, though, she is sure. All the same, Brecht manages to persuade her that it would be better for their relationship if she aborted their baby. Margarete obeys his logic tearily, as is evident from some lines of poetry she writes at the time:

Even the greatest love has no
Advice for us when bread is rare.
When out of work we must ensure
That there is no child in our care.

Brecht makes sure of things after his own fashion. He writes lengthy letters to Helene telling her not to overcomplicate matters, that he will love her for ever and so forth. What's more, he says, he has a lot of work right now and is 'scared of private conflicts'. These are the typical male conflict-avoidance strategies he serves up to his wife. And to his lover, as a reward for the abortion, he delivers an appointment for an operation on her tuberculosis-ridden lungs with the famous Professor Franz-Ferdinand Sauerbruch at Berlin's Charité hospital. Thus she enters the years of darkness childless but breathing slightly more easily. And Brecht sticks to his motto: 'In a storm, keep your head down.'

For the Nazis, Dr Charlotte Wolff is the incarnation of the trinity of all evil: not only is she Jewish but a socialist and a lesbian too. She is therefore forced to quit her job providing birth-control advice in Berlin's public health system. Her boss regretfully informs her that he can no longer defend her employment due to the political situation. She subsequently tries to make ends meet by working at an electrical physics institute in Neukölln. Very soon, though, she is staring out of the window of the institute in shock as hordes of young men in Nazi uniforms march along the road outside, brandishing long banners with the unambiguous message 'Death to the Jews'.

Henceforth Charlotte, who knows that she is 'unmistakably Jewish in appearance', feels safe only indoors or beside her partner, Katherine, who is tall, blonde and German. They never hold hands in public, though. Berliners might have tolerated this in the late twenties, but in 1932 it would be unpredictably provocative. Together they attend a palm-reading course; as their country undergoes increasingly radical change, they learn that each person's hands are a landscape whose lines never change. Can Charlotte read the signs of their approaching farewells in Katherine's palm? Katherine's father is urging her to leave her Jewish lover as soon as possible to protect herself, and she follows his advice, leaving Charlotte stumbling through the final weeks of 1932 in a state of numbness.

Robert Musil writes in his diary: 'I am the man without qualities, but no one can tell. I have all the good, conventional feelings and of course I also know how to behave, but there is no inner identification.' His wife tries her best with positive psychology. If he sits down at the dinner table with a sour expression on his face, Martha cries, 'Try a smile!' But although Robert is such a brilliant exponent of irony, the laughter muscles are the only ones he has never exercised. Yet despite his aversion to life, despite his writer's block and despair and unexperienced feelings, he sends the first volume of his novel *The Man Without Qualities* to the Berlin publishing house Rowohlt in the autumn of 1930. When he gets back from the post office, Martha detects a flicker of a smile on his face.

One year later the Musils move from Vienna to Berlin. Robert correctly suspects that he may rediscover there the unrest of 1913 that he depicted in *The Man Without Qualities*. He and Martha live, or rather survive, at the Pension Stern guesthouse on the Kurfürstendamm: they don't have any money. She tries to rustle up a meal while he sits at the desk and smokes (he has switched to nicotine-free cigarettes). As in Vienna, Martha is housewifely, warm and quiet; and as in Vienna, he is depressive, cold and irate. She makes him feel self-conscious and inhibited. At the same time, she protects his sensitive nerves from the strains of the outside world. He loves her.

In the dim light of that Berlin guesthouse, with Martha asleep, Musil grants his hero Ulrich a new form of love when his sister, Agathe, comes onto the scene. Sometimes, as Musil admits to the psychologist René Spitz during this time, there is a fraternal aspect to his love for Martha. In December 1932, the second volume of

The Man Without Qualities is published. The publisher's blurb says of the hero, Ulrich: 'The question of finding the right path leads him into the thousand-year empire of love, where the author recreates the myth of forbidden love, the archetype of all mysticism, in the experiences of the siblings Ulrich and Agathe.' And how! Ulrich explains to his sister that 'at least half the history of the world is a love story'. To which she replies to her dear brother that their story 'is the very last love story there can be. We will be something like the last Mohicans of love.'

November 1932 in Berlin. Sleet, wind, cold. The political news is more and more calamitous. SA troops march through the streets. Jewish intellectuals openly discuss emigration. 'The abhorrent complexity of the situation. Hitler still has a big mouth,' notes Klaus Mann on 7 November in his dark, stuffy room at the Fasaneneck guesthouse in Charlottenburg.

He is in a lethal mood, drifting around the bars and brothels, living on cold sausages from a jar, meeting up with past lovers and searching manically for cocaine. When one night he goes to the Six Days of Berlin track-cycling race, he catches sight of his old flame Gustaf Gründgens but looks away before the actor can recognise him. It's no good, though. At night he dreams 'tenderly' of him, his one true Mephisto. The next day his sister Erika and Annemarie Schwarzenbach, who is hopelessly, desperately in love with her, come round and they go to the Hotel Kempinski to eat oysters and live the bohemian lifestyle as a means of warding off the demons that are slowly gathering over Berlin like a black storm front.

That summer they were in Venice at the posh Grand Hotel des Bains, recovering together from the shock of their dear friend Ricki Hallgarten's suicide, smoking and drinking and swimming. But Klaus and Annemarie couldn't cope with their sadness either there or here in this drowning city. Klaus Mann wrote a poignant text about Ricki Hallgarten titled 'Radicalism of the Heart'. It is, in fact, a self-portrait: 'But he thought that life itself was a curse he could no longer bear. And yet he still loved life. He tried with all his might to ensure that this love prevailed over this darkness.'

Even in these dark November days, Klaus and Annemarie are trying to ensure that life and love prevail in Berlin. It is not easy, and so after cocaine, the younger Manns introduce Annemarie, this inconsolable angel, to morphine. 'Big session at E.'s,' Klaus repeatedly notes after visiting Erika. It binds the three of them ever closer – Erika, the strong one, always in the middle; Klaus and Annemarie, sinking on either side of her. Although it seems easy to take drugs together at night, each faces the harshness of life alone the next morning.

Alma Mahler-Werfel sums up the offspring of great German writers like this: 'Thomas Mann's children homosexual, lesbian; Wedekind's daughter a degenerate slut; Wassermann's children wastrels and whores.'

It is 8 November 1932 in Moscow and a light snow is falling. Inside the Kremlin, Nadezhda and Joseph Stalin prepare in different manners for that evening's dinner to celebrate the fifteenth anniversary of the Russian revolution. Stalin and Molotov sign lists of the rebels, traitors and suspects to be liquidated the next day; Nadezhda takes a bath. She even applies make-up, something she rarely does, puts on the black dress embroidered with red roses that her sister Anna has brought her from Berlin. She performs a twirl in front of the mirror. Anna claps and sticks a red rose from the garden in Nadezhda's dark hair.

After completing his work, Stalin comes to the meal with his close entourage. He is wearing a threadbare uniform jacket and his grey hair is a mess as he sits down sullenly at the table. Georgian food is served in his honour: lamb, salted fish, a little salad. After spotting his wife at the table, he takes no further notice of her. At this, she starts flirting with her neighbour and loudly discussing how deeply she feels for the Ukrainian farmers who are dying of hunger.

Stalin sits opposite her, tossing back one vodka after another. Then he too begins to flirt, with Galia Yegorova, who is visibly flattered and doesn't object when he starts to roll little balls of bread and flick them down the front of her dress.

Nadezhda watches all of this in horror from the other side of the table, her anger rising. She speaks more and more loudly about her husband's brutal treatment of the farmers. Desperate to interrupt her, he raises his glass and cries, 'To the extermination of all state enemies! *Na zdvarovje!*' All the other dinner guests immediately raise their glasses – all apart from Nadezhda. He calls out to her, 'Hey, drink with us!' To which she responds, 'My name is not Hey.' Icy silence. Everyone freezes. Nadezhda gets up and storms out of the room. Molotov's wife hurries after her to calm her down while, inside the room, the men trade loud laments about the moodiness of hysterical women.

Late that night Joseph Stalin goes back to their apartment. No one knows for sure whether he spent the intervening hours with the lady next to him or carrying on the party with his guests at a dacha. All we know is that he is so drunk he collapses onto the camp bed that he, the ruler of a gigantic empire, loves to sleep on, far from his wife's bedchamber. When he emerges from heavy dreams at eleven o'clock the next morning, the maid tells him that his wife has shot herself during the night.

His legs almost give way. He runs to her room at the other end of the hallway and finds her dead on her bed, still wearing the black dress with red roses on it. Blood is trickling from her mouth. Beside her lies the small Mauser pistol her brother brought her from Berlin, and on the floor is the wilted rose that fell out of her hair.

'I couldn't save you,' he is reported to have sobbed at her graveside. He doesn't feel guilty, just betrayed. 'She deserted me like an enemy,' he says. 'The children forgot her within a few days, but I will be scarred for my whole life.' The humiliation he feels after his wife's suicide destroys the last vestiges of humanity inside him. From 9 November 1932 onwards he sees everyone as a plotter to be eradicated.

Alma Mahler-Werfel accompanies her husband Franz on his

reading tour of Germany. She hates him with increasing fervour for his Jewishness, his slenderness and his slowness.

On their arrival in Breslau on 10 December 1932 she meets a man more to her taste – Adolf Hitler, who is holding a rally the same evening. Alma asks her husband to do his reading without her. She takes a seat in the hotel dining room, empties a bottle of champagne and then goes to see Hitler. 'I waited for hours to see his face. And rightly so – what a face! No Duce – a stripling.' In the hotel lounge Alma raves about Hitler's speech late into the night after her husband finally gets home from his reading. They run into Hitler, who is staying at the same hotel. Alma's eyes light up and she asks Franz, 'So, what do you think of him?' To which he replies, 'Not particularly nice.'

Heinrich Mann is at last leading a more relaxed life since moving to Fasanenstrasse 61 in Berlin with his lover Nelly Kröger in December 1932. *The Blue Angel*, the film adaptation of his novel *Man of Straw*, has brought him fame and a trickle of money. He is writing the life story of a barmaid – the poorly disguised life story of Nelly Kröger, in fact. He wants to call the book *A Serious Life*. Nelly irons his suits and shirts, but he'd rather not be seen with her at his side when he's wearing them – no, that would be a little too embarrassing. Nelly often goes off to see Rudi Carius, a twenty-five-year-old Communist, in Berlin-Wedding. Heinrich is aware of this and apparently glad not to have to take care of *everything*. He's sixty now and a little tired.

In December 1932, Marguerite Respinger marries not Ludwig Wittgenstein but Talla Sjögren. Wittgenstein had accompanied Marguerite to the post office in Constance on 28 September 1930, to mail him a parcel containing two jumpers. Ludwig felt a first pang of jealousy then – and justifiably so, as it turns out. An hour before the wedding he pays Marguerite a visit at her home in Vienna. 'My despair reached its climax,' Marguerite later writes, 'when Ludwig sought me out and said, "You're going on a voyage, and the sea will be rough. Always stay in touch with me and you will never drown."

For years I had been like soft wax in his hands that he wanted to shape into his ideal.' Now the candle has gone out.

In the summer of 1932, Ise Gropius and her lover Herbert Bayer revealed their affair to her husband Walter, with the express wish of continuing to see each other. Gropius, the old Bauhaus master, has dealt with the situation brilliantly, showing great consideration and full sympathy towards all involved. Towards his wife. Towards his rival and close friend. Towards Bayer's wife, who is so furious that she wants to take their three-year-old child away from him. He keeps telling his unfaithful wife how sorry he is about the difficult situation in which her lover finds himself, having deceived both his wife and his mentor.

In December 1932 Walter Gropius and Ise go off to the snowy slopes of Arosa. She likes it so much there that she asks her husband if she can stay on for four more weeks with Herbert Bayer. Of course, Walter says, but maybe only for a fortnight? Married life is a matter of making the right compromises, and Walter, who was once married to Alma Mahler, is battle-hardened in that regard.

June Miller comes back to Paris at the end of 1932, but it isn't clear whether she's intending to save her marriage or to destroy it once and for all. She moves in with Henry in Clichy, but prior to her arrival he takes his diaries and manuscripts to his friend Anaïs Nin's so his wife can't read them. Henry and June row until dawn; Anaïs joins them once and lies on the bed fully clothed, watching the couple become increasingly drunk and insulting.

It is here that June Miller finally draws the line. While Henry is sleeping off his drunken stupor, she writes him a note on a piece of toilet paper: 'Please file for divorce as soon as possible.' He sticks this in his notebook alongside a 799-franc receipt for passage on a ship to New York, paid for with money from Anaïs. On seeing his notebook with this farewell collage, June picks up her suitcase, walks to the door and proclaims scornfully, 'At last you've got the final chapter of your book.'

1933

When Margarete Steffin awakes from her troubled dreams on a private ward at Berlin's Charité hospital on 1 January 1933, she is greeted with a cup of coffee and a brusque 'Happy New Year'. She picks up a pencil and a piece of paper and writes a sonnet for her lover: 'Today I dreamt I lay beside you'. But in her dream Brecht first seduced her, then he ran off.

We must pay a visit to a second patient this New Year's Day. Ruth Landshoff is lying impatiently in a Swiss sanatorium.

Landshoff embodied 1920s Berlin like no other woman. Born into an upper-middle-class family as Ruth Levy in 1904, during that period she was everything at the same time. First, she posed for Oskar Kokoschka and later for the avant-garde photographer Umbo; she was a dancer, a regular at the Romanisches Café and in Schöneberg's gay bars, a racing driver, an actress in *Nosferatu* and a journalist. Then she wrote *The Many and the One*, a novel about the thrill and the shimmering spirit of the decade of which she was the true heroine.

She played croquet with Thomas Mann and cards with Gerhart Hauptmann, and had affairs with Charlie Chaplin and Mopsa Sternheim, with Oskar Kokoschka, Annemarie Schwarzenbach and Erika Mann, as well as flings with Josephine Baker and Karl Vollmoeller, who was the secret impresario of Max Reinhardt and Josef von Sternberg, whose flat on Pariser Platz was a focal point of Berlin culture. Her closest female friends were the three most eccentric European noblewomen of the late 1920s: Marchesa Luisa Casati in Venice, Maud Thyssen in Lugano and Princesse de Polignac in Paris. The photographer Marianne Breslauer belonged to her circle, as did that dazzlingly glamorous couple, Lisa and Gottfried von Cramm, and the publisher Samuel Fischer was her uncle.

Following a broken engagement with an English aristocrat, Ruth met a posh banker from the Reichs Credit Society at the Hotel Adlon, a man with a very long name: Hans Ludwig David

Wilhelm Friedrich Heinrich Graf Yorck von Wartenburg. On only their second date she started calling him Sonny. They got married in 1930, their best men the Swiss art dealer Christoph Bernoulli and Ruth's old friend Francesco von Mendelssohn, who was involved with Gustaf Gründgens at the time.

In autumn 1932, however, Ruth's whirlwind of a life came to a juddering halt. She developed bone tuberculosis and excruciating pains in her spine. First she was admitted to a hospital near St Moritz and then she was moved to a specialist clinic in Leysin, south-east of Lake Geneva, where she has had to lie still for weeks on end. Occasionally, parcels of chocolate arrive from her friend Annemarie Schwarzenbach. It is here, in a remote corner of Switzerland, racked with pain and short of hope, that Ruth Gräfin Yorck von Wartenburg lies on 1 January 1933, waiting for the future finally to begin.

On the evening of 1 January, Erika Mann's cabaret, The Peppermill, is having a party at the Bonbonnière in Munich, next door to the Hofbräuhaus, a pub frequented by Nazis. The whole programme mocks the small-minded Nazi worldview. Among the guests are Erika's parents, Thomas and Katia, and her brother Klaus. While Erika and her girlfriend Therese Giehse are performing, Klaus notices 'three stupid Nazis in the corner', noting everything down.

Helene Weigel is less scared of the end of the Weimar Republic than the end of her thousand-day marriage. She senses that Brecht is serious about Margarete Steffin. In his letters to Helene, however, her husband continues to tell her bare-faced lies: 'As I told you, housing Grete was purely pragmatic. At no moment was it about having her close.' Helene doesn't seem entirely convinced, which is why Brecht lays it on thicker a day later: 'Dear Helli, you shouldn't make a big thing of it. I am extremely reluctant to be influenced by the gossip or to pay attention to the imaginings of a few bourgeois, as you know.' (The whole theatre scene is alive with whispering about the lewd sonnets being passed back and forth between Steffin and Brecht, and probably about her pregnancy too.) The main thing Weigel knows after four years of marriage is that her husband is extremely resistant to the influence of anyone other than himself.

The first émigré of 1933 is George Grosz. He has immortalised the Weimar Republic in his drawings and paintings – the fat bellies, the top hats, the naked dancers, the madness and the poverty. Someone who has kept such a close eye on the age is able to sense when it is over. When he returns to Germany from a short-term teaching job at the Art Students League in New York, he tells his wife right there on the quayside in Bremerhaven, five minutes after coming ashore, that he plans to leave again, and this time for good. The art school has offered him a full-time job – with a salary of 150 dollars per month! Eva has noticed that her family has less and less space to breathe. As they sit in the train and George talks in glowing terms about their future in New York, she throws her arms around him and says, 'Yes, let's go.'

Barely have they arrived in Berlin when they start emptying their large apartment in Trautenaustrasse and his studio in Nassauische Strasse. They pack everything they might need into boxes that will be sent by sea and give the rest away. The clock is ticking. 'It was like before the premiere of a great play or the beginning of a battle,' George Grosz will later say. 'You were constantly clearing your throat and glancing nervously at the clock because every day the newspapers would announce that it was a few seconds before midnight. There were only allusions to what might happen after twelve, but it was clear it would be nothing uplifting or welcoming for me and my friends.' And so Eva and George Grosz frantically bring down the curtain on their life in Berlin.

On 11 January, they take three-year-old Martin and five-year-old Peter to Eva's aunt with the intention of fetching them in the summer; the next day they board the Norddeutscher Lloyd steamer *Stuttgart* in Bremerhaven and make the crossing to America. For ever. This is what they are thinking as the engines purr and the foaming water rears up behind them and the flat German landscape shrinks to a line on the horizon before disappearing completely.

Victor Klemperer writes these desperate lines in his diary in Dresden on 14 January: 'The miseries of the new year the same as before: the house, the cold, lack of time, lack of money, no hope of credit, Eva's obsession with building the house and her desperation, still growing. This business will really be the end of us. I can see it coming and feel helpless.' The saddest thing for him is that his beloved wife, a magnificent singer, never opens the harmonium they bought at great expense to sing along to. She has fallen silent.

After Josef von Sternberg set off on a European trip, leaving Marlene Dietrich feeling neglected in Hollywood, she began an affair with the successful dancer (and less successful scriptwriter) Mercedes de Acosta. To Hollywood insiders, Mercedes is known first and foremost as Greta Garbo's lesbian friend. The real attraction for Dietrich appears to be putting ever bigger spokes in the wheel of an even more famous actress. In her men's suits and men's underwear, Dietrich deliberately toys with sexual identity. Mercedes is very susceptible to such things – all the more so now that Garbo has set off on an extended trip back to Sweden. Marlene cooks for Mercedes (she loves to treat her new lovers to roast potatoes) and sends her white flowers almost daily. Mercedes finds tulips too phallic, so Marlene switches to roses. In addition, she sends her bathrobes and lingerie, hair ointment, soap and cakes. On 16 January, Mercedes writes to her that it has been three months 'since that sacred and passionate night when you gave yourself to me'.

Garbo's return from Sweden puts an end to these divine weeks. Mercedes is drawn back to her and tries to explain her motivations to Dietrich. Garbo is, she says, 'a Swedish maid with a face touched by God's radiance, interested only in money, in her own health, sex, eating and sleeping'. However, Mercedes had made this woman into an icon. 'I love only this person I have created,' she says, 'not the real person.' To Dietrich, this sounds suspiciously like

Sternberg's feelings for her. He too is just back from Europe and has reignited his courtship.

When Dietrich discovers that her lover is spilling details from their pillow talk about her film shoots with Sternberg, her patience snaps and she sends a card brusquely cutting short this particular flick.

Still, Mercedes de Acosta, the woman who seduced both Greta Garbo and Marlene Dietrich, is beset by suitors, both female and male. After the war Truman Capote will be especially fascinated by her extravagant sex life. He will come up with a game called International Daisy Chain that counts the beds linking specific people. Mercedes is the trump card because 'you could get to anyone from Cardinal Spellman to the Duchess of Windsor'.

At the premiere of *Faust Part Two* at the Schauspielhaus am Gendarmenmarkt on 21 January, Max Liebermann sits two seats away from Bertolt Brecht. Every representative of Berlin's cultural scene seems to have gathered one last time to see Gustaf Gründgens in his greatest role, as the whispering devil Mephisto. The audience is beside itself with both excitement and inner turmoil at Goethe's nightmarish new man – the 'homunculus'. They cheer the personification of duplicitous evil, 'hell's headhunter'. Gründgens' Mephisto, Alfred Kerr writes in the *Berliner Tagblatt*, displays the 'most intense psychic force and mental power'; indeed, 'Gründgens is increasingly turning into the fallen angel'. How wrong can someone be? Gründgens' ascent into the thespian firmament of the thirties is just beginning, and only three weeks later Kerr will have to leave Germany for ever, his wings clipped.

When Joseph Roth leaves Berlin on the night train to Paris on 25 January, he too is bidding a final farewell to the city. However, unlike the people who pitch up temporarily in France, Roth is used to the game of musical chairs between nations. He knows his way around Paris's cheap lodging houses and how to live on nothing but baguettes and cheap red wine. If he manages to earn a bit of money from his articles or books, he sends what he doesn't spend on drink either to Vienna, where his wife, Friedl, has been admitted to the Am Steinhof psychiatric clinic, or to Berlin, where his lover Andrea Manga Bell lives with her two children. She may not be Jewish, but her father is Cuban and being Black makes life in Berlin hard. She follows Roth first to France and then to Switzerland, where they meet Klaus Mann, who is passing through. Mann notes in his diary: 'Joseph Roth (very drunk, pro-monarchist and nuts) with the lovely Negro.'

All Quiet on the Western Front is a huge irritant to the Nazis, and its author even more so. On 29 January 1933, the day before Hitler seizes power, Remarque, who earlier bought a house in Ticino, loads his luggage into his Lancia and drives from Berlin to the Swiss border. It is snowing there, and when he shows his passport to the officers, they eye him warily but let him through. As the snow starts to thicken, Remarque feels a huge weight lifted from his shoulders. Spotting the first car park on the Swiss side of the border, he pulls over and lights a cigarette. The smoke mingles with the snowflakes. He doesn't really know what the future might hold, but he knows that things should be quieter on this southern front.

When the age of catastrophe finally dawns on 30 January, the young associate professor Dietrich Bonhoeffer is lecturing in the main hall of the Friedrich Wilhelm University on Berlin's central avenue, Unter den Linden, about the creation of the world. Incredibly, he is speaking about the Creation and the Fall exactly halfway between the Reich Chancellery and the Reichstag. As he reaches the point when Cain kills his brother and becomes, in Bonhoeffer's words, the 'first destroyer', German president Paul von Hindenburg is appointing Adolf Hitler the new chancellor.

Reading between the lines, Bonhoeffer's speech refers to the beginning of the Thousand-Year Reich. '[The] boast that we are masters of a new beginning can only be achieved through lies,' he says. Humans must put up with the humiliation of not being able to begin everything anew; this is another lesson of the Fall of Adam and Eve. Bonhoeffer appeals to a nation on the brink of doom and argues against the idea that humans can create a New Man. When the bell rings and Bonhoeffer and his students step outside, they are confronted with triumphant torch-bearing SA troops marching towards the Brandenburg Gate, celebrating the day they believe they will be able to create a New Man. Naked horror flickers in Bonhoeffer's eyes as he watches the uniformed masses carrying torches and pouring through the streets like lava.

The Fall makes a fleeting re-appearance on earth, whether by chance or divine intervention. In Tamara de Lempicka's Paris studio, a particularly gorgeous model is so exhausted that she asks if she can take an apple from the fruit bowl in the kitchen. She walks over to the bowl completely naked, picks up an apple and is about to bite into it when Lempicka shouts, 'Stop! Don't move! Now we need an Adam.' The artist remembers that a good-looking policeman is directing the traffic outside her studio. She walks outside in her painter's smock and wins him over by telling him about the beauty of the Eve he will soon embrace. He comes inside with her, undresses, places his revolver on his folded uniform, puts his arms around Eve and allows Lempicka to paint him for the next two hours.

Adam and Eve is her finest picture, simultaneously hot and cold. And the knowledge that there's a loaded revolver near the couple makes it a very modern Fall of Man. Behind the naked man and woman, the world's first lovers, skyscrapers pierce the sky, casting, as the artist puts it, 'ill-fated shadows on this divine moment in paradise, threatening to engulf it without being able to destroy it entirely'.

Late in the evening of 30 January, Joseph Goebbels writes in his diary: 'Hitler is chancellor. Like a fairy tale.'

Late in the evening of 30 January, Klaus Mann writes in his diary:

'Hitler Reich Chancellor. Shock. Never thought it possible. The land of boundless possibilities.'

In late January, the writer and journalist Wolfgang Koeppen is in Munich, writing a play for Erika Mann and Therese Giehse's Peppermill cabaret. The woman he adores, the twenty-three-year-old actress Sybille Schloss, has joined the company and asked him for some satirical song lyrics. After months of pursuing her in vain, he interprets this as a sign of erotic interest and immediately writes a funny text with the fitting title 'Complex'. Its subject is psychoanalysis, Freud and sex appeal.

Detecting on the eve of the premiere that Sybille Schloss is still reserving her sex appeal for others, Koeppen travels back to Berlin empty-handed. On the train, he writes her a letter that he never sends: 'After I left you and was waiting outside the State Theatre for the tram to the station, the opportunity was gone. I stood there drained, hollowed out, spent with suffering, insentient in my muffled pain and turned to stone.' The letter ends: 'Tomorrow I will start to write a book.' Unlike all the other books Koeppen announces after the war, he writes this one. Well, he doesn't actually start it 'tomorrow' but a year later. It's a desperate book about Sybille Schloss and that missed opportunity, accurately entitled *A Sad Affair*.

In New York, the painter George Grosz is staying at the Cambridge Hotel after emigrating with his wife. He and Eva sometimes spend their evenings wondering whether their hurried departure for a strange country was really necessary. Grosz's teaching salary barely covers the cost of their accommodation; they miss their sons, and the commissions for illustrations from American newspapers have not yet started to flow. But when he receives letters from his neighbours in Berlin in late January reporting that the police and the SA came looking for him at his empty flat and vandalised his studio, he knows how right their decision was: 'I offered secret thanks to my God for watching over and guiding me so providently.' Within weeks Grosz is officially stripped of German citizenship. Another 553 public figures will soon follow him in being proclaimed non-Germans.

The Jewish composer Friedrich Hollaender, the man who made Marlene Dietrich famous with his songs in *The Blue Angel* and now runs the Tingel-Tangel theatre, arrives from London at Berlin's Anhalter Bahnhof with his wife, Hedi. At first everything seems quite harmless. As always, he tells the taxi driver to take them to Cicerostrasse 4, but when they reach their building, his mother-in-law leans out of an upstairs window and gives them a very strange wave. She shakes her head and shoos them away before shutting the window.

The Hollaenders stand on the pavement in bewilderment as the mother-in-law comes down to meet them, and the three of them go to the café on the corner. 'They're up there,' she says. 'The Gestapo. Rummaging through everything, tearing up books, cutting up pictures. First Liebermann, now Kollwitz. The postcards from Else Lasker-Schüler with the star of David on your cheek.' 'So, what do we do now?' Friedrich asks. 'Get out of here right away!' his mother-in-law says.

They call a taxi and go to Friedrichstrasse station – that seems like the shrewder move. On the way there, though, their path is blocked by a horde of young SA fighters. Hollaender's heart sinks into his boots but Hedi pushes him down onto the back seat, hides him under her winter coat and winds down the window. When she shakes her blond curls and shouts 'Heil, lads!' they let her through.

At the station they see that the night train to Paris is due to depart in eight minutes; they purchase two first-class couchette tickets and clamber on board. The conductor has a long stare, first at their faces, then at their tickets and finally at their passports. He shows them to their compartment but holds on to their passports. As the train pulls out of the station they have no idea why the conductor has kept their passports. To feign calm they order a bottle of Riesling and two glasses. They have a drink and lie down on their berths in their coats, prepared for any eventuality. After a while they fall asleep in the darkness to the sound of the train's rhythmic rattle.

They are awakened by the early-morning sun and carefully push back the curtain. Suddenly they see French signs – *Dames*, *Liège* – and can hardly contain their joy at crossing the border. As they roll on towards Paris, the conductor returns their passports. It was merely a courtesy, he says, so they wouldn't be woken for border controls during the night. 'Of course,' Friedrich says, trying to conceal his relief.

At Gare du Nord they disembark dizzily, hearing French voices. They have actually made it. They head to the Hôtel Ansonia, 'a luxury night-time asylum with its crystal chandeliers and worn-out corridor rugs, a hive of exiles'. On the staircase the Hollaenders meet Billy Wilder with Hella Hartung. He says he's staying on the third floor, adding that he sewed his banknotes into the seams of his suits and now wants to go out and spend them in the best restaurants in Paris – 'as if he were totally convinced that new money would only come when the old stuff was gone'. On the fifth floor of the Ansonia, Friedrich meets the actor Peter Lorre and his wife Cilly; the composer Franz Wachsmann and his girlfriend Alice are in the room diagonally opposite. Things are clearly tense between the residents. 'However,' Friedrich notes, 'the barometer of the mood in the whole colony was continuously and oddly suspended between salvaged humour and newly acquired irritation.'

Whenever tedium and helplessness get the refugees in Paris particularly down, they could, Hollaender reports in his peculiar way, go and see a red-haired prostitute at the Café Montparnasse on Avenue de Wagram: 'She does a special rate for emigrants. You can lie all night with her and talk about Bayreuther Strasse and little Lake Grunewald.'

Alfred Kerr, the Weimar Republic's leading theatre critic, knows exactly when his final act has begun: when the phone rings on the bitterly cold afternoon of 15 February. His daughter, Judith Kerr, later recalled:

> He was warned in February 1933 that they wanted to take away his passport. I don't know who rang him that day. Someone from the police. He was in bed with flu at the time, but my mother quickly packed a suitcase for him and within two hours he had driven across the border to Czechoslovakia, still running a high fever.

A few days later he travels on from Prague to Switzerland, where he meets up with his wife Julia, and their children Michael and Judith, who was forced to leave behind the pink rabbit after which she would later name her poignant novel. The four of them then emigrate from Switzerland to Paris. Gründgens' *Faust, Part Two* is the last play Alfred ever saw and reviewed in Germany.

The poet Else Lasker-Schüler, a friend of Franz Marc, Karl Kraus and Gottfried Benn's, and the creator of beautiful love poems that are imbued with an unshakeable belief in reconciliation between Judaism and Christianity, is beaten up by two young SA fighters in the streets of Berlin in February 1933. She bites her tongue, almost severing it, and blood trickles from her mouth. She has to go to hospital, where her tongue is stitched back together, leaving her unable to speak.

Thomas and Katia Mann set off on a lecture tour to Amsterdam, Brussels and Paris, where Thomas gives a speech to mark the fiftieth anniversary of Richard Wagner's death. He doesn't know that this tour also spells the beginning of the couple's exile, although he might have guessed as much upon reading the following in the *Völkischer Beobachter*: 'Thomas Mann is a Francophile, mission-driven, Marxist, Centre-Party-ogling, pacifist, Jew-miscegenated thinker.'

*

When Heinrich Mann is forced from his post as head of the literary division of the Berlin Academy, he knows he will soon have to flee. However, it is not until a former Prussian junior minister tells him on 19 February that his name is on the Nazis' 'kill list' that he realises he has no time to lose. The next day he prepares his escape with Nelly Kröger.

The following morning, they put their plan into action. Taking only his umbrella as a walking stick, Heinrich proceeds to the Anhalter Bahnhof. His ticket is valid only to Frankfurt, but Nelly had boarded the waiting train in advance and stowed his suitcase on the luggage rack. She quickly leaves the train and waits on the platform for him to arrive. Running over to him, she whispers in his ear that everything is in place, but then her voice fails her and she begins to sob. Heinrich caresses her cheek and, when the conductor gives the signal, boards the train. He slumps down in relief below his luggage.

He stays overnight in Frankfurt to make it look like a domestic trip, then travels on the next morning to Kehl via Baden, where he alights. With his suitcase in one hand and the umbrella in the other, he walks across the French border on 22 February. 'Pont du Rhin crossing' reads the stamp in his passport. He has nothing to declare at customs, and the border guards have no idea who has just slipped through their fingers. They say 'Heil Hitler' and usher him into the land of their arch-enemies. As he sits in the French train that will carry him to Toulon, Heinrich writes a single word in his diary on the date of his emigration: 'Departed.'

When the *Völkischer Beobachter* gets wind of his escape, it prints the following comment: 'For instance, the former trumpet-major of the November Academy has vanished without a trace.' In the diary of his friend Wilhelm Herzog, who meets him off the train in Toulon, it says: 'Toulon. Heinrich Mann. Successfully escaped the Third Reich. Laughing and rejoicing like a child.' Never again will Heinrich set foot in Germany.

Departure will prove an altogether tougher proposition for Nelly

Kröger. Heinrich is barely out the door when police officers arrive to search their flat, and Nelly is arrested and questioned. She has no idea what to do and is unable to liquidate their shared belongings in order to transfer Heinrich's money to France. She's already an alcoholic, but amid the fear and panic of these days she develops an addiction to pills. When she has recovered from serious concussion sustained either in jail or from a fall while drunk (she doesn't tell even Heinrich precisely what happened), she too resolves to flee from Germany – but not alone. She sets off with Rudi Carius, her young lover and a Communist activist who is being hunted by the SA.

They hide out on his family's fishing trawler in Sassnitz harbour on the Baltic island of Rügen for a few days. Then, when they are sure that an easterly or south-easterly wind is forecast, they rent a small yacht under the pretence of going for a little jaunt, even taking a picnic for good measure. But when they reach the edge of German territorial waters, they just keep on sailing. The wind blows steadily and carries their small boat to Trelleborg in Sweden. Heinrich Mann wires some money to Copenhagen to help them travel on to France.

After his release from prison, the publisher of *Die Weltbühne*, Carl von Ossietzky, is wondering whether to divorce his alcoholic wife, Maud. He has fallen in love with Gusti Hecht, who just so happens to be the author of the bestselling *Is Divorce Really Necessary?* Eventually, however, Ossietzky heeds his girlfriend's advice and stays with his wife. On 27 February, he is in Gusti's flat, listening to radio coverage of the Reichstag fire.* She tells him to flee right away, but he says he must first go home to his wife.

When he gets there, Maud also urges him to leave Germany – his socialist and pacifist texts put him in grave danger. He has recently

---

*The arson attack on the Reichstag was almost certainly a 'false-flag' operation: the Nazis blamed it on the Communists. This paved the way for Adolf Hitler, recently appointed chancellor, to seize absolute power.

called Hitler a 'cowardly, effeminate pyjama creature' and Goebbels a 'hysterical cheese mite'. But Carl wants to wait and watch for a while. What might he be weighing? Having racked up huge debts, he doesn't know how he will pay for his family's living costs abroad. How would he afford rehab for his alcoholic wife, or is it morally acceptable for him to leave her alone with her sickness? He doesn't want to leave the city where Gusti lives, and he clings to the hope that the Social Democrats and Communists will stop the Nazis.

He's sitting in the kitchen pondering these issues when the doorbell rings. Two police detectives are outside. They let him eat some bread and butter before leading him away. 'I'll be back soon,' he calls out to Maud. He is first taken to Spandau prison before being transferred to the newly established Sonnenburg concentration camp near Küstrin* where he's beaten and tortured for weeks. Maud sends their daughter to a boarding school in England and then lets herself slip into a permanent alcoholic stupor. Gusti sets up a support group, Friends of Carl von Ossietzky, which takes financial care of Maud and their daughter as well as maintaining contact with the inmate.

One of Ossietzky's fellow sufferers in Sonnenburg concentration camp is Erich Mühsam, a Communist fighter and hero of the November Revolution. Only recently, he had come here to visit friends who were being held as political prisoners; now he is one himself. By 27 February he had scrambled together enough money to buy himself and his wife, Zenzl, one-way tickets to Paris, but on the night of the Reichstag fire, the Nazis came and captured him. Mühsam is determined to endure his suffering – the beatings, the fear of death, the torture – like a martyr. On 10 April, Zenzl is allowed to visit him in the camp for a few minutes and finds her beloved husband 'violated and battered'. She goes to see the chief prosecutor and manages to get Mühsam transferred to Plötzensee penitentiary, where he is assigned his own cell. He makes a picture

---

*Present-day Kostrzyn nad Odrą on the German-Polish border.

book for his wife; childish, naïve and expressionist, the drawings are a final evocation of the power of love.

Bertolt Brecht packs his most important manuscripts into his suitcase at Hardenbergstrasse 1a. When the Reichstag is set ablaze on 27 February, he and Helene Weigel go to Peter Suhrkamp, who puts them up in his flat. On 28 February, they take a train to Prague and another to Vienna, arriving there on Saturday 4 March 1933. They stay with Helene's sister.

Brecht heads to Switzerland to gauge the lay of the land. Lugano is attractive to him, not only for its mild climate but also because Margarete Steffin is still recovering from her operation at the Agra lung sanatorium there.

On the evening of Shrove Monday, which in 1933 falls on 27 February, the Munich Kammerspiele theatre company is holding its Carnival ball at the Regina-Palast hotel. Everyone present is in fancy dress and wearing a mask, and there's something liberating about people not knowing who their dance partner is. A smiling clown invites Erika Mann to tango with him. As they spin across the wooden floor, he suddenly whispers into her ear, 'The Reichstag is burning,' to which she spontaneously replies, 'Well, let it burn.' A few seconds later she asks the mysterious clown, 'Why is it burning?' All of a sudden, every clown, harlequin, Venetian lady or pirate on the dance floor is shouting, 'The Reichstag's burning!' Erika Mann never discovers the identity of the clown who was the first person to speak the truth that Shrove Monday, 1933.

When Alfred Döblin hears about the Reichstag fire, he packs a small suitcase. In the early hours of 28 February, he takes the train to southern Germany and keeps going until he can go no further. Then he gets out and starts walking. He strolls through the last German village and, his heart pounding, across a meadow and into Switzerland. His wife soon joins him and, later, so do his children. They travel on to Paris together.

Another who follows him to France is Yolla Niclas, his Jewish lover from the twenties, whom Erna Döblin had recently banned from entering their home in Berlin. Yolla is working as a photographer in Paris and manages to get hold of Alfred's telephone number from another émigré. When she calls him, Alfred is both delighted and perturbed. He asks her not to ring him again – he won't be able to stand the hell Erna will put him through. This is the moment when Yolla understands that even emigration cannot change the conditions in which love either flourishes or withers away.

Still intoxicated by their summer on the Mediterranean coast, Kurt Wolff and Helene Mosel endure a tumultuous winter in Berlin. Initially, they live with Kurt's ex-wife's sister. He meets up with all his former acquaintances and lovers, throwing himself into a hectic social life after those months of solitude in southern France, hoping to be appointed director of a radio station. Helene usually stays at home writing; both Rowohlt and Ullstein are interested in publishing *Background to Love*, the book she wrote in Saint-Tropez the previous summer. Yet storm clouds are looming ever more darkly over Berlin, and she writes to her brother Georg: 'What I hear, see, feel here is mass frenzy, mass delirium, mass psychosis. The mood reminds me of 1914.' This letter is dated 26 February. The next night, as the Reichstag is burning, they start packing their bags, and on 1 March they say farewell to their friends and take the night train to Paris. Kurt Wolff, publisher of Kafka and Trakl, has been forced to emigrate. For Jewish Helene, it is a matter of life and death.

They marry in London in late March, and Helene Mosel becomes Helen Wolff.

The toppling of Konrad Adenauer as mayor of Cologne is the culmination of several years of defamation; the Nazi Party has been campaigning under the slogan 'Adenauer out!' since 1929. They accuse him of having unsuccessfully speculated on the stock market, of being a devout Christian, of spending his holidays in Switzerland, of earning too much and being too friendly with Jews. The Nazi newspaper *Westdeutscher Beobachter* runs a fresh scoop every week and has intensified its attacks since Cologne's city council was declared insolvent in October 1932. In the spring, as unemployment rises and the atmosphere becomes increasingly tense, there is regular street fighting between the SA and far-left paramilitaries. When Hitler comes to Cologne for a campaign rally, Adenauer orders the removal of the swastika flags the Nazi Party has raised on the city's flagpoles.

These are the final spasms of resistance, however. None of the Nazis' opponents for the city's local elections is safe, and one candidate after another is assassinated. The phone rings incessantly at Adenauer's home, and anonymous voices tell him, his wife or his sons that they will soon all be gone. SA men break into his official residence in Max-Bruch-Strasse and take a soak in his bathtub. Now, when he and his spouse greet old friends in the street, none of them reply – Adenauer has become an outlaw in his own city.

He realises he needs to act quickly. Local elections are scheduled for 12 March; on the eve of the vote the Adenauers take their children to the Caritas hospital in Hohenlind, where they will be protected by the Catholic Church. After the Nazis' victory in the elections, Adenauer is hounded out of office. He first flees to the Berlin flat he is entitled to use by virtue of being chairman of the Prussian state council, but then he's deposed from this post as well. His old schoolfriend Ildefons Herwegen, abbot of the Maria Laach abbey, comes to his mind. Herwegen agrees to shelter him within the abbey's high walls, so Adenauer immediately catches the train back to the Eifel region, where despite being rescued he is plunged into fear and melancholy. His family continues to live in nearby Cologne.

'Were it not for my family and my religious principles,' he confesses to a friend from the abbey in 1933, 'I would long since have put an end to my life, for a life like this really isn't worth living.'

*

Victor Klemperer, who expects to be dismissed from his university post at any minute and is shunned by old acquaintances on the streets of Dresden because he is Jewish, has one last refuge: the movies. This time it is *Grand Hotel*, based on the novel by Vicki Baum and starring Greta Garbo. 'I so enjoy going to the cinema; it takes me out of myself,' he writes on 20 March. But his wife very rarely wants to be transported with him. 'It is so difficult to persuade Eva to go. And when it doesn't appeal and she sits there miserably, then I don't get any pleasure from it after all.'

Vicki Baum herself left Germany back in 1932 with her husband, the conductor Richard Lert, and their two sons. They are now permanent denizens of American hotels – and not always grand ones. By the time Victor Klemperer sees the film version of her book, however, she has settled in Hollywood. Her books will soon be banned from German libraries and bookshops; the Militant League for German Culture brands her 'the Jewess Vicky Baum-Levy' as well as an 'asphalt' or urban writer who 'whips up hatred abroad against nationalist Germany'. Simultaneously, *Vanity Fair* publishes an article about her new residence, a white house in the Hollywood Hills, referring to it as 'the German house of a German family'.

On 13 March, Erika and Klaus Mann both leave their homeland – but in different directions. The Nazis banned Erika's cabaret show as soon as they came to power, and the Nazi press has launched furious attacks on her. She has travelled one last time to her parents' villa on Poschingerstrasse in Munich to secure her father's most important documents; the opening pages of his novel *Joseph and His Brothers* are the first thing she packs. She then sets off in her car for Arosa. Her partner, Therese Giehse, flees in the middle of a Kammerspiele rehearsal, first to Austria and then on to Arosa, where she meets up with Erika.

As Erika gets into her car, Klaus is also packing his bags. He spends one final hour with his current lover, Herbert Franz, at the Manns' empty family home before catching the night train to

Paris. Arriving there on 14 March, he rents a fourth-floor room at the Hôtel Jacob for a month; he takes his diary out of his suitcase, draws a line under everything that has come before and writes diagonally across the page in defiant handwriting: 'Emigration has begun.' His first thought and his first dream in exile goes out to his sister Erika. 'Feelings of solitude only when she isn't here.' It must be love.

On 17 March, the Nazi city council of Dessau issues a search warrant for the house of the Bauhaus teacher Paul Klee and his wife. A large quantity of drawings and documents are confiscated and the studio is ransacked. The allegation is that Klee is a Galician Jew. He and Lily respond by moving to Düsseldorf, where he teaches fine art, but his professorship is revoked on 21 April with immediate effect.

On 17 March, Walter Benjamin leaves Berlin on the night train to Paris. He has spent the last few weeks incapacitated by shock, barely venturing outside and refusing to open the door to unannounced visitors. Now he has packed his bags and is on his way to the City of Light. He has also written to his friend Felix Noeggerath to ask if he could stay with him in Ibiza as he needs to get out of Germany fast.

On 23 March, Klaus Mann goes to Käthe von Porada's Parisian flat. She is throwing a small party to mark a visit by the artist Max Beckmann, of whom she is a great admirer. Beckmann bravely returns to his wife, Quappi, in Frankfurt but is immediately dismissed from his professorship at its art institute, the Städelschule. He begins work on his monumental triptych *Leavetaking*, transposing the pain of farewells into a mythological world. He holds out for a few more years before eventually leaving Germany for ever.

Bertolt Brecht lives at the Hotel Bellerive, on the lake in Lugano, with palm trees just outside. Almost every day he travels to the sanatorium in Agra where Margarete Steffin is staying. They lie side by side on the sun lounger on her balcony, and when she isn't coughing they dream of the future. It is a picturesque location with views of the lake, floating high above the world and apparently removed from its problems. Steffin lies here while Hitler becomes Reich chancellor, while the Reichstag burns, while Germany's Jewish intellectuals are forced into exile. Again and again Brecht lies here with her, and when they are separated, they write each other the most beautiful and lascivious sonnets. Not even emigration can bridle Brecht's lust.

Together they visit Hermann and Ninon Hesse in neighbouring Montagnola, Margarete smartly turned out in dress and hat, Bertolt as always in his worker's uniform, a cigar clamped in the corner of his mouth.

When Helene Weigel arrives in Ticino in early April with their children, she quickly realises that Bertolt has not ended his affair. Once again she weighs whether to demand a divorce, notwithstanding the perils of emigration. For now she responds to a friend's offer and takes the children to Denmark. What was that memorable phrase of her husband's? 'Here you have someone on whom you can't rely.'

Katia and Thomas Mann have also stopped over in the Swiss haven of Lugano, but their daughter Erika describes them as 'volatile, unhappy, bewildered'. They too meet up with Hermann and Ninon Hesse, and they entertain Erich Maria Remarque, who comes over from Porto Ronco. The only person they don't wish to see is Bertolt Brecht. He asks for a meeting, but Thomas Mann is not in the mood.

The squadron of famous men associated with Alma Mahler-Werfel – Gustav Mahler, Oskar Kokoschka, Walter Gropius and Franz Werfel – is swelled by a fifth member, remarkable on two counts. First, he is a priest, and second, he is Austria's foremost expert on marriage nullification proceedings. This surely exerted a powerful

attraction on Alma, and when Franz Werfel heads to Italy in March
to write, his fifty-three-year-old wife chooses the thirty-eight-
year-old Johannes Hollnsteiner as her confessor. She delights in
Catholicism's pendulum of guilt, the soothing alternation of sin
and forgiveness, and this young Augustinian of St Florian monastery would seem ideally placed to kill these two birds with one stone.

Yes, you understood correctly: Alma Mahler-Werfel, who
suffers on a daily basis from what she sees as her husband's Jewish
characteristics, falls in love with her spiritual confidant. She notes
in her diary: 'The unbelievably long night of this winter has given
way to southern winds bearing a whiff of spring. It is almost unbearable!' She even interrupts a sojourn with Werfel in Italy, where he is
working on *The Forty Days of Musa Dagh,* to race back to Vienna.
She proudly declares on 5 March: 'J.H. is thirty-eight and has so
far never encountered womankind. He sees me differently, and for
this I count myself blessed. He said: "Never have I been so close to
a woman. You are the first and you will be the last."'

None of this passes unnoticed. Hollnsteiner's car pulls up
almost every day outside the Werfels' house at Hohe Warte, and
when he is saying Mass, Alma attends if she can. She notes that her
confessor abides entirely in the here and now and is very understanding about her 'sinful previous life'. Indeed the priest with the
boyish features and the wire-framed spectacles appears to espouse
a fairly liberal interpretation of Catholic sexual mores. He tells
Alma that, strictly speaking, the vow of celibacy only really applies
when a priest is wearing his cassock. She gladly goes along with this:
'He has not once uttered the word sin – and ought I to be holier
than the pope? Both of us are committed – he to the Church, I to
Werfel.' These forces cancel each other out, so to speak. She writes
to him: 'I love you – I love your influence in the world and on me. I
long for you.' Once more Alma Mahler-Werfel becomes the woman
a man wishes her to be. As with Mahler, Gropius, Kokoschka and
Werfel, she leads Hollnsteiner to believe that she is the one he has
always craved. And because it is so beautiful down here on earth,
Alma asks him to hold her hand as her confessor should she ever

ascend to heaven. Does it sometimes cross her mind, perhaps, that her lover might be able to get her marriage annulled?

Seven, Lotte Lenya writes to Kurt Weill, is her lucky number. The fact that she still can't win at roulette in Monte Carlo does nothing to dislodge this belief. No, she interprets Weill's buying a house for her at Wissmannstrasse 7 as a good omen, and what is more, 1933 is their seventh year of marriage. She is full of cheer as she writes to him from the Mediterranean, where she and her lover, Otto Pasetti, are busy gambling away Weill's money at the casino table.

Meanwhile, at Wissmannstrasse 7 in Kleinmachnow near Berlin, where he lives alone, Weill receives a different kind of mail. 'We don't want Jews like you around here,' the letters read, along with many other things that he is too polite to report to Lenya. When SA thugs stop a performance of his new play *Silver Lake* in Magdeburg, Weill draws the inevitable conclusions. He spends the night in hotels in Berlin or with his friends Caspar and Erika Neher. Now that Caspar has come out as gay, his wife sees to the abandoned Weill – in every respect. On 22 March, the three of them leave Berlin by car, making for the French border. To avoid raising suspicions, Weill has to leave everything behind, including his beloved sheepdog Harras.

The house is sold later that year, and Pasetti fritters away all the proceeds at casinos in Monte Carlo and Nice. Having been unable to sell the house himself because he is Jewish, Weill had signed over power of attorney to Otto.

At the end of March, three people who have acquired a certain degree of fame back home in Germany step ashore in Ibiza. The *ménage à trois* has been captured in a photograph by August Sander entitled *The Dadaist Raoul Hausmann [with Hedwig Mankiewitz and Vera Broido]*. Such arrangements have become far too risky in Berlin, and so on 9 March the threesome fled the country. Now they want to put their revolutionary new lifestyle to the test in Ibiza. They find an old farmhouse called Can Palerm in a remote valley and set up home there. Hedwig runs the household, while her husband and his muse dedicate themselves to art.

Man Ray couldn't care less about politics; he is interested only in love. He continues to work on the painting of huge lips above his bed – the floating lips of his former lover Kiki. In the spring he notices that the painting isn't working; Kiki's lips are too regular. He starts tampering with them, but the results are terrible. After a while he tears the canvas from the stretcher frame, but then his gaze falls on a photo of Lee Miller. His eyes are drawn to those magical thin lips. He knows that these are the lips he has always wanted to paint. He begins a new painting – Lee Miller's lips, six feet long but at a slight slant, the way she liked to tilt her head, so they float across the sky. Morning after morning, before he leaves for his studio, he adds some touches to these new lips on the huge canvas above his bed, where he kissed them for the first and last time.

It is with horror that the young socialists Willy Brandt and his girlfriend Gertrude Meyer witness the boycott of Jewish shops in Lübeck on 1 April, with people spitting at Jews in the street. The next evening, nineteen-year-old Willy and twenty-year-old Gertrude enjoy one last embrace before he sets off for Travemünde, where a fishing boat is waiting to take him north to Rødbyhavn under the cover of darkness. From there he takes the passenger ship *Dronning Maud* via Copenhagen to Oslo. He hasn't brought much with him: one hundred Reichsmarks from his grandmother, one volume of Karl Marx's *Das Kapital* and an oath of fidelity from Gertrude.

He quickly joins the Norwegian Workers' Party in Oslo and writes newspaper articles about Germany. By late June he is so proficient in Norwegian that he no longer needs an interpreter. Gertrude is arrested in May for distributing anti-fascist leaflets, but on her release she sets off from Lübeck pretending to be a tourist and meets up with Willy in exile on 9 July. The couple spend several years together in Oslo and yet, to Gertrude's immense dis-appointment, Willy will not invite her to the ceremony when he is awarded the Nobel Peace Prize in 1971.

The Easter weekend forces Nina von Lerchenfeld, a Protestant, to acknowledge the priorities of her fiancé, the newly promoted First Lieutenant Claus Schenk Graf von Stauffenberg. Stauff, as he is known in his regiment, is a curious blend of poetry and precision. He plays the cello, reads Greek dramas and has no interest in the typical aristocratic pursuits of gambling, hunting and dancing. This is precisely what Nina loves about him.

On Easter Day, he leads the Catholic soldiers of his regiment to Mass and Communion in Bamberg, while she and her family attend a Protestant church service. Immediately afterwards he goes to Bamberg station and boards the train on which his beloved brother Berthold is sitting with Stefan George. George is not just a poet but a revered older figure whom a circle of young German writers, mostly homosexual, regard as their spiritual leader. They travel to Munich with him. Fortunately, Nina von Lerchenfeld doesn't just have her family to fall back on; she has her cigarettes too. She smokes three cartons over Easter.

Lisa Matthias, Tucholsky's former partner, writes about the Berlin spring: 'I felt as if I was going to fall down unconscious when-ever the doorbell rang or merely the telephone. I have barely been able to eat a thing in the past two weeks from 20 March to 4 April and have lost eight pounds.' Then there's the boycott of Jewish stores on 1 April: 'The shops were just closing as I took the tram home around seven o'clock. There were a lot of SA around. Everyone looks at everyone intently, suspiciously. Standing at the Kaiserdamm stop, I got the feeling that everyone would love to kill everyone else and that there is a kind of bloodthirstiness in the air.'

On 5 April, Lisa Matthias goes to the editorial offices at Ull-stein where she's working as a journalist. All the Jewish editors have already been dismissed or are sitting pale and anxious at their desks. There is another raid on *Die Weltbühne*, for which she writes articles; its publisher, Carl von Ossietzky, has already been detained. So far, though, no one has noted her relationship with the Jewish traitor Tucholsky in her police file. Packing her bags, she heads into Swedish exile on 5 April via Trelleborg, just like Willy Brandt and Heinrich Mann's partner, Nelly Kröger. She returns to the country where she spent her happiest times with Tucholsky – the days he recorded for posterity in *Castle Gripsholm*. Her former lover has turned his affections to other women by now, though – and anyway, he's in Switzerland. Her journey to Sweden is long, nostalgic and sad, and she's scared half to death.

Else Lasker-Schüler is still treating her split tongue with sage. But on the evening of 18 April she packs her belongings and clothes into suitcases and boxes, labels them and asks the Hotel Sachsenhof to store them indefinitely. Being Jewish, she knows she has to get out of the country as quickly as possible. A scheduled reading in her hometown of Wuppertal has been cancelled out of fear for her life.

She boards a train to Zurich on the morning of 19 April. Pale as a ghost, she has asked her remaining friends to escort her to the station. Once she's in her train compartment, she clings anxiously to her handbag for hours, not even daring to go to the toilet. On her arrival in Zurich she tumbles out onto the platform, practically unconscious. She cannot forgive herself for not having paid one last visit to her ancestors' graves in Wuppertal. Weighed down by her bags, she wanders through the cold streets of Zurich as night falls. She has nothing to eat. She begs and ends up sleeping under a tree by the lake for the first few nights, scarcely covered by her coat. Germany's greatest female Expressionist poet has reached the end of the line.

Trees are the only things from which Konrad Adenauer still derives some comfort. Although he follows political developments in the newspapers, he has otherwise escaped from the outside world into the strict rituals of monastic life at Maria Laach. Whenever possible, he slips through the gates into the countryside beyond: 'Overnight the whole beech wood has turned green. I have never seen so many forget-me-nots as in these forests,' he writes to his friend Dora Pferdmenges in Cologne. 'I am extremely moved and shaken by the incredible energy nature has deployed in these six weeks; it really is doing colossal things right now.' Yet it is nothing compared to the colossal political injustice that has been done in these six weeks of 1933, as spring spreads across Germany.

As Max Schmeling notes with mounting panic, Berlin is gradually emptying:

> Every week from the spring of 1933 onwards, another person went missing from our circle at Roxy, at Änne Maenz's place and the Romanisches Café. Moldauer was the first. Soon we searched in vain for Fritz Kortner and at some stage Ernst Deutsch also disappeared, and one day Ernst Josef Aubricht wasn't there. Then Bergner was gone, then Richard Tauber and finally Albert Bassermann. People said that Bertolt Brecht and Kurt Weill had also emigrated.

*

In the early hours of 11 April 1933, Walter Benjamin arrives in Ibiza harbour after travelling from Paris to Barcelona on the *Ciudad de Malaga*. It is 6.15 a.m., the start of a radiant spring day. Benjamin thinks back to his stay in Ibiza the previous year – that brief blissful period with Olga, here on the beach and in a boat. Right now, the blazing sun is so strong that he can suppress the memories of the dark days that followed. He lets out a deep sigh. Finally he has some time without needing to worry about Nazi goons hunting him or sleepless, panic-stricken nights in Berlin. In April 1933, the significance of Ibiza is that it is as far as possible to get from the German capital while still being in old Europe, the territory of his ancestors. He also needs a place where life is cheap enough to get by on what little money he has left, and he wants some peace and quiet. And so Ibiza, a haven and holiday home only a year earlier, is now the first stop on his irreversible path of exile.

This time, though, everything bothers him. Suddenly there are Spanish and German tourists everywhere. There's no proper accommodation for him, so he stays in a building the Noeggarths have half-finished. The wind whistles around the corners of his shack as he writes to Adorno's fiancée, Gretel Karplus, in Berlin. He couldn't possibly feel any worse. He gets up each morning at six o'clock and walks over to the deck chair he has hidden on the slope and reads in the gentle morning sunlight. At eight o'clock he opens his flask of coffee and eats some bread, before working in the dappled shade until one. But every afternoon a strong and gusty wind sets in. Again and again, it sends the handwritten sheets of paper flying through the air into the pine woods, making it impossible to do any real work. So he starts going regularly to a nearby village called San Antonio: 'Occasionally you need the sight of a cup of coffee in front of you as a marker of a civilisation from which you are otherwise at a sufficient distance,' he writes.

In the following months he writes frequent reviews for German newspapers from Ibiza. No longer are these articles published under his own name, however, but pseudonymously as 'Detlef Holz', 'Hans Fellner' or 'Karl Gumlich', which all apparently sound Aryan enough. But Benjamin is terrified for his fifteen-year-old son, Stefan Rafael, who is still living in Berlin and is not only Jewish but also an active Communist. Dora, Stefan's mother and Benjamin's ex-wife, has lost her job, and Benjamin's brother Georg is in detention. Benjamin writes a poem:

The heart beats louder and louder and louder
The sea becomes quieter and quieter and quieter.
Down to its very bottom.

*

The melancholy *Lyric Novella* is published in 1933. Annemarie Schwarzenbach's parents are opposed to her close friendship with Ruth Landshoff and Erika and Klaus Mann. She will later become a famous photographer, but this is a short book about a young woman mourning a lost love in a hotel in Brandenburg near Berlin, wandering the fields, trying to forget but incapable of forgetting. It is Schwarzenbach's attempt to process her own unhappy relationship with the London-born translator and Berlin socialite Ursula von Zedlitz, but she's still hurting as much as the day it ended.

On receiving an invitation from Klaus and Erika Mann and Therese Giehse to visit them in exile in Le Lavandou on the Côte d'Azur, Annemarie gets in her stylish car and sets off for southern France. There, they all lie on the terrace of Hôtel Les Roches Fleuries, soaking up the warm spring sun. The writer Sybille Bedford comes over from Sanary-sur-Mer, and Annemarie snaps some of her finest photographs. Young people in the blazing sun, teasing one another, relaxed after their temporary escape from doom. Even in black and white, they pulsate with emotional colour. She will never be this happy and at peace with herself, though, and repeatedly bursts into tears for no apparent reason, mid-conversation or while taking a photo.

At around 5 p.m. on 6 May, the new military commander of the Balearic Islands, General Franco, arrives in San Antonio on Ibiza. Flanked by high-ranking officers, he marches past the Noeggeraths' house to the Coves Blanques lighthouse. Walter Benjamin, who has barricaded himself in his room, takes a short peek through a gap in the shutters as Franco passes by, a yard away. Walter has read that Franco is forty, exactly the same age as him. A shudder runs down his spine. Then he sits down in his room again to read Céline's *Journey to the End of the Night*, which Max Horkheimer has sent him from Geneva. Franco, Céline, Benjamin: in the late afternoon of 6 May 1933, the lives of these three men briefly intersect at 38 degrees north. Together, their stories will sum up the cataclysms of the thirties. Seven years later, General Franco will give the order that no more refugees shall cross the border between France and Spain – with fatal consequences for Walter Benjamin.

Marlene Dietrich sits in Hollywood, unable to decide what to do. She longs to go back to her beloved Berlin, and she yearns for the laughter that sometimes overcame her as she drove her cabriolet along the Kurfürstendamm. But her mother, who still lives there, tells her not to come, and so does Josef von Sternberg, who happened to be in Berlin when the Reichstag burned. He sends her a telegram to tell her that she must keep away from Germany, which is in meltdown. Marlene is determined to travel to Europe with her daughter, though, and plumps for Paris, where Rudi Sieber still lives with his girlfriend, Maria's former nanny. Unfortunately, Paris is also home to the wife of Maurice Chevalier, the French actor with whom Dietrich has just started a half-hearted affair. So maybe Berlin and the familiarity of home would be better after all?

Rudi Sieber strikes an alarmist tone in his telegram on 8 May: 'BERLIN SITUATION TERRIBLE – EVERYONE ADVISES AGAINST IT – EVEN EDI THE NAZI FEARS TROUBLE – MOST BARS CLOSED – THEATRE CINEMA IMPOSSIBLE – STREETS EMPTY – ALL JEWS IN OUR BUSINESS IN PARIS VIENNA PRAGUE – EXPECT YOU AND MUTTI IN CHERBOURG LATER SWITZERLAND OR TYROL.' The reply that Marlene sends is surprising, as it gives the impression that she is suddenly nostalgic for her husband: 'DON'T WANT TYROL. HATE LONELINESS WANT FRENCH SEASIDE WITH YOU LONGING KISSES MUTTI-TOMCAT.'

But when Dietrich gets to Paris, she slips back into her role as an international celebrity. She wears a beige men's suit under a slightly darker summer coat, sunglasses and her inscrutable smile, and from this point on Rudi is standing next to her at the railway station and by her side. He is happy to be photographed in the knowledge that once again, just like a year ago in Hollywood, he must play the part of the faithful husband. Instead of heading to Tyrol, they move into a suite at the Hôtel Georges V near the Arc de Triomphe and then travel down to the Riviera after all. Telegrams from Sternberg arrive every day now, sometimes three of them: 'MY DEAR GODDESS EVERYTHING IS SO EMPTY' or 'I MISS YOU WITH EVERY THOUGHT' or 'YOU INCOMPARABLE WOMAN AND MOST BEAUTIFUL CREATURE'. His raptures are beginning to get on her nerves.

And so Dietrich spends the summer in Paris and various French Mediterranean resorts, one of many Germans this year, the difference being that she is not a fearful émigré but an urbane, bored tourist.

On 9 May, Klaus Mann writes a despairing letter to the author he loves more than almost any other: Gottfried Benn. Benn's behaviour at the Academy of the Arts and his positive statements about the new regime have caused huge outrage. Klaus is writing from the exile in Le Lavandou that he is sharing with his sister Erika and Annemarie Schwarzenbach: 'You ought to know that for me – and a few others – you are one of the very few people we would never want to lose to the other side. But, of course, you must know what you are swapping our love for and what significant compensation they are offering you. If I am any prophet, it will be ingratitude and scorn.' Klaus is an excellent prophet – this is precisely what happens – but Benn has become hopelessly obsessed with a fixed idea of the 'new state' and misconstrues this declaration of love as an attack. Klaus has requested that Benn send a reply to the Hôtel de la Tour in Sanary-sur-Mer, his next staging post.

Arriving there on 12 May, Klaus reads in the German papers that his books were publicly burnt the previous day in the Königsplatz in Munich: 'Barbarism bordering on the infantile,' he writes. 'But I am honoured.' He sits in his second-floor room and waits for the postman. Erika has the adjacent room. She talks to him, he writes 'about the sadness and unworthiness of emigration – though I don't feel that way'. This comes as no surprise from someone who has spent his whole life on the run from his emotions. After writing his long letter to Benn, Klaus makes a short but no less important note in his diary: 'Our motto is: Learn to hate! Learn to be unjust! You, the enemies of freedom, have taught us how to hate.'

And also how to wait, for Benn doesn't answer. Klaus watches the small boats rocking in the gentle breeze, closes his shutters in the evening and opens them again in the morning, hears the fishermen going out to sea and returning to harbour, hears the town hall's bell strike every fifteen minutes and the screech of the seagulls. But Benn doesn't write. Instead, he shouts out his reply over the airwaves on 23 May, in a riposte he calls 'Answer to the Literary Emigrants'. He asks mockingly if Mann thinks that history is 'particularly active in French seaside resorts'. He continues: 'Do you finally realise, down there by your Latin sea' that 'history is changing' in Germany and a people is determined to 'perfect itself'? Indeed, 'I declare myself personally in favour of the new state because it is my people that is now carving out its own path.'

When his response is printed in the *Deutsche Allgemeine Zeitung*, Benn seals the clipping in an envelope and sends it to Klaus at the Hôtel de la Tour in Sanary-sur-Mer. Benn's answer disgusts Klaus – strikes him dumb with horror – but it also inspires him to found a journal called *Die Sammlung* in Amsterdam. It will become the most influential German-exile magazine. A few years later, in the same room (No. 7) in this hotel, he will put the finishing touches to his novel about Gustaf Gründgens, *Mephisto*.

Meanwhile, Christopher Isherwood is sampling every aspect of Berlin life that *Cabaret*, the film adaptation of his books, will later bring to global attention. He lives in Fräulein Thurau's guesthouse in Nollendorferstrasse, teaches 'Natalia Landauer' English and meets a woman called Jean Ross, aka 'Sally Bowles', who tells him that she doesn't 'believe that a woman can become a great actress [without having] any love affairs'. He sees Nazis and Communists fighting in the streets, watches as fear insinuates itself into Berlin, and feels the growing sense of unease at his favourite haunt, Cosy Corner – a small working-class gay bar at Zossener Strasse 7, which is famous as far afield as London and New York. He spends tender moments with his youthful German friend Heinz Neddermeyer, who is always frying him schnitzel and meatballs. He writes to his friend Stephen Spender, telling him that he needs to stay in Berlin for a little while longer: 'The final part of my novel requires a lot more research.'

Then, in spring 1933, his field research is complete. *Berlin Stories* concludes with a diary entry from the winter of 1932 that describes the air as thick with fear. His Jewish friends have emigrated, his homosexual friends are interrogated and persecuted, their bars closed down. When Magnus Hirschfeld's institute is pillaged on 6 May, Isherwood knows it is time to leave. On 10 May, he sees documents from the Institute for Sexual Science being burnt alongside books by Tucholsky, Carl von Ossietzky and Erich Maria Remarque. He starts to say his goodbyes, gives away most of his belongings and packs the rest into two suitcases. He isn't taking much with him other than his great German love, Heinz Neddermeyer, for whom he has arranged a passport. By 14 May, he is ready. 'Now the day has come, too wonderful, too terrible to be true. The day I am supposed to leave Germany.' Neddermeyer comes to meet him at six o'clock in the morning. He bids farewell to his landlady, and he and Heinz take a taxi to Anhalter Bahnhof in silence, then catch a train to Prague. Heinz is a 'valet' by profession, according to Isherwood's application for a travel permit. The German border guards let them through. What neither of them yet knows is that this is the start of four years of travels through Europe and Africa.

Erich Kästner's children's books meet with the Nazis' approval, but they hate his 1932 novel *Fabian*. According to the *Völkischer Beobachter*, it contains nothing but 'crude stories' and 'depictions of sub-human orgies'. In March 1933, he and a group of other 'Communist and radical left-wingers', including the Jewish authors Lion Feuchtwanger, Alfred Kerr and Egon Erwin Kisch, are excluded from the Association for the Defence of German Authors. On 10 May, copies of *Fabian* and Kästner's poetry collections are publicly burnt. 'Down with decadence and moral decay' and 'More discipline and morals in the family and the state', shout the Nazis on Bebelplatz as they toss Kästner's books into the flames. Of the authors whose books are cast into the fire that day, he is the only one who is present, giving him insight into how hate transforms people. A female student recognises him and cries, 'There he is – Kästner!' He writes: 'She was so surprised to spot me among the mourners at what was in essence my own funeral that she even pointed at me. I must admit that I found it unpleasant.' The other students, mesmerised by the sight of the flames consuming the books, ignore the young woman's cries, however.

It is hard to understand why Kästner isn't scared out of his wits. He knows that almost every other author whose books are on that fire has already emigrated, yet he walks home, his resolve unbroken. 'I stayed', he says later, 'to be an eyewitness.'

After the public book-burning Kästner continues to go to the Romanisches Café. He keeps his vote for the Socialist Party a secret and pretends nothing has changed, even though he knows that his two most recent lovers – 'Moritz' and 'Pony Hat' (aka Margot Schönlank) – have fled to Paris. He travels with his new girlfriend, the actress Cara Gyl, to the Eibsee, a lake in Bavaria, where they eat well, hike a little and coo over each other. In between, he works on *The Flying Classroom* at a small desk outside the hotel. His secretary, Elfriede Mehring, drops in once and he poses for a picture, looking tanned and wearing a freshly ironed shirt, apparently untouchable. What was it that Else Rüthel wrote in her brilliant review of *Fabian*? That Kästner employed the 'jargon of a high-class master of ceremonies'. And it's true: he even seems to want to talk disaster away. He was in Zurich when the Reichstag burnt down, but no one could prevent him from travelling back to the German capital; it was 'our duty and responsibility', he said, 'to face up to the regime, each in our own way'.

So Kästner gets on with his new book, and *The Flying Classroom* is in bookshops by December. By the time it is published, Cara Gyl, who held his hand while he was writing it and is mentioned in the preface, is history, and Kästner has turned his attentions to the young actress Herta Kirchner. He immediately informs his mother in Dresden: 'I while away the late evening hours with a twenty-year-old blonde actress who has read me and loved me since she was fifteen.'

When Kästner tries to withdraw some of his first royalties for *The Flying Classroom* from the bank in Nestorstrasse, he discovers that the Gestapo has frozen his account. They've done the same to forty-one emigrated authors. Officers from the Gestapo subsequently arrest and interrogate him. After being released, he immediately writes a letter to calm his mother, playing the whole thing down as a minor nuisance.

It is impossible not to be irritated by Kästner's behaviour in 1933: it seems as if he's unwilling to see the sword hanging over his head. One of the arguments he makes against emigration is that his mother wouldn't have anything to do if he didn't send his dirty laundry to Dresden for her to wash and iron. It is worrying that Kästner, famously a mummy's boy, seriously considered this to be legitimate grounds for staying in Germany.

Magnus Hirschfeld went into exile before the true Nazi era even began. The legendary sexual researcher knew that being Jewish, gay and a socialist, he was the embodiment of everything the Brownshirts hated. The museum of his Berlin Institute of Sexual Science had acquired an iconic reputation among the worldwide homosexual community. He initially returned from a lecture tour of America, Asia and Russia to Ascona on the peaceful shores of Lake Maggiore, but soon decided to move to Paris.

At his side were the latest love of his life, Li Shiu Tong, who was funding Hirschfeld from his large fortune, and Hirschfeld's longstanding lover Karl Giese. The three of them pursued a close yet sometimes complicated *ménage à trois*, first in Switzerland and then in France. In May 1933, they sit in a Parisian cinema and watch a newsreel of Nazi hordes plundering and destroying their institute and its library before hurling a bust of Hirschfeld, 30,000 photographs and many important documents onto the fire as part of the great book-burning frenzy on Bebelplatz. How nightmarish to be a powerless witness to the destruction of so many years of your own research. Karl Giese and Li Shiu Tong have to support their sixty-five-year-old friend out of the cinema and into the dark, puddled streets of Paris. He is truly broken.

On 16 May, the composer Arnold Schönberg emigrates from Berlin to Paris with his wife and their one-year-old daughter after receiving a warning from his brother-in-law Rudolf Kolisch. Back in March, Schönberg was informed by the Berlin Academy of the Arts that his presence was undesired. In Paris, with the painter Marc Chagall as his witness, he reaffirms the Jewish faith he renounced in 1898. He writes to Anton Webern: 'For fourteen years I have been prepared for what has now come to pass. I have been able to prepare myself very thoroughly over this long time and have definitively cast off everything that once bound me to the West. I have long been determined to be a Jew.'

In October 1933, Schönberg and his family take the *Île de France* from Le Havre to New York.

Lion Feuchtwanger and his wife, in exile in southern France, have ended up in the cheerful resort of Bandol. He immediately instructs his secretary, Lola Sernau, to come from Berlin. On 20 May, he begins work on his novel *The Oppermanns* and notes in his diary that he has slept not just with his wife but also with his secretary. His stiff neck the following day arouses his wife's suspicions; she says he probably has syphilis. Feuchtwanger's response: Marta 'has a tendency to suspect some kind of "guilt" behind any unpleasant incident'. Things don't improve over the next couple of days. 'Trouble with Marta. It isn't easy with her,' he writes. She implements a harsh regime, making Lion jog around the new house ten times in the morning to earn some eggs for breakfast. Disciplinary measures are no remedy for jealousy, however. Lion confides in his diary that the relationship between Marta and Lola is 'unpleasant', and there's also 'trouble with the bloody car Marta bought'. This continues throughout the lovely summer, with the tide of negativity only turning on 30 July: 'Fucked Marta. Lola in a permanent bad mood.' Perhaps we didn't need so much detail, and neither does Marta. She is shocked when she later finds and reads her husband's diary – the diary of a sex maniac. 'I would write in far more tender terms, but I still cannot get over the diary. It caused me great pain and it was my sole disappointment because I never had any illusions about anyone else.'

Thomas and Katia Mann have worries of a different kind in Bandol, where they have checked into the Grand Hôtel after their restless first months of exile. They aren't really comfortable in the oppressive heat, but their children have advised them to settle somewhere along this stretch of the Mediterranean coast. They can only get to sleep at night with powerful sleeping tablets and they cannot bear the searing sunshine. They are plagued by fevers and colds, by mosquitoes and the gusty mistral that gnaws at their nerves. They cannot bear the crowds of people with whom they are obliged to eat meals and share the lift. In fact, they cannot bear this state of exile. Thomas and Katia are not suited to a life of the kind Vicki Baum portrays in *Grand Hotel*; they need to feel firm ground beneath their feet.

They are all too aware of how different they are temperamentally – and obviously, as always, Thomas suffers more than his wife. 'A feeling of my health having been jarred,' he notes. 'My nerves weak, my body unwell.' Katia tries to calm him down and suggests that the cooler climes of Normandy or Brittany might make for a better place of exile. 'It strikes me as too late for that,' he says. Then, on 6 June, Thomas's fifty-eighth birthday, 'the melancholic depression slightly got the upper hand', as he writes in his diary that evening. He notices the way Katia's features grow more serious and more concerned. Klaus and Erika come over from the neighbouring village of Sanary-sur-Mer and debate the 'question of staying here or going away' without resolving the issue. Again and again, the sound of cannon fire rings out across the sea from the nearby naval base in Toulon. Thomas concludes: 'Returning is out of the question, impossible, absurd, nonsensical and full of terrible dangers for our freedom and lives.' The Manns therefore decide to rent a villa called La Tranquille in Sanary-sur-Mer until they come to a decision.

Charlotte Wolff is dismissed from her job at the electrical physics institute and arrested in the street. The Gestapo officer explains that it is because she is dressed as a man and also that she's a spy. The head of the nearest police station recognises her as his wife's former doctor and lets her go, yet three days later her flat is searched and she is accused of spying for Russia. Charlotte knows it is time to leave, so on 26 May she takes the train to Paris via Aix-la-Chapelle. On the platform, her former partner, Katherine, squeezes her hand long and hard. Both of them have tears in their eyes. Finally, Charlotte boards the train for the longest and most agonising journey of her life. Every time the compartment door opens, she expects the Gestapo to come and arrest her. However, she makes it across the border into Belgium, and a few hours later she reaches the Gare du Nord in Paris with 'a mix of receding horror and renewed hope, the nightmarish journey occupying her mind'. She tumbles onto the bed in a cheap hotel and sleeps till the next morning without stirring. Still in a slight daze, she goes into a small café on Boulevard Saint-Michel and joyfully orders her first French breakfast: '*Café au lait et une tartine.*' Helen Hessel, her friend and an earlier émigré, soon invites Charlotte to move in with her and her sons for a while.

The big showdown between Zelda and Scott Fitzgerald occurs on 28 May 1933. In the Baltimore surgery of the psychiatrist Dr Thomas Rennie they take stock of a marriage that began so thrillingly in America before drowning in a tide of alcohol and tears in Europe. Along with the doctor, the couple have called in his assistant, who takes shorthand notes of the whole conversation, ultimately running to 114 densely filled pages. Dr Rennie supports

Scott's attempt to deny Zelda the right to write her own books, and she is initially silent – out of sheer disbelief. In fact, though she has been officially declared insane, Zelda appears to be the only one of them who is in her right mind.

Scott is angry that his wife has dared to write about her years in Europe and all the psychiatric clinics. He thinks she has overstepped the mark: 'You are a third-rate author. I am the best-paid story writer in the world.' Her response drips with sarcasm: 'Then why are you arguing with a third-rate talent? Why the hell are you so jealous?' Fitzgerald rages on, to which Zelda replies, 'If this carries on, I'll go back to the psychiatric clinic – it's more relaxed there.' Scott responds that he can't stand living with Zelda anymore; the blame she places on him for her suffering drives him to be permanently drunk. For hours on end they argue like this, back and forth. The focus keeps returning to Scott's claim that he alone is entitled to write about their shared past and Zelda's stays in clinics.

Unfortunately, the book Scott writes about their life together is miles better than Zelda's *Save Me the Waltz*. *Tender Is the Night*, published in 1934, shamelessly exploits their past, with no regard to the damage done, but it is a classic.

The summer of 1933 casts an evil pall over German culture, represented in Dresden and Paris by men who have been hounded out of their jobs: Kurt Weill and Bertolt Brecht on stage in Paris, and Otto Dix on canvas in Dresden. All of this, incidentally, has an immediate effect on the men's love lives, but we should tell this tale in the right order.

As soon as the Nazis seize power, Otto Dix is fired from his professorship at the Dresden Academy of Fine Arts. He may not be Jewish or a Communist, but his paintings are castigated as 'smut' and 'a danger to youth'. In particular, the fact that he portrays the terrors of war so unsparingly seals his fate under a regime that intends to proclaim a new age of heroism. By April, Dix's work has been labelled 'degenerate' in a municipal exhibition, while

the critic Bettina Feistel-Rohmeder denounces him in the following terms: 'Professor Dix proves in this student show that he is a
corrupter of German youth, and it should be the duty of German
women's groups to object loudly and repeatedly.'

Refusing to be provoked by these attacks, Dix seeks artistic
refuge in the good old days of German painting by harking back
to Lucas Cranach, Dürer, Hans Baldung Grien and Matthias
Grünewald. He wants to find a way to expose a regime that is
committing crimes – against art and against him. The result is a six-
foot-high wooden tablet in the style of the Old Masters showing
an allegory of The Seven Deadly Sins. Greed, Wrath, Envy, Pride,
Sloth, Lust and Gluttony are each depicted as a deformed human
being. Envy is represented as a small, angry figure with a Hitler
moustache. Death dances in the centre of the painting, with the
skeleton's limbs resembling a swastika. Resistance in oil on canvas.
An indictment – and a prophecy.

Incidentally, Lust is depicted in the picture as a voluptuous
woman with curly hair, and she has the facial features of Käthe
König, Dix's lover in Dresden. Dix knows that, along with all his
accusations against the great Nazi sinners, he is committing a personal deadly sin: revealing his continuing infidelity to his faithful
wife. But he hopes she will forgive him.

By extraordinary coincidence, a play called *The Seven Deadly
Sins* celebrates its premiere at the Théâtre des Champs-Élysées in
Paris on 7 June. This sparkling blend of ballet, song and drama
was written by Bertolt Brecht with music by Kurt Weill, sung by
Lotte Lenya. The funding for the enterprise is provided by a British
patron of the arts, Edward James, who is desperate for his German
wife, the dancer Tilly Losch, to have a starring role. She acts and
sings as one half of a split personality, with Lenya playing the other.
It so happens that the two half-women fall in love with each other
under the pretty poncho they share onstage, and they go around
as a couple during rehearsals and in the following weeks. Losch
has to keep this secret from her husband, Lenya from her lover,

Otto Pasetti (who, night after night, waits in vain for her at the Hôtel Splendide). The first person to get wind of their romance is Kurt Weill, who is feeling lovesick himself. He has been indulging in some recent horseplay with Marie-Laure de Noailles, his aristocratic Parisian patroness, but Lenya considers adultery – in her words, 'the eighth deadly sin' – barely worthy of attention. She still gets on fantastically with Weill, who has been funding her and Pasetti's dissolute lifestyle on the Côte d'Azur for so long. Her decision to push for a divorce regardless is largely down to the fact that Pasetti has now officially divorced his wife, though the arias about eternal love he sings to her over cocktails before the casinos open have certainly played their part.

'I still love you, of course,' she writes to Weill. When she asks him whether he would mind if she had a child with Pasetti, he admits with tears in his eyes that he would be very hurt. Lenya stares at him long and hard. 'Then of course I won't, dear Kurt,' she says. While the divorce proceedings continue, she manages to smuggle more of Weill's property from Berlin to France, including his sheepdog Harras. Now, after rehearsals of *The Seven Deadly Sins*, he takes an evening stroll with the dog through the fragrant fields around his rented house in the Parisian suburb of Louveciennes. These are, incidentally, the same fields that Camille Pissarro transformed fifty or sixty years earlier into probably the most beautiful Impressionist landscape paintings in history.

Shortly after the last performance of *The Seven Deadly Sins*, Edward James is rewarded for his investment in the production with a divorce request from Tilly Losch, who is hopelessly in love with Lotte Lenya. This does more damage to his wallet than to his heart, however, because James is gay.

Yet this is not quite the final word on the victims claimed by *The Seven Deadly Sins*. Brecht comes back into the frame again, bringing Margarete Steffin with him – she has been discharged from the sanatorium near Lugano after spending months there and has come to assist her friend and idol with rehearsals. After weeks of Parisian bliss with Brecht, however, her world collapses when he

reveals that he has no intention of moving in with her; he's planning to travel to see Helene Weigel and his children in Denmark.
Following Helene's example that spring, Margarete considers
breaking up with Brecht for good and writes him a sonnet. It is
titled 'Now just think if every single woman' and describes a dream
in which all Brecht's girlfriends gather around his bed:

> Those you once chose as your sport
> Play a nasty trick on you

She still cannot quite believe that her time with him is over, even
when he packs his bags and leaves for Denmark. By the time he
arrives, Helene has set up a study for him. It has three desks and a
magnificent view of the sea and is a long way from the children's
bedrooms. As he tries to give her a grateful kiss, she tells him that
he may only move in if he swears to desist from having affairs. He
swears on his mother's grave – and then writes to Margarete Steffin
that same evening to tell her how much he is looking forward to
seeing her in August in Paris.

In Dutch exile, the former Kaiser Wilhelm II, or 'His Imperial
Majesty' as his household staff continue to address him, is cross
with his wife, Hermine, who is still busy bowing to the Nazis. This
poses a challenge to the love that the old and weary monarch has
found late in life: 'She is in an absolutely intolerable state! She
means well and she cannot wait for me to be back on my throne,
but we won't achieve it her way. She's chasing after the Nazis and
doing all kinds of things in Berlin and in writing from here that are
doing more harm than good.'

   Since the abdicated emperor's own land boasts very few trees
after twelve years of his felling and chopping, he has now taken
his axe to the woods of his neighbour, a certain Mr Blijdenstein,
who is grateful to have found such a skilled, hardworking and free
assistant forester.

*

Before the Jewish-American boxer Max Baer climbs into the ring to fight the German Max Schmeling in New York on 8 June 1933, he sews a yellow star of David onto his shorts. He wants to make his position on the Nazi power-grab clear. Schmeling is the better boxer, but Baer defeats him in the tenth round by technical knockout.

Schmeling didn't stand a chance. In fact, he was lucky because Baer had recently stopped an opponent in the fifth round by technical knockout with a vicious hail of punches – and the other boxer died.

Schmeling wakes up in his New York hotel room the morning after the bout, inspects his swollen face in the mirror and wonders if he should hang up his gloves. This defeat is a humiliation. He calls Berlin and tells his girlfriend, the actress Anny Ondra, star of Alfred Hitchcock's first talkie, *Blackmail*, that she can go ahead and book a registry office ceremony. She says something like, 'Really, Max?' before the phone connection is cut. The pair are nevertheless married on 8 June.

Inspired by Schmeling, Baer, who is famous not only for his powerful right hook but also for his sense of humour, leaves for Hollywood immediately after the fight to play himself in the movie *The Prizefighter and the Lady*. Schmeling retaliates by starring as himself in the boxing film *Knockout,* in which he is filmed, fittingly enough, opposite Anny Ondra, who plays the boxer's attractive blonde bride.

No one knows how Heinrich Mann's girlfriend Nelly Kröger, and her boyfriend Rudi Carius, have managed to make their way to southern France, but they have. Quivering with joy, Heinrich welcomes Nelly into his hotel room in Bandol and they are reunited under the soothing Mediterranean sun. It's not like it was three years ago, when they watched the rough cut of *The Blue Angel*, but this is the start of their exile years together. Now Nelly resorts ever more frequently not just to alcohol but to pills – and intermittently to Rudi Carius. Heinrich Mann was aware of Nelly's cheeky young Communist lover back in Berlin, but he is irritated that Nelly has brought him along to the shores of the Mediterranean. There is a drawing from this time of the sixty-two-year-old Mann standing in the doorway of his hotel room, a little taken aback at the sight of a naked Kröger and Carius in his bed.

Margarete Steffin remains in Paris while Bertolt Brecht is in Denmark with Helene Weigel and the children. She writes him a wise letter, full of longing: 'I sometimes wonder when your various friends will tell another girl, "Yes and then in 1932/33 he was often with this girl called Grete Steffin, followed by ..."'

How right she is, but Brecht writes to her that he has no idea what she's talking about; his love for her is unshakeable. He hurries to the post office with his letter before his former lover and closest collaborator, Elisabeth Hauptmann, arrives with a large number of Brecht's manuscripts and one of Helene's favourite pearl necklaces in her luggage, all of which she managed to rescue from his apartment before it was raided. Brecht urges her not to return to Berlin, but she will not be deterred – and she is subsequently arrested. It is a good thing, then, that a new woman enters his life – Ruth Berlau, a Danish Communist famous for having cycled to Moscow. Now, though, she comes to the Brecht family on foot.

In June, Thomas and Katia Mann and their younger children move to the small neighbouring town of Sanary-sur-Mer where Klaus and Erika settled back in May, as did the Feuchtwangers. Yet it is the arrival of Thomas and his wife at La Tranquille, the villa high above the roaring waters of the bay and beneath the pine trees and cypresses, that ushers in what are perhaps the three brightest months in German exile history. Aldous Huxley finished writing *Brave New World* only a few hundred yards away the previous year, and his young friend Sybille Bedford found this villa for the Manns. Bedford is the glittering nexus of this Sanary community and develops into its singular chronicler. For the span of one warm summer, the promise of a better world order seems to come true.

In Sanary, expatriate life plays out in the open air, usually at the tables of the three cafés lining the seafront – the Café de Lyon, where the locals gather, La Marine and the bar Chez Schwob. Here, the German exile community meet up for early-morning coffee and early-evening drinks. Here, the men read the German newspapers with horror while the women buy fish on the quayside. And here, evening arrangements are made: drinks at the Feucht-wangers' magical villa above the cliffs, a reading at Thomas Mann's or a summer party at René Schickele's house with its picturesque view of the whole bay and the setting sun.

'The harbour was smiling with its bright boats, and evening descended over the "Holy Land" beyond the bay, darkening the rocky crags with its shadow,' writes Schickele, concluding: '*Il faisait bon vivre.*' The scent of mimosa hangs over Sanary-sur-Mer in the early summer 'like the breath of the gods'. German writers, artists and philosophers are dotted around the place in their rented houses and flats. Only Klaus and Erika Mann continue to stay in Hôtel de la Tour by the port, which offers them the necessary buffer of a fifteen-minute walk to their parents' villa.

La Tranquille is situated at the end of the long path leading up from the harbour to the promontory. The sea breaks against the shore on both sides, and every day Thomas Mann chooses where he would prefer to go for a swim. Before breakfast, he, Katia and their children Elisabeth and Michael take a basket down to the sea and wade out into the warm water, then dry themselves and climb back up to the house. Still, after only one week, the lord of this manor resumes his normal routine. Following his swim, he sits down at his desk and continues work on *Joseph and His Brothers*.

On 13 July, he gives a reading. It is a balmy evening and the cicadas have struck up their grotesque clamour in the canopies of the pine trees as Thomas begins to read from his new manuscript, his voice barely audible over the creatures' buzzing. A small stage has been erected at the back of the Manns' villa and he sits there on a chair, his wife behind him, his daughter Erika reverently handing him one sheet after another. Sitting in the garden, drinking in every word, is the entire German expatriate community as well as Aldous Huxley and his wife. Also present are Thomas's brother Heinrich and Nelly Kröger, whom Thomas describes in his diary as 'particularly vulgar'. What can he do, though – she's family, after all. Ashamed of her intellectual simplicity, Heinrich tells his brother that it is a result of falling on her head shortly before she fled from Berlin; she was different before her accident, he says. Thomas appears to believe this explanation (or he might just be humouring his brother). When Nelly serves herself a fifth glass of punch and starts to stagger, Heinrich suggests that they ought to be heading home.

With the exception of the steadfastly faithful older Manns, there are many facets to the erotic situation in Sanary-sur-Mer that muggy summer – and we can assume that what we know is the tip of the iceberg. First and foremost, there is Lion Feuchtwanger, whose writing and sex life are both incredibly prolific, as his diaries attest. In addition to his wife and his secretary, Lola Sernau, with whom he has cultivated an intense relationship, he is also having affairs with Bruno Frank's wife, Liesl, who lives opposite the Manns, and with Ludwig Marcuse's wife, Sascha. They are later joined by the caricaturist Eva Herrmann, as well as a string of young ladies from Sanary and the surrounding villages.

There are also a range of lesbian liaisons going on in which Sybille Bedford plays a leading role. She lives with Eva Herrmann and entertains relationships with Erika Mann, Annemarie Schwarzenbach and Aldous Huxley's wife, Maria. Helen Hessel and Charlotte Wolff also come down from Paris to Sanary for the summer. The greatest scandals, however, are associated with the American travel writer William Seabrook, who satisfies his sadomasochistic appetites in his huge villa directly across the road from the Huxleys, suspending his trussed-up girlfriend, Marjorie Muir Worthington, from the ceiling (Golo Mann* was an amused lodger in their household).

---

*Golo, Thomas and Katia Mann's third child, had fled Germany by now and was to spend the next few years teaching in France.

Then there are that summer's short-term visitors: Heinrich Mann and Nelly Kröger, Ernst Toller and Christiane Grautoff, Arnold Zweig with Lily Offenstadt, Bertolt Brecht and Margarete Steffin. The list goes on and on. The only one of them who is alone is Klaus Mann, which is why, as we know from his diary, he repeatedly drives over to Toulon late at night on the lookout for a saucy sailor. He writes a short story about this time titled *A Summer's Pain*; indeed all these people are suffering from this pain, this paradoxical situation of being a refugee in paradise. When the guests have gone home and all his children are tucked up in bed, Thomas Mann sits down in his wicker chair on the small terrace and gazes up at the sky. The cicadas have fallen silent. From below comes the crash of surf. Above him, the stars. He cannot comprehend the events that have brought him, a son of Lübeck and a resident of Munich by choice, to this small town on the Mediterranean. Ringing in his ears are Gottfried Benn's words to his son Klaus: 'Do you think history is particularly active in French seaside resorts?' He looks up at the heavens and doesn't feel so sure. On 25 August, the Manns learn that SA men have occupied their villa in Poschingerstrasse and wrecked it. Now they know that they must find a new home. When Thomas and Katia leave Sanary in September to settle permanently in Zurich, it spells the beginning of the end of the warmest, sunniest and boldest mass emigration project in German literary history.

Some people see escaping from the Nazis as a triumph, others as the opposite. 'The more emigrants I meet, the more clearly I grasp our defeat,' Golo Mann writes in his diary. During these summer days he feels very drawn to his uncle Heinrich, whom he thinks is enduring his fate 'with great dignity'. Golo contrasts this with the attitude of his father, whom he considers 'ladylike in his pain, affronted by the whole world'.

'What a strange family we are! In the future people will write books about *us* – not just about some of us individually.' These wise words are from Klaus Mann, or to be more precise from Klaus Heinrich Thomas Mann, for every time he reads his passport, both his father's and his uncle's names jump out at him. It is a miracle that he puts up with this heavy symbolic load for so long. And that, despite their fame and their stolid characters, he still loves them both so passionately.

On the evening of 16 June, Haim Arlosoroff – known as Viktor in Germany – and his wife, Sima, go for a walk along the beachfront in Tel Aviv. A splendid early summer's day is drawing to a close. A gentle breeze is blowing in off the sea, and scraps of conversation and the clatter of cutlery drift through the twilight from the restaurant terraces. All of a sudden two men step out from behind a large palm tree. One shines a torch in Arlosoroff's face while the other barks, 'Are you Dr Arlosoroff?' When he confirms that he is, one of the men opens fire with a revolver. Arlosoroff slumps to the pavement, soaked in blood. Sima lets out a series of desperate screams as the two men make off, undetected.

At the time, Arlosoroff is the unofficial foreign minister of the Jewish Agency, responsible for representing Jewish emigrants to Palestine until the state of Israel comes into being. But he also has a significant past. For many years he was the lover of Magda Quandt, who is now the wife of Joseph Goebbels, and a close friend of Adolf Hitler's – something like first lady of the Third Reich.

We do not know if it was Goebbels who had his predecessor murdered on this balmy evening in Tel Aviv. All we know is that the idea that his wife had once not only loved this Jew but also contemplated emigrating to Palestine with him has been driving Goebbels mad. We also know that David Ben-Gurion, the Zionist leader and future first prime minister of the state of Israel, sent Arlosoroff to Berlin in May 1933. Spotting a portrait of Magda and Joseph Goebbels wreathed in roses in a shop window, he tried to make contact with her by letter. In response, he received a coded message from Magda at his hotel telling him that it was too risky for her to speak to him and that he should go back to Palestine immediately if he held his life dear. He did, but it appeared that someone would be happier if there were no living witnesses to Magda Goebbels' past passion for a Jew; it is only two days after his return to Tel Aviv that Arlosoroff is assassinated.

Josephine Baker, the chorus girl with the big heart and the big eyes that she can make roll back in her head until her pupils disappear, is the richest African-American woman in the world in 1933. She has completely retired from public life after the racist abuse on her European tour and is living on her country estate near Paris. Pepito has made sure that the gigantic villa Le Beau Chêne resembles a temple to his wife. The first and second floors are plastered with photographs of Baker's stage performances, while the foyer is for some reason full of fifteenth-century suits of armour. The bed Josephine Baker sleeps in apparently once belonged to Marie Antoinette – but unlike its previous owner (and much to her sorrow), she doesn't get pregnant in it.

Josephine populates her house with more and more wildlife. There are cages for parrots and her three monkeys, and kennels for the various dogs, whose number has now swelled to thirteen. They're free to wander at will, with only the bathroom off limits. Here there are full-length mirrors on all four walls and a silver tub with gold taps; only the water that pours from them is ordinary. When the weather is warm, Josephine takes her daily bath in a huge marble-clad outside pool filled with water lilies and goldfish. She has created a miniature paradise for herself. She refuses to read any newspapers: she doesn't want to be woken from her dreams.

Ordinary life has resumed in Hermann and Ninon Hesse's house in Montagnola above Lake Lugano. The spring visits from émigrés are over; Thomas Mann, Brecht and all the others have not been granted permanent residence in Switzerland and have therefore moved on to southern France. Casa Rossa sinks back into its sluggish ways, interrupted only by cleaning routines that are increasingly taxing Hermann's nerves. Ninon runs a tight ship, and it is all too clean and posh for him. All the floors have to be mopped and polished every day, meals are served at fixed times and conform to the strictest of diets.

These are also the only aspects of his wife's character that he praises in a letter to the Austrian illustrator Alfred Kubin: 'I am grateful to this woman for leading me once more into temptation and seducing me once more on the verge of old age, for managing my household and feeding me light and wholesome food.' This doesn't sound much like passion. She's young enough to be his daughter but she acts like his mother. One of his young lovers, Elisabeth Gerdts-Rupp, visits him in Montagnola and is horrified by what she finds: 'The worst thing is that it confirmed everything his friends told me in advance, namely that his relationship with Ninon is proving to be a graver error with every passing day.'

The problem is that it isn't only Hesse who seems unhappy; running a tight ship is all too much for Ninon. Hesse writes to her: 'I have frequently been mystified by your states of sadness and disinclination and your often fanatical devotion to taking care of the floors and the meals.' She sometimes mystifies herself. When she hears that her ex-husband has remarried, she wonders if she was right to pressure Hermann into this marriage, right to give up her doctoral thesis and her dreams of having children to run this household. He escapes into the garden every day for hours to weed and also takes the waters at Baden two or three times a year. Ninon travels alone to Italy, as she did for her honeymoon. Somehow, though, the two of them grin and bear it.

The newly wed Kurt and Helen Wolff want to settle close to Hermann Hesse in Ticino after fleeing from Berlin. However, they feel unwelcome there, so they too head for southern France and the wonderful cabin that Helene has rented for the past two summers. Now, in the summer of 1933, in the very place where they discovered their love for each other, they are exiles. Katia and Thomas Mann come over from Sanary-sur-Mer to visit, and Thomas describes it in his typical style: 'Tea with Wolff and his ladies in the garden of his primitive home, a farmer's retirement dwelling.'

That is one way of looking at it, but for the Manns' hosts this is a special place. Not a retirement home but a fountain of youth. For Helene it is also the blissful setting she immortalised in *Background to Love*. In these June days she falls pregnant, and despite the oppressive situation abroad, this happiness fills her and Kurt with cautiously hopeful thoughts about the future.

The love story of Anaïs Nin and Henry Miller has long since entered literary lore as a result of her *Henry and June* and his *Quiet Days in Clichy*. Unfortunately, though, their *amour fou* is interrupted that summer by the reappearance of another of the men in Anaïs Nin's life: her father.

All her therapists and lovers have heard how much she suffers from the fact that her father, the proud musician Joaquín, abandoned her and her mother. Now, in June 1933, there is an opportunity to heal this open wound. Having just turned thirty, she travels to Valescure to see her fifty-four-year-old father, who intends to spend the summer holidays there without his new wife. To break the ice, Joaquín Nin tells his daughter how wild and passionate her mother was. In return, Anaïs describes her usual strategy for seducing men. Impressed, he confesses that he goes about things much the same way. Then he puts it into practice with his daughter, telling her, 'You are the synthesis of all the women I have loved.' She lets him caress her foot and he tells her that he dreamed he kissed her 'like a lover'.

Then he tells her, 'I don't feel towards you as if you were my daughter.' Anaïs replies, 'I don't feel as if you were my father.' On 23 June 1933, they sleep together for the first time.

Anaïs starts writing a new journal, which she calls *Incest*. It contains all the quotations above and a great many sexual details besides. It also describes her greatest source of pleasure – her ability to turn a story on its head. At last it is not she who is afraid of her father leaving her, but he who is scared she will leave him.

After two weeks she returns to Paris, with several full diaries but free of guilt. Her husband is pleased to see her rosy-cheeked and writes: 'Anaïs has come back looking radiant because she has found her father again. She has always dreamed of her father.' Hugo writes a horoscope for Anaïs and her father, but he cannot interpret it properly. Only his wife can: 'Father's moon is in my sun – the strongest attraction between man and woman,' she writes. 'When Hugo showed me this, fatalism choked the last vestiges of my sense of guilt.'

Dora Benjamin, freshly divorced from Walter, manages to escape from Berlin with their son, Stefan Rafael. They establish a small guesthouse in San Remo called Villa Verde. Meanwhile, Walter is living in penury in Ibiza; none of the fees for his reviews are reaching him. He looks more and more bedraggled. He wanders around San Antonio and reads one Simenon crime novel after another to distract himself. He falls out with the Noeggeraths and moves to a half-finished building with no windows. He roams around restlessly all day long, sleeping on a simple sheet spread on the floor and washing in the sea. The villagers nickname him El Miserable, The Wretched One. Benjamin finishes a draft of his essay 'Experience and Poverty' and writes to his friend Gershom Scholem that he is seriously considering emigrating to Palestine.

All year Pablo Picasso paints Marie-Thérèse Walter. He no longer paints his wife. When he, Olga and their son visit his family in Barcelona, Picasso sends a letter to Paris on the very first day: 'My adored lover, I am coming back. I will soon be in Paris again. I am so happy that I will see my love. Forever yours, P.'

Céline, who is acclaimed in France for *Journey to the End of the Night*, writes to his German girlfriend, Erika, in Berlin on 27 June: 'Once the Jews have been chased out of Germany, there will be jobs for the other intellectuals there! Heil Hitler! Take advantage.' To his Jewish girlfriend, the gymnastics teacher Cillie Pam, with whom he spent two passionate weeks in September, he writes soon afterwards: 'The Jews are in some danger, but only a little bit, and I don't think things will ever get bad.' There are much more important things to do, he thinks: 'How are you? Are you making babies or revolution? And how are you dealing with your libido?'

The twenty-ninth of June is Victor and Eva Klemperer's anniversary. He writes in his diary: 'Of the twenty-nine June 29ths of our life together, this is basically the most dismal, but we have fairly successfully endeavoured to get through it calmly.' He notes the new words he wants to record in his 'lexicon' of the Nazis which, as *The Language of the Third Reich*, will one day make him famous: 'Schutzhaft' and 'gleichschalten'.* His only source of hope, along with cinema, are his two cats, which rub themselves calmingly against his legs as he writes his despairing diary entries.

Nineteen thirty-three is the year when Meret Oppenheim makes art history. She becomes the muse of two great artists, but first she turns the ear of another artist into a sculpture. First she draws it, over and over again – because she is unable to soften his heart, Meret is forced to target a different part of Alberto Giacometti's body. He doesn't reciprocate her love and introduces her instead to Man Ray, still wallowing in sorrow over the loss of Lee Miller. Man Ray persuades Meret to pose naked for him next to an old printing press and paints her arm black. Published in the Surrealist magazine *Minotaure* as part of his *Érotique voilée* cycle, this photo makes her an overnight celebrity.

Soon after that, Meret meets the Surrealist Max Ernst and falls in love with him on the spot. She is only twenty-two; he has just turned forty-two and is living with his second wife, Marie-Berthe

---

*The Nazis used the euphemistic term *Schutzhaft*, or 'protective custody', to denote the extra-judicial arrest of political opponents, Jews and other downtrodden groups. *Gleichschalten*, or 'to co-ordinate', describes the process of establishing totalitarian control.

Aurenche, who watches him like a hawk. Still, Max becomes inflamed with passion for Meret, writing: 'Dear Meretli, I can tell you completely unsurrealistically and unplatonically that your sudden disappearance has left me feeling barely alive.' Then the following lines the next day: 'Tell me you love me' and 'You are beautiful, very beautiful in my memory'. We can guess that the two lovers enjoy a joyous and completely unsurrealistic autumn in Paris.

Gussie Adenauer repeatedly travels by train from Cologne to Andernach and from there by bus to the abbey at Maria Laach. Ten-year-old Paul stays with his father there for a few weeks in July. Konrad Adenauer finds it helpful to have someone to distract him in his despair. In his letters he calls Maria Laach his place of 'banishment' and even 'my exile'.

After their wedding at the village church in Bad Saarow on 8 July, Max Schmeling and Anny Ondra hold the reception at the nearby Hotel Esplanade. Guests have been asked to bring their bathing costumes, and some of them swim in the pool before dinner. The young married couple then spend their honeymoon in Heiligendamm.

Just as the Prussian diplomat and writer Karl August Varnhagen von Ense had no access to the spiritual and intellectual riches of his wife, the great Jewish salonnière and even greater letter-writer Rahel – the subject of the biography Hannah Arendt is writing – so Hannah's husband, Günther Stern, lacks any sensitivity for the inner thoughts of his wife. Hannah doesn't need to try very hard to imagine her subject's estrangement from her husband; she can draw on her own experience. 'The more August understands, the more Rahel is compelled to keep things from him. She doesn't hide anything specific, only the uncanny uncertainty of her nights and the disquieting twilight of the day.' Arendt can never confide in her husband as effortlessly as she did in Martin Heidegger.

However, the cause of the final breakdown of her marriage is pleasingly Freudian – cigars. A box of dark Habanos, a gift from Arendt's friend Kurt Blumenfeld, enrages Günther. His angry reasoning is that, first, cigars are for men and, second, they stink. Hannah serenely lights one, waves the match out and exhales the heavy smoke into the upper reaches of their flat in Opitzstrasse.

Even though she has been predicting Hitler's rise for years and considering emigration, even though she is the one who finds their marriage claustrophobic, ultimately it is Günther who emigrates to Paris first. As a member of the left-wing circles around Bertolt Brecht, he is concerned that the Nazis might scour the playwright's address book for political opponents to round up. Arendt leaves only later, after supporting Zionists in Berlin to document every-day antisemitism 'because if one is attacked as a Jew, one must defend oneself as a Jew'.

All the same, when she is released, entirely due to the goodwill of an inexperienced police officer, after eight days in custody on charges of conducting illegal research at the Prussian State Library, she is not inclined to tempt her luck a second time. She is horrified that even Berlin's intellectual elite – including her friends – are going along with the Nazis. She cannot believe her ears when she hears that Heidegger has celebrated 'the grandeur and honour of this national awakening' in his speech upon being elected rector of Freiburg University.

She travels with her mother to Dresden and on to the last station into the Erzgebirge, mountains close to the Czechoslo-vakian border. She knows of a sympathetic German family whose house is situated on the border itself; they spend a day sheltering there. That night, under the cover of darkness and out of sight of border patrols, they walk out of the house into Czechoslovakia and freedom. Hannah had been determined to remain faithful to her mother tongue, and to German philosophy and literature, but she now knows that she has to leave Germany behind.

She reaches Paris via Prague and Geneva, constantly campaigning for the Jewish community, writing speeches and helping refugees to emigrate to Palestine. In Paris, she meets Günther again and they even live together, but they both know that their marriage is over – not even the pressure of emigration can patch up their relationship. Her official name is still Hannah Stern, though, and she has also smuggled her husband's most precious belonging out of Berlin for him – the manuscript of his thousand-page novel *The Molussian Catacomb*. It had initially been confiscated from Stern's publisher by the Gestapo; then Brecht kept it hidden until Arendt finally wrapped it in a dirty sheet, hid it in her suitcase and transported it with her to Paris. Rarely has she experienced such gratitude from her husband as in the instant when she opens the suitcase and hands him the manuscript. In fact, he is almost happier about being reunited with the book than with its bearer.

After her mother has returned to Germany to be with her second husband, Martin Beerwald, Arendt sets about forging an independent life in France. She takes Hebrew lessons because she says she wants to 'get to know her people' and finds a job with a Jewish charity called Agriculture et Artisanat.* Mainly, though, she writes. Slowly but surely, Hannah Stern reverts to Hannah Arendt.

Prior to emigrating she had hurriedly tossed into her suitcase all the manuscripts, excerpts and notebooks relating to her book about Rahel, and all made it safely across the border among her underwear. Now she continually detects in her subject her own fate and the failure of the assimilation that seemed achievable to Rahel in the 1810s and 1820s. Yet in her portrayal of the life of a woman who was full of spirit and warmth, Arendt manages to turn the historical figure into her contemporary, in part because she so closely identifies with Rahel's romantic ups and downs. Rahel suffers greatly from pain and abandonment, and while Arendt writes, she is palpably digesting the end of her relationship with Heidegger; her descriptions of her subject's dreary marriage

---

*Agriculture and Handicraft.

also allude to her barren years with Günther. Great minds feel
alike.

Käthe von Porada's Parisian friends urge her to go to Berlin and
find out what has happened to Gottfried Benn. Why is this dis-
tinguished man of letters lending his support to the brutal new
regime? She is to tell Benn how horrified Germans abroad are by
his stance, but she doesn't accomplish her mission. Instead, she is
stupid enough to fall in love with the man she's supposed to be
interrogating. They meet at Benn's surgery-cum-apartment in early
July. Porada's aim is to introduce Benn to Max Beckmann, whom
she adores. The poet and the painter, as similar in physiognomy as
they are in their affinity for Greek and Roman mythology and pondering life's great questions, have never met, but Porada also fails in
this mission. The two men keep postponing the meeting and eventually Benn cancels due to an unfortunate cold. Her conclusion:
'Never again did I try to bring two heroes together.'

Things are working out much more smoothly between Benn
and Porada. She is smartly turned out, five years younger than him,
well-educated and divorced, while Benn's evenings are not fully
booked – despite his work as a doctor and his affairs with Tilly
Wedekind and Elinor Büller. After their second meeting, they go
on a date to the cinema. Afterwards, Benn writes to her that he
cannot for the life of him remember what the film was about. 'I
do, however, remember everything about the charming creature I
worship so much and whom I consider to be the most delightful
and most cultivated lady by the Tyrrhenian Sea. I prostrate myself
before her as her faithful St Bernard, G.B.' This delightful and cultivated lady stays in Berlin for two weeks and they embark on an
affair. He begs her not to say anything to the Parisian friends who
sent her to see if Gottfried Benn was still in his right mind. 'Would
you please not disabuse anyone about me? I really don't care. Let
me be your private affair.'

To his private affair Benn dedicates the poem 'Through Every
Hour' to her: 'Poem for Kati – 14.8.33'. That same day a card lands

in his letterbox from Tilly Wedekind, the playwright's widow. She writes: 'I love you, Benn! With head and heart, body and soul, with my whole being, I am yours! Tilly.'

To make sure he takes her at her word she pulls up the next day outside No. 12 Belle-Alliance-Strasse and honks her horn. Benn comes down, and they drive out to a lake to swim, sunbathe and eat ice cream.

What about Käthe? Her dilemma is that soon after returning to Paris she happens to run into Klaus Mann, the loudest critic of Benn's aberrations. He takes her out for dinner and she has to bite her tongue all evening to avoid giving herself away. She is finding it increasingly hard to justify to herself why, instead of accomplishing her mission in Berlin, she ended up jumping into bed with the accused.

Meanwhile, also in Paris, Tamara de Lempicka is fighting off the advances of the filthy-rich Baron Raoul Kuffner. As we know, she has recently pinched him from his mistress by painting a grotesquely distorted portrait of her. Kuffner has been in love with Lempicka ever since – and all the more so since she painted him in an especially flattering, virile and dapper pose, hiding the fact that his hair is thinning and his features far flabbier than she depicted. Now, in the summer of 1933, his wife having died the year before, Kuffner writes to Lempicka to say that since the mourning period for his wife is over, he would like to marry her. Tamara replies: 'Please do not put pressure on me. I don't have time to get married right now. I have to paint.' Maybe, she adds, she will have time for a wedding in 1934.

Walter Benjamin is still living in his half-finished accommodation in Ibiza, penniless and scared. His daily routine consists of brooding and writing, followed by more brooding. He shuns the sun, which suddenly seems as cruel as his fate. One morning, however, he notices that a young Dutch woman has moved in two doors down from him. Anna Maria Blaupot ten Cate is a thirty-year-old artist who witnessed the book-burning in Berlin that May and has made her way to Ibiza from Italy. She is here because, unlike Benjamin, she envisions living in bohemian freedom under the blazing sun.

What is bound to happen, does. Once more Benjamin falls head over heels in love with the wrong woman. He doesn't pen a single letter or a single review in August 1933 – Anna Maria blocks out everything else. They walk through the pine woods, sit under fig trees and bathe in the warm blue sea; they sail out into the night on the langoustine fishermen's small boats, they talk, they sit in silence and they make love. He tells her, 'You are all the things I've ever been able to love in a woman.'

On 13 August, Walter offers his beloved an autobiographical essay, 'Agesilaus Santander'. It opens with the words 'When I was born' and ends with the fateful encounter with Anna Maria, to whom an angel led him as a reward for his patience: 'And so, though I had only just seen you for the first time, I travelled back with you to where I came from.' Benjamin the troubadour has found a new object of his love, his 'new angel'.

In September, he writes to Gershom Scholem and asks him to send his poem on Paul Klee's *Angelus Novus,* which is hanging on the wall in Benjamin's Berlin flat. 'I have met a woman here who is his female counterpart,' he writes. Anna Maria becomes his incarnation of the Angel of History, and he writes his own poem for his adored:

> as the first woman on the first day
> you stood before me and ever so
> now you'll hear my beseeching's echo
> which has a thousand tongues. It says, stay.

Maybe it all gets to be too much for Anna Maria, because she doesn't stay. Rather fittingly for an angel, she floats away in September, first from the island and then out of Walter's life. After her departure he suffers several severe bouts of fever. Arriving in Paris via Barcelona, he is diagnosed with malaria.

*

In September, Bertolt Brecht travels from Denmark to Paris, and from there, now accompanied by Margarete Steffin, to Sanary-sur-Mer to see Lion and Marta Feuchtwanger. Marta has to be taken to hospital because she forgets to put on the handbrake when she parks their car and is run over as it rolls backwards. Brecht, on the other hand, engages in five weeks of furious lovemaking with Margarete. As she sleeps he writes to Helene in Denmark: 'It's boring here by the Mediterranean.'

Kurt Tucholsky spends 1933 in Switzerland. He continues to live with Hedwig Müller in Ticino and at Florhofgasse 1 in Zurich. In March *Die Weltbühne* was banned, in May his books were burned and in June he is stripped of his German citizenship. He's an unhappy man, and being unable to publish his thoughts drives him crazy, particularly when it comes to addressing events in his homeland. To the poet and playwright Walter Hasenclever in southern France he writes: 'I do not need to tell you that our world has ceased to exist in Germany. For that reason I shall hold my tongue for now. You cannot hold back an ocean by whistling.'

Not that Tucholsky is able to whistle – his sinuses are so inflamed with ulcers that he has to undergo a series of operations, though they fail to cure him and he suffers terribly. His friend Carl von Ossietzky is in a concentration camp, all his major fellow intellectuals have emigrated to Paris, the singers for whom he wrote his songs are no longer permitted to sing and the newspapers he loved writing for are no longer allowed to print his articles. So he writes dozens of letters every day. He's as witty as ever, though the humour turns increasingly dark. It is as if, with every passing month, the clouds are closing more tightly over his heart. This is partly because he must divorce the one woman he truly loves – Mary. He knows he has to protect her. Remaining married to a pacifist, left-wing Jewish journalist who has been stripped of his citizenship could be her death sentence.

On 21 August, they are officially divorced. As he writes in *Rheinsberg: A Storybook for Lovers*, 'There is no blame. There is only the course of time. These streets intersect in infinity. Everyone carries the other around with him or her. Something always remains.' Lisa Matthias, his lover from *Castle Gripsholm*, sensed that he would never entirely break with Mary: 'You just won't let Madame be free. When you are away, even when you are with me, you are worried about "what she's up to". So you still love her: that's my conclusion.' She was absolutely correct. After the divorce Tucholsky leaves Switzerland and travels back to Sweden, where he is living in exile.

On 18 September, Klaus Mann is overcome by an unfamiliar urge at his luxury hotel in Zurich: 'Fancy writing a love poem. How melodramatic. Despairing tenderness – in the midst of disaster.' He sits down, opens his notebook and sharpens his pencil, but finds no inspiration.

On 18 September, the dissolution of Lotte Lenya's marriage to Kurt Weill is officially pronounced. Although the official grounds for divorce is her affair with Otto Pasetti, that relationship has long been on the rocks. As for Kurt, he only got together with Erika Neher because he didn't want to wait around for Lotte. It is therefore the divorce of two people who still love each other. Lotte will spend the rest of her life regretting her decision.

Else Lasker-Schüler has found accommodation at Zurich's Augustinerhof hostel, the cheapest place in town. She lives from hand to mouth – her tongue has healed – trying to sell her poems and drawings, trying to make contacts in political circles and with Jewish groups. On 19 September, she meets Erika and Klaus Mann and goes to the cinema with them – a rare treat. Klaus notes in his diary: 'Lasker-Schüler (distracted and desperate) shows us some pretty pictures of American Indians that she produces to keep herself calm.' She sits in her tiny hostel room for days, moving down to the big stove on the first floor when it gets too cold; sometimes, she says, 'I consider my frugality like nirvana.' But it's impossible to find light if you study only darkness.

Marlene Dietrich returns to Hollywood in September. At some point life in Europe simply became too tedious for her, or perhaps too stressful. Being in the same city as her mother, her daughter, her husband, his lover and her own lover's wife, added to the stream of émigrés from Berlin who arrive at her door because they've heard about her generosity and are hoping for a handout, all under the gaze of the international press – this is beyond even Dietrich's considerable capabilities.

Luckily, the shooting of her new film, in which she is to play Catherine the Great, is slated for September. Josef von Sternberg wants to transform his muse and lover into the most powerful woman in human history; his relationship with Dietrich has progressed from admiration to love and now obsession. After her arrival back in Hollywood he addresses her exclusively as 'Beloved Goddess' and makes her two gifts – a new, even more magnificent mansion and an even more elegant Rolls-Royce. Oh, and a gold cigarette case studded with rhinestones and diamonds that will whisper its engraved message every time she opens it:

MARLENE DIETRICH
WIFE, MOTHER AND PERFORMER LIKE NONE OTHER
JOSEF VON STERNBERG

This is the final straw. Marlene Dietrich belongs to no one but herself. What's more, she can't help but notice that her besotted director's movies are receiving worse and worse reviews. She acknowledges that he created her, but now she wants to live without him. Very soon Dietrich will shoot her last film with Josef von Sternberg, the significantly titled *The Devil Is a Woman*.

*

On 26 September 1933, Claus Schenk Graf von Stauffenberg and Nina von Lerchenfeld get married in St James's church in Bamberg. He wears his uniform and a steel helmet after explaining to his bride that a wedding service is just that – service. Not that she expected anything else. After their wedding reception at the Bamberger Hof hotel, their honeymoon is to take them to Rome. The big attraction is an exhibition to mark the tenth anniversary of Mussolini's rule, and they also want to admire Caravaggios, Raphaels and Michelangelos.

On the morning after the wedding, they board their south-bound train, and Claus's brother Berthold travels with them to Bellinzona, where he gets off to see his greatest love, stefan george, the upper-class man of lowercase letters.* Berthold had really wanted to get married like his brother, but the poet wants him all to himself, voicing repeated objections to Berthold's potential union with Maria Classen, to which Berthold loyally acquiesces (at least while George is alive). As is expected of people of their social standing, Claus and Nina conceive their first child during their honeymoon trip to Mussolini's Italy.

On 29 September, Erika Mann and Therese Giehse open their Peppermill show for the second time. Thomas and Katia Mann and Liesl and Bruno Frank take their seats in the audience for the premiere, just as they did back on New Year's Day. This time, however, they are all in Switzerland, driven out of the country by the inhumane policies this cabaret seeks to expose.

While Berlin's entire intellectual community seems to have fled to southern France or Paris, two intellectuals make the oppo-site journey in autumn 1933. Endowed with an Institut Français research grant, Jean-Paul Sartre has come to Germany to study

---

*Stefan George (1868–1933) espoused an aristocratic ethos but also experimented widely with punctuation and typography, largely eschewing the conventional initial-capitalization of German nouns.

with Edmund Husserl, the great phenomenologist philosopher. His most important impetus lies elsewhere, though: 'I reconnected with the irresponsibility of my youth.' Even as swastika flags wave over Berlin and all the country's great authors are fleeing to Paris, Sartre recognises Berlin as 'the city of love'.

First of all, he rushes to restaurants that serve hearty German food; he loves dark beer, pork, sauerkraut and sausages – the kind of food he would eat when he stayed with his grandmother in Alsace. Then he sets out to enjoy Berlin's nightlife. He can't speak a word of German and so, to his regret – he actually came here to 'experience the love of German women' – he has to take 'a French girlfriend'. He later wistfully recalls a Hungarian admirer of Simone de Beauvoir who could barely speak French and whom she rejected. This encourages him to consult a German dictionary and write her the following words: 'If you only knew how witty I am in Hungarian.'

So Sartre studies German philosophy and German nightlife in Berlin in the company of a Frenchwoman called Marie Ville, the dreamy wife of a staff member at the Institut Français. When he tells de Beauvoir about this, she once again notices what a strain their strange honesty pact and Sartre's absence place her under. She obtains sick leave from work and goes to Berlin. Sartre's ill-judged response is to introduce her to his new lover on her very first night in town. He tells her she has nothing to fear; Marie Ville is just a minor fling. He even puts a wedding ring on Simone's finger – but only so she can pose as his wife and rent a small flat near the Institut Français for the duration of her stay.

But de Beauvoir would rather be Sartre's wife for real. She is hurt by this 'contingent love', the term Sartre uses for his extramarital affairs, in parallel to their own 'necessary' love. De Beauvoir travels back to Paris and starts writing a novel about the conflict between love and independence. Sartre stays in his French microcosm in a posh villa in Berlin-Wilmersdorf and fails to notice anything about the age of hate that has commenced.

*

The same cannot be said of Heinrich Mann. He is an extremely sensitive man, which is why the book he wrote during his first summer of exile in France, now published by Amsterdam-based Querido, is called *Hatred*. His experiences at the Berlin Academy in February and what he can tell from people's faces and the newspapers is all the evidence he needs to know what's coming. Fifteen years later, Lion Feuchtwanger will say of this book: 'Heinrich Mann predicted the Germany of the last decade earlier and more accurately than any of us. He described it from its first stirrings, long before it became a reality.'

One of the most peculiar couples of an age in which they were not exactly in short supply, Salvador Dalí and Gala, spend a blissful summer in a small fisherman's hut in Portlligat on the Costa Brava.

When she was Paul Éluard's and Max Ernst's partner in 1920s Paris, Gala's forthright sexuality had driven the Surrealists to distraction. Dalí – who prefers voyeurism to active sex and ties himself in knots fighting his homosexual tendencies – appears to see in Gala's femininity a means of self-liberation. This may not be logically or even psychologically comprehensible, but it clearly works. Gala's love allows Dalí to discover the genius and uniqueness of his art. Incidentally, throughout their decades-long relationship, the two of them have sex either once (according to Gala) or never (according to Dalí). 'Fear', Gala explains, 'is the fundamental trait of Dalí's character.' When she informs him that an operation on her womb has left her unable to have children, he registers the news with intense relief. He wishes to remain her only ward.

Gala's dominance makes her the polar opposite of the giggling, capricious, moustachioed oddball, and he is delighted to subjugate himself to her governance for the rest of his life. Although Gala and Paul Éluard officially divorced back in 1932, Éluard still worships her – despite his longstanding relationship with the generous and mysterious actress Maria Benz. He tells her so in passionate letters: 'Gala, nothing I do is detached from you.'

But Gala is already closely attached to Salvador Dalí. She won't leave his side for as much as a single day. To demonstrate that Gala is his, Dalí paints an unusual portrait of her. He places two pieces of meat on her shoulders and makes her pose for hours. After working on the painting for a few days, he proudly presents her with *Portrait of Gala with Two Lamb Chops in Equilibrium on Her Shoulder*. It is only now that he has this woman by his side that Dalí is able to express his wildest fantasies on canvas. Thanks to Gala, his motto that beauty should be edible finally comes true. Accordingly, his second great portrait of Gala from 1933 is called *The Sugar Sphinx*.

Day by day, Victor Klemperer continues to compile his lexicon of the language of the Third Reich, though he no longer believes that he will ever be able to publish it. On 9 October, his birthday, he notes a few wishes in his diary: 'To see Eva well again, in our own house, at her harmonium. Not to have to tremble every morning and evening in anticipation of hysterics. To see the end of the tyranny and its bloody downfall ... No pains in my side and no thoughts of death. I do not think that even one of these wishes will come true for me.'

Otto Dix flees with his wife and children from the growing hostility in Dresden to Schloss Randegg near Lake Constance in southern Germany. Looking out of the small castle's windows, he sees extinct volcanoes with names like Hohenkrähen, Hohentwiel, Hohenstoffeln and Hohenhewen. The presence of these peaks may well have helped a humiliated man like Otto. The first thing he does after arriving is paint Randegg's old Jewish cemetery – as both an accusation and a warning. Beyond the cemetery, among the tall fir trees, lies the Swiss border.

The castle is the Dix family's haven in the storm. It belongs to Martha Dix's first husband, Hans Koch, who married her sister after their divorce. So the Dixes and their children, Nelly, Ursus and Jan, move into Martha's sister's castle. They live in the south tower, which adjoins a huge room that Dix uses as his studio. Inside, the easel; outside, the soft hills rolling off into the distance. Otto Dix has stopped painting war, deadly sins and people. Instead, he paints enchanted valleys and gentle mountain slopes in the autumn, winter and spring, emigrating into the landscape.

After having an affair with her own father, Anaïs Nin rekindles her previous Parisian liaisons – first with her husband, second with her therapist and lastly with Henry Miller. Things are a little complicated right now with Hugo; having thrown himself into astrology, he has discovered that as an Aquarius he is far less compatible with Anaïs, a Pisces, than the Capricorn Henry Miller is. Miller, on the other hand, continues to live off the money Nin gives him and continues to enjoy the sex. Her therapist, René Allendy, gets both these things from her, but unlike Miller pays for them with a guilty conscience.

Miller also gives astrology a try and comes to the conclusion that he is probably going to die in 1933. He draws up a will appointing Nin his sole heir, which in this case equates to asking her to pay off his $3,600 of debt. Mostly, though, he is preoccupied with turning his tangled love affairs with Anaïs and June into *Tropic of Cancer*.

Anaïs has generously rented a flat for him at 4 Avenue Anatole France in Clichy, where he lives with his friend Alfred Perlès. This is also the setting of *Quiet Days in Clichy*, his novel about sex and Paris. Miller smokes Gauloises all day, listens to music and acts the writer, sitting in a vest by his typewriter with a bottle of wine. He is glad when Anaïs comes by to tidy up the kitchen. He doesn't tell her how much he is thinking about June back in New York. He continues to exploit these resurgent memories so he can get on with writing *Tropic of Cancer*. International politics, Hitler and the German émigrés flooding into Paris are of no concern to Henry Miller.

Vladimir and Véra Nabokov are sticking it out in Berlin for the time being, though their financial difficulties have obliged them to move in with Véra's cousin Anna Feigin in Nestorstrasse. Vladimir gives occasional tennis lessons to local boys on a neighbourhood court. More importantly, he pours his novel *Invitation to a Beheading* onto paper in a two-week spurt of creativity. He is disturbed by the increasing violence in Berlin. Véra loses her job when the Nazis close down the offices of a Jewish law firm where she earned the money to pay their rent. When the Nabokovs are later asked why they didn't leave straight away in 1933 – Véra is, after all, Jewish – the author answers: 'We were always lethargic. Nicely lethargic in my wife's case, terribly lethargic in mine.'

But Nabokov can see what's going on around him. On the shore of Lake Grunewald he writes the short story 'The New Neighbour'. Two workers in Berlin first harass their new neighbour, Mr Romantovsky with the thick Slavic accent, then torment him and finally murder him, for absolutely no reason. The story is about Nabokov's paralysing anxiety. 'At the time I came up with those two thugs and poor Romantovsky, Hitler's grotesque and evil shadow lay over Berlin,' he later says. Against this oppressive background something improbable takes place that autumn in Nestorstrasse: with a slightly surreal smile Véra announces to Vladimir that she is pregnant. Their son, Dmitri, will be born in May 1934.

Having arrived back in his exile home of Paris and almost fully recovered from malaria, Walter Benjamin is reacquainted with his great summer love, Anna Maria Blaupot ten Cate. We don't really know what happens, but we do know that their love gradually evaporates into the air. She moves to the south of France, where she marries the Frenchman Louis Sellier in 1934. In August, Walter had written: 'In your arms, fate would never affect me again,' a prophecy which comes true. When Anna Maria puts her arm around another man, fate comes back to strike Walter with a vengeance.

*

Marlene Dietrich has now also grasped that the threat is beginning to spread from Germany across Europe. On 7 November, she writes a letter to her husband in Paris that offers a glimpse of what's behind her cool façade. She asks him for a new jar of night cream with the explanation: 'I'm getting old.' Then, in a sudden fit of concern and fear, she adds: 'Do me a lovely favour. Go out and buy some big suitcases tomorrow to put all your things in and get out of there. You know there's always a shortage of suitcases at the last minute.' Suddenly changing tone, she beseeches Rudi's lover: 'Please, Tami, help me to get him ready to leave Paris in a few hours, if possible. There are always ships.' And to crown the absurdity, she concludes the letter to her husband and his lover with this wonderful farewell: 'You are the best and truest of men. I love you, your Mutti.'

A very special love affair ends in 1933: the relationship between Nancy Cunard, the eccentric Englishwoman from the noblest of backgrounds, and the African-American jazz pianist Henry Crowder. On the streets of Paris, people mutter under their breath as they walk past, she in glittering robes and jangling ivory bracelets, he dressed to the nines in an impeccable three-piece suit.

Nancy writes an incendiary essay titled 'Black Man and White Ladyship', which her mother considers scandalous and so reports her daughter to the police. She seems determined to breach all her country's class divisions and racist prejudices. In Paris she runs The Hours Press for avant-garde literature and is the first to publish James Joyce, and Ezra Pound's *Cantos*.

Like Picasso, Cunard is a compulsive collector of African tribal art; her Paris flat is filled with sculptures, masks and weapons. She's also writing an ambitious book about Black culture intended to demonstrate that it has equal value with white culture. Despite all her intelligence, what she fails to grasp is that her partner, though Black, identifies less with his African ancestors than he does with his parents from New Orleans, with African-American culture and with jazz. With the creeping feeling that Nancy loves him not as an individual but as a symbol, he heads back to America.

In 1934, after he has left her, Nancy's *Negro Anthology* comes out. It teems with literature, music, culture and history; a thousand-page album of love and a manifesto against hatred. She has dedicated the book to Henry Crowder, the love of her life.

Down in Ticino, where it can be warm even in December when the wind drops and the sun breaks through the clouds, Stefan George enters his final days.

Under one of his Aryan-sounding pseudonyms, Walter Benjamin offered George birthday greetings in the *Frankfurter Zeitung* in July and dubbed him a prophet. In his poem 'A Young Leader in the First World War', George had predicted that a 'Second World War' would follow. Benjamin noted: 'Stefan George has been silent for years. In the meantime we have acquired a new ear for his voice.'

Klaus Mann sees things slightly differently. In his émigré magazine *Die Sammlung,* he responds with an essay titled 'Stefan George's Silence'. It is an expression of hope that George not be taken in by Hitler and the new Reich: 'We hope that his silence stands for resistance. If he wants to end the way he lived – with an infallible knowledge of purity, integrity and authentic nobility – then he should persist in the same attitude to the new Germany as the old one compelled him to adopt: averting his gaze.'

Stefan George reads these lines in Minusio in November 1933. He is on a strict regimen: mostly raw vegetarian food, no cigarettes and no alcohol. However, on 26 November, he defies these injunctions. For breakfast he has several bread rolls with sardines and ham; for lunch there is duck breast with turnip and mashed potato, followed by rice pudding and sweet white wine. He obviously overdoes it: 'Straight after his final mouthful, as the dishes were being cleared away', he slumps back in his chair unconscious, according to his faithful disciple Frank Mehnert. A doctor is called and he administers some injections, but the next day George collapses again, loses consciousness and is transported in his wicker chair to the Sant'Agnese clinic in Muralto. Mehnert sends telegrams to the elderly author's closest friends in Germany to inform them of George's condition. They all head south, including Claus and Berthold von Stauffenberg, to witness the master's last breaths. On Monday 4 December 1933, Stefan George's heart stops beating.

Claus von Stauffenberg, the rigorous first lieutenant, draws up a precise roster of which disciple will keep watch over George's body at which time in Minusio's cemetery chapel. As George is lowered into his grave at 8.15 a.m. on 6 December – and with him 'Secret Germany', the poet's esoteric circle – the weak December sun is rising over the high mountains opposite. In the valley below, Lake Maggiore lies black and silent. The next day, a large laurel wreath with black, white and red ribbons and two swastikas, sent by the German embassy in Bern on behalf of the new regime, is laid on his grave. Not even Stefan George could choose his admirers.

Ernst Jünger and his wife, Gretha, want to escape from Berlin. Following their friend Erich Mühsam's internment in a concentration camp, the Gestapo raided their flat in search of connections to the disgraced Communist. Their friendship with the sadomasochistic artist Rudolf Schlichter and his wife Speedy, who works as an escort, is also feeding rumours about them. So Jünger burns his diaries from the past fifteen years, his poems and letters and political writings, and turns down membership of the re-formed German Academy of Literature. He and Gretha decide to leave Berlin, especially as she is pregnant again and doesn't want to have to push their pram through SA marches and running battles. Ernst also desperately needs a change of air: 'These Bohemian faces disgust me.' And so they move to Goslar on the edge of the Harz Mountains in December 1933, hoping for 'a quiet life, away from the confusing and numbing rhythm that has invaded Berlin'.

Ruth Landshoff, that restless soul, loses her wedding ring in a train toilet on her way to Paris. She knows it is more than bad luck.

For a long time now, she has been more deeply in love with the English baron Bryan Guinness than with her husband, Graf Yorck von Wartenburg. Guinness has given her a pair of ground doves, and she takes the caged birds everywhere she goes. In return she sends him her 'Emigrant Novella' from Paris, but he is unable to get it printed in *Harper's Bazaar* or taken on by a literary agent. It has never been published, and yet Landshoff is the first writer to put the shameful silence of the émigré into words. Her desperate and nameless hero 'hated speaking and he hated looking because it bothered him to live in yearning. The emigrant loved his country very much. No one had forbidden him to love his country, but he was forbidden to live in his country.'

On 12 December, four years after Aby Warburg's death,* his great love leaves Germany. The freighter *Hermia* carries from Hamburg to London not only the Jewish art historian's legendary library but also his photo collection and his *Mnemosyne Atlas*. One of the greatest intellectual treasure troves of the 1910s and 1920s thus escapes destruction. Warburg's widow, Mary, dies in Hamburg soon afterwards.

On 18 December, his fifty-fourth birthday, Paul Klee receives a temporary residence permit from his hometown of Berne, and with it a chance to leave Germany legally, along with his wife Lily. They abandon most of their books and furniture in Düsseldorf. Klee cuts his right hand while packing and it turns septic – a final affliction on German soil. On 23 December, the Klees and their cat, Bimbo, depart Germany for good. Lily writes to her son, Felix: 'I am now heading out into the world and am homeless for the first time. It was a bad year. I look back on it with horror.'

*

---

*The German art historian and theorist Aby Moritz Warburg (1866–1929) was known for his private cultural studies library.

The songwriter Bruno Balz is arrested by the Gestapo on charges of breaching Section 175 of the German Criminal Code, which penalises homosexuality, owing to his connections with Magnus Hirschfeld's Institute for Sexual Science. Back in 1924 he co-produced one of the very first gay songs, 'Bubi lass uns Freunde sein' ('Boy, Let Us Be Friends'). He now starts writing innocuous tunes for UFA talkies, for example 'Kleine Möwe, flieg' nach Helgoland' ('Fly to Heligoland, Little Gull') and he will soon create a safe space for himself with clearly heterosexual lyrics for the Swedish-born singer and actress Zarah Leander. They're so good that UFA, and thus the Nazis, cannot do without him. He senses that songs about love could be his salvation.

On 19 December, the abstract painter Wassily Kandinsky and his wife, Nina, give up their Berlin apartment and emigrate to Paris.

On the morning of 24 December, Gussie Adenauer and her children board the train in Cologne for the Maria Laach abbey. There is snow on the ground as Konrad meets her at the gates, and she folds him gratefully in her arms. They eat a light meal in the refectory and sing a few carols in his cell. The children have brought along some small presents for their father. Later, they go to Mass. Surrounded by his family and transported by Gregorian chants, Konrad feels tears running down his cheeks.

Bertolt Brecht has bought a second house to go with the one by the Ammersee. The new one is at 8 Skovsbostrand in Svendborg on Denmark's Baltic coast, its purchase funded by the fee for his *Threepenny Novel** and money from Helene Weigel's father. Also

---

* *Threepenny Novel* was one of only three prose works written by Bertolt Brecht. Set in London at the turn of the twentieth century, it explores financial machinations and – like the more famous *Threepenny Opera* that preceded it – features the gangster character called Macheath, subject of the song 'Mack the Knife'.

in Denmark is Margarete Steffin – still seriously lung- and love-sick – who has travelled up from Paris. Brecht has asked his future lover Ruth Berlau if she wouldn't mind detaining his clingy lover in Copenhagen so his wife doesn't fly off the handle. Helene is somewhat mollified to know that Steffin is a five-hour drive away in Svendborg.

Margarete, however, is crying her eyes out with Berlau; she senses that Brecht is beginning to cut her adrift. What she doesn't yet suspect is that the real reason for this growing distance is right before her. Only Elisabeth Hauptmann manages to extract herself from Brecht's manipulative games. After she has spent months making every effort to save his manuscripts in Berlin, including going to jail, Brecht accuses her of laziness and ineptitude. She writes to him that she can only be happy 'by breaking off all contact with him'. And how does he react? He takes it in his stride. What was it he wrote in his sixth sonnet to Margarete Steffin? 'Men's lust is not to suffer.'

On New Year's Eve, Thomas Mann comes up with a fairly benign summary of a year of emigration in his new home in exile, Küsnacht near Zurich: 'My homesickness for the old circumstances is, incidentally, limited. I feel it almost more for Sanary, which in hindsight appears to me to be the happiest stage of these past ten months, and for my small stone terrace in the evenings when I sat out on it in a wicker chair and watched the stars.' The heavens are still smiling on him, at least.

AFTER

In January 1934, First Lieutenant Claus Schenk Graf von Stauffenberg poses in a deserted barn in Bamberg for the sculptor Frank Mehnert, a fellow disciple of Stefan George. Stauffenberg is modelling for Mehnert's monument of an SA soldier, but he refuses to don an SA uniform for the session. He writes: 'I have not yet fully come to terms with my immortalisation as an SA man, of all things, but I console myself with the thought that it is far worse for the Nazis than for me.' When Mehnert visits the apartment of the newly wed Stauffenbergs, Nina, the lady of the house, has to wait in the dining room while Stauffenberg continues to pose for the sculptor in his study. Stefan George was always determined that his disciples should have no contact with their friends' families, Stauffenberg tells his wife, and Nina accepts this rule. She is five months pregnant with their child.

Women are like cities, Ernest Hemingway thinks as he arrives back in Paris; you love them initially for precisely the things you will later hold against them. He writes a short snapshot of the current situation in the city that will appear in *Esquire* in February 1934. And what is the situation? It is devastating. 'What makes you feel bad is the perfectly calm way everyone speaks about the next war. It is accepted and taken for granted.' Then he addresses his American compatriots: 'All right, Europe has always had wars. But we can keep out of this next one ... If kids want to go to see what war is like, or for the love of any nation, let them go as individuals.' He describes his love for Paris and recognises that it is he rather than the city that has changed.

> Paris is very beautiful this fall. It was a fine place to be young in and it is a necessary part of a man's education. We all loved it once and we lie if we said we didn't. But she is like a mistress who does not grow old and she has other lovers now. She was old to start with, but we did not know it then. We thought

she was just older than we were, and that was attractive then. So when we did not love her any more we held it against her. But that was wrong because she is always the same age and she always has new lovers.

And then, autumnally and sincerely, he writes: 'But me, I now love something else.' He does say what that 'something else' is.

Man Ray has worked on his magnum opus for eighteen months. Now his eight-foot painting of the lips of Lee Miller is finished – it is called *A l'heure de l'observatoire, les amoureux.*

The first part of the title refers to the observatory he sees every day on his way to work and which he has inserted in the bottom left-hand corner of the painting. It is also an allusion to Miller, who lives in a different, American time zone; 'United States Observatory Time' is what people hear when they call the American talking clock. Finally, *les amoureux,* or *the lovers*, is a tender nod to the time they shared together. The lips flying across the sky look like two bodies cuddling in a kind of cosmic ecstasy. It is a miracle that the result of all these symbols isn't kitsch. 'Love', Man Ray later says, 'takes on universal dimensions in this work that was painted at a time when the mounting tide of hatred was about to engulf Europe.'

The former general and German chancellor, Kurt von Schleicher, and his wife, Elisabeth, are granted just two years of marital bliss before five men break into their house in Neubabelsberg in Berlin in the middle of the night of 30 June 1934 and shoot them. The general dies on the spot, his wife soon afterwards in hospital. Both corpses are impounded by the Gestapo to prevent any speculation or investigation, and the 'burial' at Lichterfelde Park cemetery takes place without the bodies of the deceased. It is clear that the SS carried out this double murder, but what remains unresolved to this day is whether the order was given by Hermann Göring, Heinrich Himmler or Adolf Hitler himself. Another squad of men with pistols turns up at the Schleichers' house on 1 July, but all they find are the former chancellor's mourning relatives. Joseph Goebbels notes in his diary: 'According to plan in Berlin. No mishaps apart from Elisabeth Schleicher dying too. A pity, but nothing to be done.'

Such was Goebbels' comment on the killings that have gone down in history as the 'Night of the Long Knives', when Hitler ordered a murderous purge of the entire leadership of the SA. It should be noted that Curzio Malaparte had predicted an incident like this in his 1932 book *Coup d'État: The Technique of Revolution*. Hearing about Kurt von Schleicher's assassination in his Dutch exile the next morning, Kaiser Wilhelm II gives up all hope of the monarchy being restored.

All of a sudden, on a hot Bastille Day in 1934, a new couple sails into this book. It is early evening at the Wannsee in Berlin; the sun is slowly setting over the lake and a cool north-north-westerly breeze is rising. Twenty-year-old Libertas is standing in a bikini top and loose-fitting red trousers on the prow of *Haizuru*, a sailing boat that belongs to her friend Richard von Raffay. Then a rowboat emerges from the reeds and heads in their direction. Sedately and yet as if magnetically attracted to the yacht, a young man with long, flowing hair steers through the clusters of waterlilies. When he introduces himself as Harro Schulze-Boysen, an adjutant at the Ministry of Aviation, it is love at first sight. Richard can tell that some kind of magic is in the air, so he hops discreetly onto the Blue-Red Yacht Club jetty, leaving the two lovestruck creatures to their own devices.

The warm July night began to fall
It was so full of tenderness,

Libertas writes about that fateful day.

But when she removes Harro's shirt, what she sees makes her shudder. His skin is covered in welts and scars, and swastikas have been branded on his thigh. He confides to her that a year earlier the Gestapo held him in their underground torture chamber and used whips and thumbscrews to make it clear to this firebrand publisher of *Der Gegner* magazine how the new regime would deal with anyone who opposed it. They murdered his Jewish colleague and friend Henry Erlanger right in front of him. He will avenge all this, he tells her, his voice calm yet resolute. His scars and stories jolt Libertas from her daydreams. This is the moment, Norman Ohler writes in his book *The Bohemians: The Lovers Who Led Germany's Resistance Against the Nazis*, when she begins to think and Harro begins to heal. A shiver runs down her spine as she realises that the man she is holding in her arms was tortured by the Gestapo at Prinzalbrechtstrasse 8 in Berlin. She used to play hide and seek in those very rooms when it was still the Museum of Arts and Crafts and her father was head of the fashion department.

It is not just a wonderful love affair that begins in the summer of 1934 between Libertas, granddaughter of Count von Eulenburg, and Harro, great-nephew of Admiral von Tirpitz.* They also form the core of the resistance group that the Gestapo will later dub the 'Red Orchestra'.

For now, Harro and Libertas live life to the full and move into Richard von Raffay's flat. Libertas works as press secretary for the Hollywood film company Metro-Goldwyn-Mayer, and when Harro gets home from the Ministry of Aviation, she drags him off to see one of the latest movies starring Greta Garbo and John Wayne. After the film they go dancing at the Jockey-Bar, and if it's too hot for the cinema, Richard lets them take his boat onto the Wannsee. The couple buy an Opel and name it 'Spengler' after the author of *The Decline of the West*.

---

*Botho Graf zu Eulenburg (1831–1912) was a Prussian statesman who, as a member of the notorious 'camarilla', had homoerotic links to Kaiser Wilhelm II. Alfred von Tirpitz (1849–1930) served as secretary of state of the German Imperial Naval Office.

Why does the writer Wolfgang Koeppen have to flee Germany so suddenly in the summer of 1934? He is neither Jewish nor a Communist, nor has he ever picked a fight with the Nazi regime. The answer is very simple: because he is in love with the wrong woman.

When Koeppen returned to Berlin from Italy in March, he took up a seat in one of the cafés lining the Kurfürstendamm, keeping watch for signs that the world really had changed. One lovely April day he met a young woman on the terrace of the Hotel Bristol. She was wearing loose summery clothes and a large hat and had two enormous dogs, a pretext for Koeppen to get to know her. He found out that she was just eighteen and the wife of an SS leader.

The SS leader's wife loses her heart to the young author. She goes to his place late in the evenings and slips away again at dawn. Sometimes she leaves her dogs behind, as a kind of deposit – he knows she'll be back the next evening to pick them up. 'What developed between me and the beautiful yet entirely amoral girl', Koeppen says, 'was a novel.'

When the Röhm purge happens in late June and the Nazis undertake their first murderous rampage through Berlin, Koeppen asks her: 'Has your husband been shot?' To which she replies: 'No, he's doing the shooting.' But the unfaithful young woman's husband has evidently found out about his rival. Koeppen is forced to leave Berlin, with no time to pack his bags, and seek his salvation in exile in the Netherlands. Only four years later, when he is sure that the Charlottenburg SS leader's wife is out of the frame, will he dare to return to Germany.

Salvador Dalí and Gala finally get married in 1934; immediately afterwards her ex-husband Paul Éluard weds his lover, the twenty-eight-year-old actress Maria Benz. For her part, Lee Miller returns from America and marries the Egyptian Aziz Eloui Bey, who commissioned her to paint a portrait of his then wife two years earlier.

Tamara de Lempicka, the eccentric Paris-based Polish painter, also gets married. Only last year she told her suitor, the deep-pocketed Baron Raoul Kuffner, that she didn't have time for a wedding. After catching a glimpse of his bank balance, however, she has come to her senses. It is therefore a marriage both of convenience and of good taste; she admires him for his aristocratic manners, and the only drawback she can see is that he is far too fat.

Other couples, Simone de Beauvoir and Jean-Paul Sartre for instance, would agree with her that sexual satisfaction is to be sought outside the marital bed. 'I loved my husband', Tamara de Lempicka later says, 'but I needed other men around me for inspiration. I liked going out at night, and that required a good-looking man to be available and tell me what a great artist I was and stroke my hand.'

Even our most beautiful fairy, the ever-lost and ever-longing Annemarie Schwarzenbach, is looking for a groom. She gets engaged to Claude Clarac, a French gentleman of sublime elegance who is his country's ambassador in Tehran. Claude gives her a new sportscar, and in 1935 she moves into his villa on the edge of Tehran, which is so luxurious that even the daughter of a rich Swiss industrialist is impressed. It has huge grounds, a swimming pond and countless servants who buzz around Annemarie all day, tending to her every whim.

Well, not quite *every* whim, for each evening when the sun sets over Tehran, she craves drugs: morphine and Veronal. Even here, she manages to get her hands on some; soon she is back to living in a twilight state, but ensconced in luxury. She hardly ever sees her husband, which suits her just fine. As a homosexual, he urgently needed a spouse to gain acceptance in this Muslim country. But Schwarzenbach hides away in this remote corner of the world, feeling anxious. 'I'm scared of going back,' she writes. 'I believe in nothing and no one, and I have doubts about my life. That is why I am tempted to stay here, far from the world.' Erika Mann, for whom Annemarie has long harboured unrequited romantic feelings, writes brutally about her to her brother Klaus: 'There is something peculiar about the child, and sadly she will never come to anything.' Thank goodness Annemarie never reads this criticism of her despair. But now that we can see how productive she was, as a writer and photographer, we know that she came to far more than Erika Mann could imagine.

On 28 April 1934, the French author and antisemite Céline writes to his Jewish lover, Cillie Pam: 'Humanity will be saved by its love of thighs. Everything else is just hate and boredom.'

And how are things with Erich Maria Remarque? All quiet on the romantic front. He becomes fearful when women get too close to him, only to miss them when they're gone. Now Jutta Zambona, from whom he is finally divorced, spends her life sitting on his lap in his magnificent house in Porto Ronco. Outside, the gentle waves lap at the shore of the lake and the palm trees stretch their limbs in the warm breeze; inside, a suntanned émigré couple while away the time amid maximum wealth and minimal excitement.

When the luxury liner *Île de France* sets sail from Cherbourg for New York, there are a large number of émigrés on board, as well as two people searching for someone or something. On the very first evening, neither of them can sleep and, opting for a view of the dark expanses over the emptiness of their cabins, they bump into each other on deck.

For Marlene Dietrich and Ernest Hemingway, it is love at first sight, but a love that seems to have remained platonic. They exchange countless letters over the following years. He gives her the nickname 'Kraut' because of her German origins, while she calls him 'Papa'. Hemingway's explanation is that the feelings between them are an 'unsynchronised passion'. This means that whenever he is violently in love with Dietrich, 'the Kraut was deep in some romantic tribulation, and on those occasions when Dietrich was on the surface and swimming about with those marvellously seeking eyes of hers, I was submerged'. It is almost touching to read this about two lovers who otherwise ploughed through the late twenties and the entire thirties without giving any consideration to whether their other passions were properly synchronised. With each other, though, they were clearly cautious – perhaps because they were so alike.

After the suicide of his second wife, Nadezhda, Joseph Stalin becomes increasingly close to her brother Pavel and his wife Zhenya, as well as to Zhenya's sister Anna and her husband Stanislas. The most powerful man in the Soviet Union, unable to trust anyone, is consoled by talking to them about his grief, while they lovingly care for Stalin's two children in the Kremlin's spacious hallways.

In summer 1934, Zhenya starts to spruce herself up. She wears Nadezhda's clothes, and sometimes when Stalin is having dinner with his family and the light strikes her in the right way, he thinks that she even resembles her sister-in-law. She is the only person in his entourage who doesn't fear him. On the other hand, Stalin will never forgive Stanislas for bringing home from Berlin the revolver with which Nadezhda shot herself – and he will never forgive Anna for dolling her up that fateful evening. In any case, Stalin strikes up a relationship with Zhenya, more out of nostalgia than anything else, but also to avoid spending his nights alone.

For a while, everything is fine. It will not be until 1938 that the whole lot of them – Zhenya, Pavel, Anna and Stanislas – are murdered by Stalin's henchmen.

In spring 1934, Henry Miller has moved from Clichy to a magnificent old apartment nearer the centre of Paris; 18 Villa Seurat is in the fourteenth arrondissement, where Antonin Artaud (who was briefly one of Anaïs Nin's lovers) once lived for a short time. On the day that he moves in, Miller receives, hot off the press, a first copy of *Tropic of Cancer*. This marks a turning point in his life. He is now a writer, visibly, publicly. And after years of vagrancy and parasitism, he at last has a fixed address, even if it is paid for by

Anaïs – or, more accurately, by her husband. When the divorce papers arrive from New York confirming that June is finally willing to draw a line under their turbulent marriage, Henry writes a single word in his diary: 'Hurray.'

Now that June is no longer a threat to his independence, he can tackle her in his fiction. He begins a new novel, *Tropic of Capricorn*, which tells the story of their marriage. While he sits at his typewriter in his vest with Bach or jazz blaring from the nearby gramophone, Anaïs lies on the sofa. Later, however, when he gives his muse the manuscript to read, she reacts with outrage, criticising his reduction of women to sexual objects.

'You simplify the world,' she tells him, calling his attitude to lesbian love 'simply very primitive'. Miller listens without flinching and doesn't alter a word. 'I want to become the monster I am,' he tells her.

The roguish Surrealist Max Ernst is certainly the most underrated heartbreaker of the early thirties. The year 1934 begins for him with a passionate, red-hot relationship with Meret Oppenheim, the young Swiss artist who has already turned the heads of Alberto Giacometti and Man Ray. Only Max Ernst feels able to go toe to toe with her. He writes to her almost every day. Once: 'Meretli, Meretli, Meretli, I love and kiss you, your Max.' Two days later: 'I'm unshaven, I'm prickly, so if you will put up with this, I will kiss you all over.' Next: 'Meretli, I have to think of you continuously. If you have not forgotten me, tell me so. Again and again, I am astonished by your beauty.' For the first time in her life, Meret feels that someone loves her, body and soul. Max writes with excited flippancy: 'I am true to you, in the very best sense of the word. The mouse of Milo cannot goad me, let alone the Venus of Montmartre. You alone do I love and desire. If war were to break out, come hither at all speed so we can go to the same concentration camp and not just play chess.' This goes on throughout the winter, spring and summer.

But then, on a scorching hot Parisian day in late summer, she tells him out of the blue in a café called La Rhumerie Martiniquaise that she doesn't want to see him again. Max is stunned. For him, he writes, it is like 'a natural disaster'.

Meret, however, is certain that she can no longer allow herself to be trapped in love with this man if she wants to be not constantly in his shadow. She doesn't want to be a muse – she wants to be an artist, and she doesn't believe she can do that with Max. She dreams up the fur-covered cup, saucer and spoon, one of the greatest Surrealist works of all. In the same way that this cup protects the hot liquid with fur, she has wrapped her steaming heart in a cold farewell. Max writes: 'Who covers the soup spoon in russet fur? Little Meret. Who has outgrown us? Little Meret.'

Meret knows that even if the Bible portrays them as being incapable of it, since the Fall women have had to seize their opportunities to outdo men. She writes: 'According to the patriarchal perspective only the man sins, namely by biting into the apple. His sin is that he is able to judge his own acts; Adam does not believe Eve capable of this, even though she bit into the apple first.'

After the loss of this apple-eating Eve, a stunned Max goes looking for a replacement. It seems unthinkable to return to his cosy home, his spouse and their child after so many blissful months with such an intellectually vivacious young woman. And so it is a happy coincidence when he gets to know Lotte Lenya while working for the Schauspielhaus theatre in Zurich. Lotte has gone off her tenor, Otto Pasetti, whose promises of hitting the jackpot seem to ring less and less true. She hasn't yet fallen back in love with her first husband, Kurt Weill, and it is while she is in this limbo that Ernst meets her; they grant each other a few months of romance, erotic letters and weekend escapades all over southern Europe. She savours the imaginative prowess Ernst deploys in his letters, skills he first honed on Gala and more recently on Meret Oppenheim. She revels in his attention and feels desired, loved and titillated by his words. Weill is dutifully informed that a new beau has burst onto the scene, so what does he do after financing his Lotte's dissolute life on the Riviera for so many years? He finances that of her new conquest, moving heaven and earth to persuade people to buy Ernst's paintings. Is this madness or love? He writes to Lotte: 'Now live, little one. Lots of kisses from your Knuti.'

Nineteen thirty-four is a year of frank discussions between Ernest Hemingway and Scott Fitzgerald. After a string of letters from Scott about not being able to get down to writing and how much he is suffering from Zelda's bouts of schizophrenia, Hemingway writes back:

> Of all people on earth you needed discipline in your work and instead you marry someone who is jealous of your work, wants to compete with you and ruins you. It's not as simple as that and I thought Zelda was crazy the first time I met her and you complicated it even more by being in love with her and of course, you're a rummy. But you're no more of a rummy than Joyce and of course most good writers are.

These are the home truths Scott has to read about himself as *Tender Is the Night* is published.

Zelda, on the other hand, spends the whole of 1934 in clinics: from 2 January to 12 February in Sheppard Pratt Hospital near Baltimore, until 8 March at Henry Phipps Psychiatric Clinic of Johns Hopkins University, until 19 May at Craig House psychiatric clinic in Beacon, New York, and until the end of the year back at Sheppard Pratt. She makes several suicide attempts.

In these hospitals, between bouts of depression, she works on a text called 'Show Mr. and Mrs. F. to Number—'. It is published in the June edition of *Esquire*. The text consists of descriptions of all the hotel rooms the Fitzgeralds have stayed in since their arrival in Europe in 1921. It is a nod to their years of travel and also a terrifyingly, fascinatingly detailed act of reckoning. Only in a psychiatric institution in the middle of an American nowhere is it possible to remember so precisely the smell of the sheets in the hotels of Juan-les-Pins and how it differed from that of the pillows in Monte Carlo. She knows every bit as clearly as her husband does that the thirties are picking up the tab for the twenties – in general, but also in the specific case of Zelda and Scott Fitzgerald.

To their daughter, Scottie, who is growing up in the exclusive care of her nanny, Scott writes about Zelda: 'But the insane are always mere guests on earth, eternal strangers carrying around broken decalogues that they cannot read.' Then he gives her a piece of forlorn advice: 'You had in your parents two extremely bad examples. Just do everything we didn't do and you will be perfectly safe.'

The countryside is basically the *Background to Love*, as Helen Wolff wrote in her 1932 novel, and she and Kurt have stuck to this precept. From Nice, where their son is born, they move to the hills near Florence, where they run a small guesthouse, producing eggs, vegetables and figs for themselves and their guests. When Mussolini's Italy declares German-speaking Jews *personae non gratae*, they head for Paris. There they acquire the necessary passports and visas to flee to America, where they will become famous for introducing American readers to the best literature old Europe has to offer via their publishing house, Pantheon Books. Uwe Johnson will dedicate his *Anniversaries* tetralogy to Helen, and Günter Grass will mourn her death. First, though, she and Kurt have to battle their way through the endlessly oppressive thirties.

This is the beginning of many restless years in exile for Klaus Mann, even after all his previous flights from his inner demons. The only fixed address he has ever had is his parents' house in Poschingerstrasse. His poem 'Greeting to the Twelve-Hundredth Hotel Room' is legendary, but he reached that number back in 1931 at the tender age of twenty-four. He has been running away his whole life, fuelled by his hatred of the Nazis, near-daily injections of barbiturates and a frenzied pursuit of one-night stands. 'He never sat down properly,' Elias Canetti later observed. 'He slid back and forth, leapt up, walked away, addressed one person and then the next, looked past him and talked to someone else whom he didn't really see either. He saw so much that he didn't seem to want to see anyone.'

Klaus Mann spends most of his time in Amsterdam, where his exile magazine *Die Sammlung* is published. He travels to Paris regularly and visits his parents in Zurich. Yet he can also be found in London, Prague, New York and Moscow. Intermittently, there is respite on the beaches of the Mediterranean from where, according to Gottfried Benn's accusations, it may be hard to judge the situation inside Germany. Klaus proves Benn wrong, however. Wherever he is, he is an incisive analyst of the crimes committed by the Third Reich against the German intellectual spirit and by the traitors who support them. The institution that hosts a speech he gives in Brno heralds him thus: 'Klaus Mann – son of the Nobel Prize winner Thomas and nephew of Heinrich, but even in the shadow of these titans he has matured into a powerful literary figure in his own right and developed into a combative future leader of German youth abroad.'

During these years, authors such as Robert Musil and Stefan Zweig and even his own father refuse to write for his magazine, knowing that to do so would mean having their books banned in Germany. Klaus is forced to accept that many people he admires and even one person he loves have other priorities. He does gain a close new friend in Fritz Landshoff, though, the brains behind the Amsterdam-based exile publisher Querido (and Ruth Landshoff's cousin), with whom he spends every evening chatting, drinking and working.

Amsterdam is also home to the German exile publisher Allert de Lange, where Hermann Kesten and Walter Landauer are in charge of the German list. 'We held joint evening meetings to define the two publishers' catalogues,' Fritz Landshoff writes, 'while by day we struggled to maintain the façade of being competitors.' In the thirties the two houses publish books by émigré writers such as Heinrich Mann, Lion Feuchtwanger, Anna

Seghers, Joseph Roth, Ernst Toller, Vicki Baum, Alfred Döblin, Erich Maria Remarque and Irmgard Keun. German literature is in exile.

The Jewish Communist Erich Mühsam strikes the wardens at Oranienburg concentration camp as too proud and too dignified, and so he becomes a special target of SA abuse. They are determined to break him.

A year earlier, Mühsam was one of the few at the final meeting of the Association for the Defence of German Authors who could see what was coming: 'Not all of us gathered here will see one another again,' he said. 'We are a company fighting a losing battle. Even if we have to die a hundred miserable deaths in the prisons of the Third Reich, we must tell the truth today and cry out in protest. We are doomed.'

When the SS take over the Oranienburg camp in June 1934, Mühsam's death sentence is confirmed. On 7 July 1934, the new commandant advises Mühsam that if he doesn't kill himself in the next two days someone will lend him a helping hand. On 9 July, his fellow inmates find him hanging in the latrine – murder, although his death is reported as suicide in the *Berliner Tagblatt*, the newspaper for which he was writing only a year ago. When his wife, Zenzl, hears the news, she collapses.

A narrow house with a sea view, 121 Promenade des Anglais in Nice hosts a special collection of literary housemates for six months in 1934. Heinrich Mann and Nelly Kröger are living on the third floor, with Joseph Roth and Andrea Manga Bell beneath them, while the first floor is home to Hermann Kesten and his wife, Toni.

When they sit together or stare out at the sea from one of the balconies, there is only ever one subject of conversation. As Kesten records: 'Joseph Roth told a love story from Podolia, Heinrich Mann a love story from Palestrina, and Mrs Nelly Kröger brazen stories from her younger years on the Kurfürstendamm.' She recalled 'how they would go out dancing in pairs, or with the

first boy you spotted. Stories full of giggling, cuddling and kissing.'
The three couples seek to forget the hardships of life in exile by
thinking of former lovers, but this becomes more challenging as
the months pass and their relationships are corroded by fear, dep-
rivation and incessant motion – and by the alcohol they drink to
deal with these torments.

One of the most gruelling passages in Anaïs Nin's diary is the one
about her abortion in September 1934. She is pregnant but has no
idea who the father is; in the relevant period of February she had
been intimate with Henry, Hugo and her psychiatrist Otto Rank.
There is no question of keeping the baby because her vocation is
to fulfil the role of lover – 'I have too many children already,' she
writes. She wishes to continue caring for the men around her, not
a child whose habits she doesn't understand and who might take
control of her.

On 17 September, she finds a Jewish doctor who has escaped
from Berlin and will carry out the abortion, despite her being in
the sixth month of pregnancy. She writes in her diary that while the
doctor is trying to exterminate the life inside her, she 'seduced him
into a conversation about the persecution of the Jews in Berlin';
she turns even this rare moment of dependency on a man into a
demonstration of her power.

After studying the foetus – a girl – she puts on her makeup and
a silk jacket to receive the various possible fathers – first Miller,
then Rank, then Hugo. When Miller tells her that the publication
of *Tropic of Capricorn* is imminent, Nin replies: 'Now that's a birth
that interests me much more.' When he has left, she drinks a glass
of champagne with Hugo.

The years after his return from Berlin are the worst Jean-Paul Sartre
has ever experienced. He has grown fat in Germany and he hates
the prospect of swapping the metropolis for provincial Le Havre,
where he'll teach adolescents about the great questions of Western
philosophy.

His self-esteem has suffered other blows. First, the shock of realising that he is going bald – an indisputable sign of advancing age. Then there's the humiliation of having worked on his book *Nausea* for four years, only for Gallimard, his dream publisher, to reject it. Last but not least, his Berlin lover, Marie Ville, has gone to Paris with her husband and wants nothing more to do with him.

An even greater disappointment is his unsuccessful wooing of a young Russian woman called Olga, a former pupil and the current lover of his wife, Simone de Beauvoir. Day after day he tries in vain to catch her eye. It all culminates in a genuine crisis of virility for him in 1935. He tries injecting himself with mescaline, but this only brings hallucinations. For months afterwards lobsters suddenly appear before his eyes or houses start wobbling as in a fever dream.

On one of these melancholic days, Simone visits her husband in Le Havre. They sit out on the terrace of their favourite café, Les Mouettes, staring sullenly at the sea while Sartre complains about the tedium of their lives. He tells de Beauvoir that they are prisoners of the bourgeois world, forced to teach and act responsibly. They are not even thirty but already has-beens. The next great event in their lives will be retirement, he says; he knows he will feel it before he even feels it. He may look like an emotional person, but in reality he is a desert.

He goes on and on in this vein. The gulls disperse, the sea turns darker and tears well up in Simone's eyes as she sits there in silence.

Once Joseph Goebbels has married Magda Quandt, his sometime lover Olga Bronnen is left entirely to her husband, Arnolt, and their marriage quickly grinds to a standstill. One day she walks into the offices of Funk-Stunde, the broadcaster where the former playwright now works, and pulls out a revolver. As she is about to shoot him, however, a good-looking racing-car driver by the name of Manfred von Brauchitsch leaves the recording studio where he has just given an interview. Olga puts away her gun, starts flirting with Brauchitsch and leaves the building with him for a coffee.

Olga's psychological state is worrying, but physically she is still

extremely attractive – and active, though only away from the conjugal bed. Her husband has therefore begun to show an interest in
his younger female colleagues and in particular his twenty-three-
year-old secretary, Hildegard von Lossow, a tall, elegant blonde
woman from a good background. Hildegard quickly takes over the
role of housewife in the flat in Helmstedter Strasse. On 11 April
1935, the first warm day of spring, Arnolt and Hildegard are sitting
outside a nearby café when they spot Olga striding past. They say
hello, and Olga walks on to the flat, where she turns on the gas.

Upon arriving home, Arnolt tries to revive her; he opens the
windows and calls the doctor in a panic. Olga, so devoted to him
despite her constant infidelity, dies in his arms in the same apartment where, five years previously, they had plotted with Goebbels
to cut short Thomas Mann's speech and Erich Maria Remarque's
film premiere.

The next year, Arnolt and Hildegard wed. They give up his old
life and the flat in which Olga died for a bungalow in Kladow.
When Hildegard enters Arnolt's study on their first evening in
their new home, she notices that he has hung a huge gold-framed
photograph of Olga above his desk, her lips in a sensual pout.
Feeling a rush of jealousy and anger, she leaves the room, takes a
knife ... and cuts an extravagantly blooming rose in the garden. She
takes the flower up to her husband and places it in a vase in front of
the photo of the late object of his worship. 'That was my sacrifice
to the gods,' she later says. After this act she resumes unpacking.

The couple soon have daughters, despite Gottfried Benn having
diagnosed Arnolt as infertile – perhaps because Benn would have
liked to marry Hildegard von Lossow himself. Yet all he needs is
patience, for the gods are preserving this silently devoted aristocrat
for him.

Magnus Hirschfeld is a broken man. His Institute for Sexual
Science has been destroyed, his lover Karl Giese has been expelled
from France, the country where they sought refuge, and his health
is poor. He draws up a will that divides his estate equally between

Giese and Li Shiu Tong, his two close confidants, who are jealous rivals, before travelling to Nice.

On 14 May 1935, he celebrates his sixty-seventh birthday. At ten o'clock in the morning he's reading his birthday cards; by noon he is dead.

Dietrich Bonhoeffer teaches preaching for the Confessing Church in Finkenwalde in Western Pommerania – the first attempt to establish a Protestant form of monasticism. Eleven-year-old Maria von Wedemeyer is attending church one day when Bonhoeffer delivers one of his fiery sermons. She has come with her grandmother Ruth von Kleist-Retzow, one of Bonhoeffer's most passionate sponsors. Little does Bonhoeffer know that ten years later he will write to Maria: 'Safely shielded by benevolent powers, calmly we await that which may come.'

For now, in 1935, someone completely different catches his eye. Eberhard Bethge is the gentle, slender son of a pastor. Within the space of a few days, twenty-nine-year-old Bonhoeffer and twenty-six-year-old Bethge have become inseparable. Stunned, Bonhoeffer writes in his diary that he has never experienced such closeness to any person, especially not to any woman. In the evenings after class, he plays the piano while Bethge sings Handel in his bright tenor. When the preaching course is over, the two of them share Bonhoeffer's room in his parents' house as if it were the most natural thing in the world. Soon they have a joint bank account and sign their Christmas cards 'Dietrich and Eberhard'. Bonhoeffer feels less attracted to marriage, he writes, than to 'uncompromising friendships' – though we have no idea how much the two Protestant monks compromised in this case. Whatever may have taken place, Bethge later marries Bonhoeffer's niece, and Bonhoeffer discovers his profound love for Maria von Wedemeyer.

Erika Mann, who is still with the actress Therese Giehse, writes to her ex-husband, the artistic director of the Prussian State Theatre, to request that he send her their divorce papers – she's planning to marry the gay British poet W. H. Auden as a means of acquiring British citizenship. Klaus initially pointed her towards Christopher Isherwood, but Isherwood felt anxious at the prospect and suggested that Auden might be more suitable. There are some slight complications at first because the groom cannot tell Ledbury registry office either his bride's age or if her surname is still Gründgens or has reverted to Mann. The official remains calm, however, and urges Auden to check with his future wife; they are married on 15 July.

There is a touching wedding photo of the two of them in tweed jackets and ties, smiling uncertainly. Erika looks delighted to have a passport again, a British one this time, and Auden is filled with pride at having personally contributed to the fight against the Nazis. Straight after the ceremony and the photographs he hurries off to The Downs School, where he teaches English, while Erika takes the train back to London.

Unlike many other married couples, the newlyweds remain on good terms after the ceremony. Yes, W. H. Auden later lives with Erika's brother Golo in an illustrious communal living arrangement in Brooklyn that includes the composer Benjamin Britten, Paul Bowles and the American author Carson McCullers, who falls in love with Erika's friend Annemarie Schwarzenbach (no, the romances of the thirties don't get any easier to follow). Faced with his wife's festering rage against the Nazi regime, Auden gives a wise piece of advice: 'Don't hate too much.' He also manages to find a suitable husband for Therese Giehse: his gay friend, the author John Hampson.

Bingo! In 1936, the lovers Erika and Therese possess British passports, thanks to their double marriage of convenience to the cream of English literature. They greet this farcical circumstance with the good humour that has always united them.

*

Now just think if every single woman
You'd ever had should gather by your bed

So begins the sonnet that Margarete Steffin has written in despair to Bertolt Brecht. A consummate repressor of nasty thoughts, he decides not to imagine such a scene, but Max Beckmann does. In 1935, he is sitting in his Berlin studio in a permanent state of fear, having been driven out of his professorial post. Artistically he retreats into the ancient world, devising enormous mythological triptychs in which he depicts the calamities of the present as divine ancient tragedies. It is not only a surge of images that assail him, though, but a surge of temptation.

When he closes his eyes, five women who have left a lasting imprint on his life appear in his mind; he sits down at his easel and begins his great autobiographical painting *Five Women*. Rarely has an artist laid bare his complex love life so. On the left is Lilly von Schnitzler, Beckmann's feisty and courageous Frankfurt patron, wife of the head of IG Farben and a leading society figure who even invited Joseph Goebbels to dinner to convince him of the quality of Beckmann's supposedly degenerate art. Next to her, Beckmann places the posh Käthe von Porada, and at her right is Hildegard Melms aka 'Naïla', the most passionate of his former lovers, most influential muse and model for many of his works. His first wife, Minna Beckmann-Tube, whom he cannot get out of his mind, is also there, crouching in the foreground. And in the centre of the picture is the self-confident Quappi, Beckmann's current wife, in the role of sensual seductress.

The actress Brigitte Helm ends her career as spectacularly as she started it. As a seventeen-year-old virgin and boarding school pupil she tasted triumph in Fritz Lang's *Metropolis*. Her role as the 'Maschinenmensch', the film's robot in shimmering gold armour, stands as an iconic image of early German cinema alongside that of Marlene Dietrich lounging on a barrel wearing lingerie and a top hat in *The Blue Angel*.

But whereas Dietrich cultivated her status as an icon her whole life long, after an equally meteoric rise to fame Brigitte chose a different and far more radical path. She is German cinema's vamp, combining, as Fritz Lang commented, 'virgin and hetaera, the wild and the chaste'. UFA studios stakes everything on the wild side of her character, her pulsing beauty and golden hair, in the lineage of Lulu, the heroine of Frank Wedekind's 1895 play *Earth Spirit*. She is henceforth always cast as the 'sinful, devilish, slippery snake', as the magazine *Der Film* describes her career. Her early fame from *Metropolis* hangs over her like a curse. In her twenty-eight films, twenty-four different directors seek to be for her what Josef von Sternberg was for Dietrich.

Brigitte gives a very unusual interview in which she rails against the roles she is offered and judges herself to have been reduced to a sex object: 'My wish would be for 1935 to remember that I might be capable of a bit more than only playing feckless and reckless stupid women. My greatest wish would be to play a truly maternal woman.' What Brigitte Helm hasn't yet understood is that the film industry isn't interested in fulfilling its leading ladies' dreams, only those of their audience.

Helm therefore has to take things into her own hands. Fate determines that the shoot for her final movie, *An Ideal Spouse*, coincides with her long overdue divorce from her not-very-ideal first husband, Rudolf Weissbach, who has spent the intervening years frittering away his wife's film earnings on the Riviera and the Baltic coast in the company of other women.

In spring 1935, Brigitte marries again, this time to the industrialist Dr Hugo Eduard Kunheim, one of Berlin's most sought-after bachelors. They move to a gigantic villa at 2–4 Am Grossen Wannsee. On 28 August, *Die Filmwoche* announces to its astonished readers that 'Brigitte Helm can be seen on screens for the final time now in *An Ideal Spouse*. She has stated that she now wishes only to fulfil her duties as a wife and housewife. We shall see ...'

But what everyone thought was impossible turns out to be true. As abruptly as her film career started, it is over. Throughout her time in front of the camera she has felt constricted, as though she had never shed the steel corset she wore in *Metropolis*. So she steps out of the limelight and into the freedom of a conventional life, ceasing to be a star overnight. Journalists are left aghast until she explains, 'I am turning my back on film without regrets and despite the pleasure it has given me because I am thinking of all the happiness I shall find in my private life.'

The most incredible thing is that she really does find happiness. Her husband loves her and vice versa. Immediately after the wedding she falls pregnant with their first child. Pieter is born in 1936, Viktoria the following year, then Matthias and finally Christoph. They live an upper-class family life shielded from the tempest of the Third Reich before retreating to Switzerland. Pieter will later say that her children never knew Brigitte Helm; to them she was always Brigitte Kunheim.

After visiting Zelda, who has now succumbed to mental derangement, in the clinic in Baltimore, Scott Fitzgerald writes to a friend: 'It was wonderful to sit with her head on my shoulder for hours and feel as I always have even now, closer to her than to any other human being ... And I wouldn't mind a bit if in a few years Zelda and I could snuggle up together under a stone in some old graveyard here. That is really a happy thought and not melancholy at all.'

In a few years they actually will lie in a grave together in Old St Mary's Catholic Cemetery in Rockville, Maryland. Inscribed on the gravestone are the final words of *The Great Gatsby*: 'So we beat on, boats against the current, borne back ceaselessly into the past.' These rowers are like Walter Benjamin's Angel of History: they move forwards while simultaneously looking back.

The eternally homeless Kurt Tucholsky returns from Switzerland to his Swedish exile, but he senses that even here he will never truly settle. 'It isn't nice to be always searching. One would occasionally like to go home,' he writes in his diary on 3 June.

In July, Joseph Goebbels spends two weeks holidaying alone on the Baltic coast. He goes swimming, walks in the beech forests that two decades earlier inspired Rainer Maria Rilke to write songs in their praise and talks to his ministry and inner circle every day by phone. Magda, now pregnant, will join him later.

In the meantime, Goebbels has invited the Austrian actress Luise Ullrich along to forestall loneliness, and she spends four days with him at the seaside. She appears to have behaved – that autumn she gets her first major role in *Regine* for UFA, which is ultimately under Goebbels' control.

It is almost impossible to keep up with Bertolt Brecht, so restless are his years of exile. There is one constant, however: wherever he pitches up to direct a play, one of his devoted women is waiting for him. In Denmark, Helene Weigel stands by him although he has been cheating on her for a decade; in America, Elisabeth Hauptmann welcomes him with open arms even though he hasn't written to her for months. Yes, wherever he goes one of his women is there to take care of him and welcome him into her bed. Everywhere these ladies make a home for a man who is permanently on the run.

The message Brecht gave every woman he was involved with was: 'Here you have someone on whom you can't rely.' Nevertheless, each of them is confident that one day she will be the one to save him from his troubled fate. When he is with one woman, he writes to the others to tell them how bored he is and how he longs to see them, and these distant lovers either believe him, or want to – in times of exile, it often amounts to the same thing.

The thirties are a decade of never-ending torture for Margarete Steffin. Ever since Brecht has traded her love for Ruth Berlau's, she is rarely allowed an audience with the master, even as tuberculosis eats away at her auditory canal, her gut and her lung. Her life has been reduced to shuttling from hospital to sanatorium and back again, hoping all the while that Brecht will send her a few comforting lines. But he doesn't have time for that.

In summer 1935, Frau Dr Kluge travels from Halberstadt to Stuttgart to pick up her chic white two-seater Mercedes cabriolet. It is an automobile for eternity. There is a little money left over, so she fixes a plaque to the dashboard with a passport photo of her on it and the engraved words: 'Think of me and drive carefully.' Her husband has always driven carefully, though.

At the court of the erstwhile German kaiser Wilhelm II in Huis Doorn, life follows a routine. At nine o'clock there is breakfast, with bread, jam and coffee, followed by prayers. Empress Hermine then does a few laps of the extensive grounds on her newly acquired Dutch bicycle. With his hands folded behind his back and leaning slightly forwards, the emperor goes for a stroll in the opposite direction. When their paths cross, they give each other a little wave.

'Married couples', the empress knows, 'must learn to leave each other alone at certain times.' After these constitutionals, however, it is only half past ten. She 'would like to offer him some of the affection withheld from him by his misguided people'. Her husband isn't particularly in need of affection, however – he's happy in his own company, which she finds bothersome in the extreme. She goes into the drawing room and contemplates whether she can think up anything else to do. Manage the household perhaps, but it already runs like clockwork. At least her three faithful dachshunds seem to need her.

After lunch she will feed the ducks on the pond, but other than that Her Imperial Majesty has nothing more to do than to eat a light dinner with her husband. After that he reads a few articles from the foreign press aloud to her before taking his leave and ascending wearily to his bedchamber.

She justifies their exile with what the great Leibniz once supposedly said, that the soul has no windows and we are 'all nomads'. In fact, Leibniz was talking about 'monads', the elementary particles that make up the universe. Hermine entertains a special relationship with Africans, whether nomads or otherwise. She usually wears her favourite ivory necklace with a small elephant hanging from it – a wedding gift from an African tribal chieftain in the former colony of Togo who still regards the German Kaiser as his master and her as his mistress.

For Pablo Picasso, it is a year of extremes. He is acclaimed for his minotaur etchings, especially *Minotauromachy*, his most ambitious graphic work. It is a timeless piece about an old god and his lust for young goddesses – a picture about transience, temptation and humankind's inability to liberate itself from the net of antiquity's threats. This is, of course, a self-portrait. After all, Picasso is not only facing the outrage stirred up by the memoirs of his ex-girlfriend Fernande Olivier,* but on top of this his beloved muse Marie-Thérèse is carrying his child.

When Olga sees Marie-Thérèse's round tummy during a visit to Picasso's studio, she makes a scene and moves out with their son to a hotel. It is, Picasso says, 'the worst time of my life'. He rents a flat very close to his studio, in Rue La Boétie, for Marie-Thérèse and their daughter Maya, who is born that September. All the foundations for a new life would seem to be in place, but it is the biological facts that finally convince Olga that their marriage is over. She unleashes a divorce war, while Picasso locks up his studio and stops painting so as not to create even more objects of value in their now-soured 'community of accrued gain'.

He is emotionally incapable of creating anything. Indeed, he will not paint a single picture until the new year. Even the newborn Maya can only arouse him occasionally for a few minutes from his midlife crisis, which his lover's baby and his wife's departure have laid bare.

In spring 1935, Gottfried Benn the doctor diagnoses Gottfried Benn the poet: 'Drained, empty, urgently requires a change of scene.' He takes a position with the army in Hanover or, to be

---

*Fernande Olivier (1881–1966) changed her name from Amélie Lang after running away from her abusive husband to Paris at the age of only nineteen. She was Picasso's lover and model from 1904 to 1912, and he later hired lawyers to ensure that only six instalments of her serialised memoir of their time together were published.

more precise, he becomes head of Section IVb of the Alternative National Service Inspection Unit. But before he leaves, he prescribes himself a double dose of female company. On the last two days of March, he says goodbye to his Tilly Wedekind and Elinor Büller. Early on the morning of 1 April 1935, he boards the express train to Hanover and then walks for fifteen minutes through the pouring rain to his digs at a certain Fräulein Sattler's house.

However, he can't sleep there – the room is too bright, the coffee is bad and there is no telephone, so he moves out to Breite Strasse 28. It is hard to imagine a more desolate life than the one Benn leads in military administration. On duty from 8 a.m. to 2 p.m., then freefall through the emptiness of the long afternoon – and in Hanover to boot. He is haunted by his deluded welcoming of the Nazi regime in spring 1933, which he garnished with terrible essays, but the Nazis have forgotten all that and start persecuting him for his early Expressionist poems. Benn is also tiring of his two lovers, finding that all the sneaking about saps his energy. He asks them both – Tilly Wedekind alias 'Tillerchen' and Elinor Büller alias 'Morchen' – how they would react if they were to find a second lover weeping by his graveside. He receives their answers the next day. Tilly replies: 'I think the shared grief would unite us.' And Elinor writes: 'You despicable scoundrel.'

He often tells both women that he is busy at the weekend, before taking a seat alone on Sunday in the omnibus after a meagre breakfast and driving out with other bored citizens to the Harz Mountains or Lake Steinhude for 6.50 marks, which includes coffee. It seems as if he deliberately wants to manoeuvre himself into a state of soul-destroying desolation. He goes to beer cellars called Knickmeyer's, Kasten or Kröpcke, and they are as ugly as their names. Everything about Hanover is dull: the flat countryside, the standard, accent-free German, even the weak beer. Benn becomes increasingly obsessed by this monotony, like a form of monastic asceticism. His mantra is: 'Write little and cry in your sleep.'

For a poetry collection to mark his fiftieth birthday, Benn reviews the material of the past fifteen years and is shocked by its deterioration in quality. The poet who was, along with Trakl and Heym, the greatest exponent of pre-war German Expressionism comes to the painful realisation that he didn't write a single poem of note throughout the entire Roaring Twenties. He writes in his notebook: 'Infinite shame at my decline.'

He sits in a large beer garden called the Stadthalle each evening after the temperature rises, sipping lager. Water patters from a fountain, the waiter carries out drinks and plates of bread and dripping, and the band plays 'I Fancy Erica Like Columbus Does America'. It is the same every evening through May, June and July that year. After he gets off duty, he slips into a semi-conscious stupor.

But then a miracle occurs. After struggling in vain for two decades to regain his poetic powers, they strike like a thunderbolt from the dull grey Hanoverian sky. He feels the first gusts of a cold wind approaching in the distance, a first tentative sign of autumn, and he begins to compose a poem. 'Day which marks the summer's end,' he writes on the back of a menu, then: 'Heart to which the sign came. The flames have all been spent, the high tides and the game.'

He finishes the poem, puts it in an envelope and addresses it to Friedrich Wilhelm Oelze in Hartwigstrasse, Bremen, the man whom Benn calls his 'production manager' and gentle motivator. Soon afterwards, on a postcard sent from the Stadthalle, he asks Oelze not to write to him for a while but to check his letterbox every morning. Benn senses after decades of waiting that the muggy monotony of the Hanoverian summer is finally transforming into poetry all the emotions inside him that can make him feel as if he has a slab of lead on his heart.

Every morning throughout the first days of September 1935, Oelze walks along his rhododendron-lined gravel path and retrieves a piece of great literature from his letterbox. 'Day Which Marks the Summer's End', 'Oh, the Noble', 'Asters' – verses that make him one of the greatest German poets of the twentieth century – all make their way by post to Bremen on the back of menus.

What thoughts must have gone through Oelze's head on those

mornings? He sees what he is holding and knows that for years, potentially for decades, he will be the only person who will see these lines. 'Needs no particular response,' Benn writes under one poem. Benn knows that what is currently pouring out of him is greater than himself. Here in Hanover, far from Berlin and far from his loved ones, in the solitude he both craves and curses, Benn writes amorous verse of fantastic, even unreal poetic force: 'Never Lonelier Than in August', of course, but also 'Three', in which he overcomes his *ménage à trois* with Telly Wedekind and Elinor Büller:

Onto your lids slumbers I send,
Onto your lips a kiss I've sown,
While I must bear without a friend,
The night, the grief, the dream alone.

*

On 4 September, Kurt Weill and Lotte Lenya board the RMS *Majestic* in Cherbourg together to cross the Atlantic.

The first night in their double berth, Weill reaches out and, still reeling with disbelief, really does touch Lotte, two years divorced from him but apparently newly in love with him again. He considers it a good omen that the two of them are travelling to America to stage Franz Werfel's *The Eternal Road* with Max Reinhardt. It is a magnificent and aptly named play about the triumph of the Jewish people and the existential threats they face.

For the first time after a decade of travelling, disappointments, emigration and hope, after *The Threepenny Opera* and *The Seven Deadly Sins*, after Otto Pasetti and Max Ernst, Kurt and Lotte have the gift of time. During the six-day Atlantic crossing they review their past, all its highs and its lows. Many tears are shed to the hum of the ship's engines, but a little more each day, the tears are succeeded by caressing, kissing and lovemaking. By the time they step ashore in New York, they are a couple again. 'It really takes time to be able to speak of love,' Lotte Lenya will later say.

*

Kurt Tucholsky has lost his elixir of life – writing. He is only able to produce if he knows that his work is going to be printed immediately, but the newspapers he used to write for no longer exist, and the publishers who used to print them are all in jail. He describes himself as a 'former author'. Even women no longer really exude any attraction for him. In Sweden he sinks into depression and inactivity, reads, writes letters and gradually goes to seed.

On the evening of 21 December 1935, Tucholsky takes his life with an overdose of Veronal. There is no money in his wallet, only the touching farewell letter his wife, Mary, sent him when they split up seven years earlier: 'Will come if needed and called – that is my message to you. Your Meli.' On the table in the deserted house in Hindås is another farewell letter, this one addressed to Mary. But Gertrude Meyer, who finds it, also reads the written instruction only to deliver the letter to Mary if 'she is not married or seriously committed'.

This letter contains Kurt's greatest declaration of love – one that it seems he could make only after putting the greatest possible distance between himself and its object. Of their love he writes: 'Had a gold nugget in his hand and bent down to pick up a penny; didn't understand and made stupid mistakes; may not have betrayed but did cheat, and didn't understand.' He thanks Mary for her 'loving patience in going along with this lunacy and the restlessness; the patience to live alongside a man who constantly acted as if hunted, who was constantly afraid, no, terrified.' And then, in conclusion, he calls Mary 'him' to maintain a certain distance: 'If love is the thing that turns one upside down, makes every fibre crazy, then it is possible to feel it here or there. If, however, true love also requires that it lasts, that it keeps coming back, again and again – in that case, one has loved only once in one's lifetime. Him.'

Tucholsky's will is opened in January 1936. For the first and only time, all the women in his life are gathered together – on seven sheets of paper. Hedwig Müller, his Swiss lover, receives his ring engraved with the words '*Et après*'. Gertrude Meyer, who chose his burial place in Mariefred cemetery in the shadow of Gripsholm Castle where he first fell in love on Swedish soil – albeit with Lisa Matthias – is entitled to pick her favourite books from his library in Hindås. His sole heir, however, is Mary. After it is made public, she changes her surname back to Gerold-Tucholsky and devotes herself entirely to honouring the newly restored component. Kurt's mother accepts with gritted teeth the share her son has granted her, even though he has added that he hopes she has the decency to forgo it, in the name of a relationship so dysfunctional that he called his lovers 'Mummy' while he was alive. Lisa Matthias, Tucholsky's 'Lottchen', does not get a mention in the will. Apparently the dedication of *Castle Gripsholm* is sufficient.

On 21 December, as Tucholsky is slipping out of life, Klaus Mann also takes Veronal at his parents' house in Küsnacht near Zurich, 'but somewhat reluctantly, only because there happened to be some in the room'.

And what about Else Weil, aka 'Claire' in *Rheinsberg: A Storybook for Lovers*, who was Tucholsky's first wife? She worked as a doctor in Berlin until 1933. After Hitler takes power she, like all the other Jewish doctors in Berlin, is dismissed – or rather, in line with the usual bureaucratic methodology, her health coverage is revoked. She also has to move out of the palatial apartment at Wielandstrasse 33 and take work as a nanny in Grunewald for a family with the name of Hoffnung. She will flee to France via Holland but will lose her cabin booking for the crossing from Marseilles to America when her visa doesn't arrive on time. Soon afterwards she will be murdered in Auschwitz.

Heinrich Blücher followed in Hannah Arendt's footsteps by escaping from Berlin to Paris via Prague, but they only meet for the first time in Montparnasse in the spring of 1936. He is a committed Berlin Communist and a tried-and-tested street fighter in the tradition of the Spartacus League,* but in exile he adopts the disguise of an aristocratic tourist: a three-piece suit, with a hat and cane.

Blücher and Arendt collide in a whirlwind of desire, which in their case means physical and intellectual passion. Hannah Arendt will later say, with exaggerated modesty: 'It was thanks to my husband that I learned to think politically and see historically.' What is certain is that it was thanks to him that she expanded her conception of love – beyond St Augustine and Heidegger to the miraculous paradox by which 'love of the world' and the unworldliness of love can simultaneously exist.

On 8 May 1936, Oswald Spengler dies alone in his flat in Munich. The author of *The Decline of the West* does not have to witness it.

On 22 May 1936, shooting begins for Leni Riefenstahl's film *Olympia*. Riefenstahl intends to film the lighting of the Olympic torch and the first runners as they set off across Greece. Light floods the pathways and bounces off the white walls of the stadium, illuminating the shadows. Anatol Dobriansky, the son of Russian immigrants from Odessa, is to be the first runner in the movie. Of the 'young, dark-haired Greek, maybe eighteen or nineteen' Riefenstahl writes in her autobiography: 'We got on very well.' In other words, she takes him as her lover so that she doesn't have to sleep alone during filming.

This young Greek falls hopelessly in love with her, and when Riefenstahl dumps him after finding another young beau while on location in the high dunes of the Curonian Spit, poor Anatol tries to shoot himself. Riefenstahl's genial cameraman, Willy Zielke, is able to prevent this but can't stop Anatol becoming a scruffy

---

*The Spartacus League was originally founded as the International Group in 1914 by Rosa Luxemburg, Karl Liebknecht, Clara Zetkin and other Social Democrats. Its later goal was the establishment of a German-wide Soviet republic, and it was absorbed into the German Communist Party in 1919.

shoelace hawker in Berlin after the shoot. What lives on nonetheless is a striking photo of him as Greek javelin thrower, a harbinger of the future. It was taken by Zielke, but Riefenstahl is determined to claim it as her own.

She implements a cunning plan to get her way, telling Zielke's wife that she noticed during filming that her husband was bisexual. She whispers a word here and there, and Zielke is soon diagnosed as schizophrenic and admitted to Haar psychiatric hospital, where he is declared insane. Riefenstahl drives out to see his wife and takes all Zielke's photos and negatives into her possession, then issues them under her own name. Zielke is also forcibly sterilised at the hospital. (A few years later, with every other cameraman fighting at the frontline, the diabolical Riefenstahl will fetch this broken man from the hospital to help her shoot *Lowlands*.)

Erich Maria Remarque's reputation as a connoisseur of art precedes him. For years he has been compensating for his bouts of depression and fruitless quest for true love by buying French Impressionist paintings. Every new transfer of royalties for *All Quiet on the Western Front* adds a new Cézanne or Monet to the walls of his villa on Lake Maggiore.

When he and his lover Margot von Opel make a trip to Budapest in May 1936, he is among the very first people to see one of the major works of art of the nineteenth century. Accompanied by the author Sándor Márai, Remarque and Opel attend a small reception hosted by the Baron Ferenc von Hatvany. While the ladies are distracted in the drawing room, the baron takes his guest to a back room. There he opens a cupboard and takes out a picture with a mixture of pride and embarrassment. It is Courbet's *The Origin of the World*, the most gigantic leap towards Modernism in French portrait painting – a direct view of a woman's vulva. (Remarque notes in his diary that evening: 'A somewhat swinish but good Courbet.')

When they have re-joined the ladies, the baron attempts to kiss Margot von Opel behind a curtain. Later, Remarque confesses that he cheated on her the day before with a pretty Danish woman. Margot weeps, and Remarque feels ashamed; for him, *The Origin of the World* will remain the origin of desire and of suffering.

With her second marriage and the knowledge that she is financially set for life, Tamara de Lempicka's creative flow dries up. For ten years she has painted the figureheads of an epoch in Paris as Art Deco icons, but now she spends very little time in her studio and far more in sanatoriums, trying in vain to cure herself of her depression with diets and spa treatments. The demons of her troubled childhood and youth in Russia are gaining the upper hand; she can no longer maintain a glamorous façade. In Paris she paints two careworn émigrés and calls the picture *The Refugees*, but this reckoning with reality only deepens her depression.

In her desperation she travels to an Italian convent near Parma and asks to be admitted, determined to leave her wild bisexual life behind. When she meets the mother superior, Lempicka is so fascinated by her face that she decides to remain an artist. This will be the last picture of her golden age; the tears she paints on the dignified nun's cheeks are her own.

She begins the painting in Europe and completes it at the Ritz in New York. She has managed to persuade her husband, the sugar-beet baron Kuffner, to sell his Hungarian estates and emigrate to America with her, first to Manhattan and then to Beverly Hills. This move saves their lives, but they will not find happiness on the barren slopes of the Hollywood Hills.

Hannah Arendt and Walter Benjamin play chess for hours in their Parisian exile. Usually Arendt's queen checkmates Benjamin's king, but the situation in Arendt's home is very different. Friends describe her life with Heinrich Blücher as a 'dual monarchy': two proud and self-assured thinkers, independent and yet profoundly devoted to each other. It is true that this pair of philosophers develop a form of love in 1930s Paris that seems much more humane than the famous 'pact' between Jean-Paul Sartre and Simone de Beauvoir a few arrondissements away. Arendt and Blücher require none of the extramarital erotic freedoms that Sartre regards as a precondition.

No, they approach each other slowly in their letters and their conversations, knowing that detours give you a better understanding of the terrain. Arendt says in one letter that she is inspired by the 'outrageous hope' that she 'can demand anything' of him, meaning that she can 'treat you as I treat myself'. To which Blücher replies: 'My darling, I can breathe again, deep inside, and fill myself with your love.' Then, very tentatively, he adds: 'Now that you are my wife, may I be so soft as to tell you that I desire you?'

He always signs 'Your husband' now, even though he knows she is still married to Günther Stern. And on 24 August 1936, she sends him her profession of love – and doubt: 'That I love you – you knew that in Paris, as did I. And all that I can say about that today is: let us try – for our love's sake. I don't know if I can be your wife. My doubts have not been swept away. Nor has the fact that I am married. (Forgive me, my most beloved, for so much brutal bluntness – if you can.)' She soon confesses to him what a bad state her marriage is in: 'I didn't notice much of the hell it was being at home because I was working like a horse. I maintained my passive resilience as much as the other person maintained the notion of being married to me.'

These touching letters fly back and forth between Arendt and Blücher in the early days of their love, usually when she is away in Switzerland. The two of them defy the constraints of exile, the terrible news from their homeland and about the persecution of the Jews, and together they find a language for their feelings, falteringly at first but more forcefully with time. There is no pathos, just great earnestness – and many liberating jokes. Arendt soon knows that she wants to dissolve her marriage in order to be with Blücher. She has to be 'his wife', as she has in fact long been in practice. He also has to officially end a previous marriage. On his French divorce papers, incidentally, he gives his occupation as 'puppet master' – a bold move, given that he is consistently suspected of being a spy.

*

Just when Pablo Picasso has been openly united with Marie-Thérèse Walter and they are wheeling their daughter through Montparnasse in her pram, a new person enters his life. He spots Dora Maar sitting at a table in his favourite café, Les Deux Magots in Saint-Germain-des-Près: 'She was wearing black gloves with small pink flowers embroidered on them. She took off the gloves and picked up a long, sharp knife, which she stabbed into the tabletop between her fingers to see how close she could get to each finger without actually cutting herself. From time to time she missed by a fraction of a centimetre, and before she had finished the game, her hand was covered in blood.' Picasso stares at her wide-eyed, then goes over to her table and asks for her gloves. She tosses them to him. He places them in a display case as if it were a shrine.

Within a few days, Dora Maar becomes Picasso's lover. Marie-Thérèse and little Maya move to a house twenty-five miles from Paris, in Le Tremblay-sur-Mauldre. Picasso manages to pack off his wife and son to his château in Normandy so that he has a free rein in Paris; he will leave them the castle as part of the divorce agreement.

Picasso looks for a new studio in which there's nothing to remind him of his past life torn between two women. He finds a bright space in Rue des Grands-Augustins in Paris, and Dora Maar moves into a flat next door. There are incredible jealous scenes between the blonde, natural Marie-Thérèse and Dora, the dramatic, incisive Spanish Communist.

And what about Picasso, such a powerful artist and such a weak man? He says, 'I wasn't interested in making a decision ... I told them to sort things out between themselves.' Dora Maar emerges victorious from this battle. When Picasso paints the spectacular *Guernica* in the summer of 1937 – named after the Spanish city that has just been bombed by the Germans – he positions a mythical 'torch-bearer' in the centre of the picture. In *Minotauromachy* two years earlier, a similar figure bore Marie-Thérèse's features. Now, however, the woman has black hair and Dora Maar's distinctive nose. Whoever holds sway over Picasso's body and his desires also holds sway over his art and his eye.

Klaus Mann has had a love–hate relationship with Gustaf Gründgens since the two men were close in the twenties; how close remains unknown, but we do know how hurt Klaus was that his sister Erika picked Gründgens to be her husband. In 1932, in his novel *Meeting Point in Infinity*, Klaus settled his score with Gründgens – and he will continue to do so for the rest of his life. In his diary he asks himself: 'Why do I think of him so much and with such dislike?' Gründgens keeps appearing to Klaus in dreams during his exile in Paris and Amsterdam. He watches his former friend's meteoric ascent to artistic director of the Prussian State Theatre in Berlin, then turns his story into a novel named after the greatest dramatic character Gründgens ever played: Mephisto, the devil in Goethe's *Faust*.

The title thus alludes to the real-life model for the character of Hendrik Höfgen and his seductive powers. The novel, as he admits to his mother, promises to be 'of a certain hateful buoyancy'. His only dilemma is how to deal with his depiction of the relationship between 'Hendrik' and 'Barbara', who 'should not be Erika and yet of course she is'.

In the end Barbara turns out to be perhaps the most affectionate portrait of his beloved sister that Klaus ever paints: 'She had experience of other people's pain, but since early childhood she had failed to take her own pain and her own helplessness seriously, or to tell others about it.' There is only one person in the world who knows about 'the fragility of her inner state', he writes – the father whose love he so craves.

Mephisto is published in the summer of 1936, first serially in the émigré newspaper *Pariser Tageblatt* and then in book form in Amsterdam. The response is mixed. Thomas knows his son, and also his son's literary flaws. *Mephisto*, he writes, is problematic when it strives to be fiction because 'a work that is so closely bound up with reality is most at risk and, in a sense, at a loss when it tries to deviate from that reality and to deny it.' Unfortunately, he is right.

Providence determines that Gründgens is wed on the very day the book is published. Rumours about his homosexuality have grown so strident in Berlin that he can retain his position as artistic director of the State Theatre at Gendarmenmarkt only by entering into marriage; he does this with Marianne Hoppe, a twenty-seven-year-old actress who is, like him, more interested in her own sex.

In 1936, they take up residence on a small country estate in Zeesen that has been expropriated from Jewish refugees. After their wedding at the registry office, the young couple travel to their new home. Marianne goes for a swim and Gustaf takes a nap. A few guests join them that evening, but Gründgens has to return to Berlin for a performance. When he arrives back in Zeesen after the play, the guests have all left and Marianne is asleep. As a result, Gustaf also emerges from his second wedding night unscathed. The wags of Berlin come up with a nice rhyme: 'Hoppe Hoppe Gründgens, they can't have no childrens; and if Miss Hoppe does have sons, they will not be Gründgens' ones.'

During the summer of 1936, the Belgian town of Ostend witnesses a three-character drama with an all-star cast. In this windswept place appear the authors and friends Joseph Roth and Stefan Zweig, the former having succumbed irredeemably to drink during his exile, the latter mentally polishing *The World of Yesterday*, as his most famous book will be called. They are joined by thirty-one-year-old Irmgard Keun, the novelist who shot to fame in 1930s Berlin with *The Artificial Silk Girl* and has now left Germany for good.

Joseph and Irmgard recognise in each other the same delicate despair, the same silent hope. Together they embark on a shared frenzy of writing, living and drinking. Roth's soulmate Zweig discreetly withdraws, packing his bags and advising the blissful couple to 'take all the good you can still get'. Joseph and Irmgard board a train; giving Germany a wide berth, they travel to Galicia and the sites connected to his Jewish ancestors. 'I have to see it all once more,' he tells her. For two years they are the most peculiar and poignant couple in the German émigré community, descending together into the destructive pit of drink.

In Paris, the cast of another, long-running drama of the thirties briefly expands when Gonzalo Moré, a bold and bohemian Peruvian, joins the *ménage à trois* of Anaïs Nin, Henry Miller and Hugo Guiler.

On 14 September 1936, Henry Miller is hopeful that Anaïs will spend the night with him in his new apartment, as she does every Saturday. On this particular Saturday, however, Gonzalo becomes so jealous that he says he will leave Anaïs if she doesn't come to his flat instead. She slips some powerful sedatives into Henry's tea so that he dozes off early in the evening, then she tiptoes from the house and spends a night of passion with Moré. At six in the morning, she hurries back and sneaks into bed with Henry at Villa Seurat, where he is snoring away, blissfully unaware of her absence. After a nice breakfast she goes to see her husband in their own splendid new flat, bringing with her a bunch of flowers. That evening she notes in her diary: 'No blame. No pity, no guilt. Only love.'

Nineteen thirty-six is a decisive year for Libertas and Harro Schulze-Boysen. They marry and move into a new apartment at Waitzstrasse 2 in Berlin-Charlottenburg, which quickly becomes the secret headquarters of their elite resistance group of doctors, artists and professors.

To ensure that Harro can gain access to essential information, his wife puts into action a plan to facilitate his promotion to lieutenant. Libertas makes a last-minute trip to her parents' home in Schloss Liebenberg, where Hermann Göring is spending the weekend hunting fallow deer. Satisfied with having shot two fine stags, Göring is about to go up to his room when his hosts' charming daughter tells him that because of some errors her husband made as a young journalist, he is sadly being denied a position of responsibility at the ministry. Göring promises to take care of it, little suspecting that he will be personally promoting a resistance fighter to officer rank.

Audacious Libertas plays her part to perfection, even handing back her Nazi Party membership card. 'As a wife,' she dissembles to the party leadership, she must devote herself fully to her husband and household. The Nazis have no option but to accept this logic, but in reality her behaviour enrages both her mother and her mother-in-law. The twenty-two-year-old has no intention of slaving over the stove for her husband. No, she wants to be a journalist and writer and live a life of her own choosing by his side, as if this were still the Roaring Twenties.

When Libertas sets out alone on a rusty freighter from St Pauli for the Black Sea with her accordion, her Leica and her notepad, Harro has to explain to his mother: 'I want Libs to travel, precisely because I wish my wife to get used to existing independently of me.' Not that this appeases his dear mama one bit.

Harro sees things very differently: 'What do you know about the exceedingly subtle laws under which a happy marriage can flourish? I am still man enough to have a continual need to win a woman over and assert my love against all the odds. And since I am not a sexual pirate and love my own wife infinitely, I do not want to place the adventures and obstacles outside my marriage but bring them inside.'

These are fine words, especially as Harro knows that the Nazis have created an almost insurmountable impediment to his marriage. His kidneys are so damaged from the torture he endured in the summer of 1933 that he cannot carry out his 'marital duties' as he would wish. But Libertas writes to him from her voyage to the Black Sea, surrounded by sailors: 'As far as staying faithful is concerned, my boy, you have nothing more to fear.'

In August 1936, in Sanary-sur-Mer, Lion Feuchtwanger and Aldous Huxley, the British author of *Brave New World*, are vying for the attentions of the gorgeous artist Eva Hermann, who lives on the edge of town with her girlfriend Sybille Bedford. Hermann solves the problem in her own fashion. First, she sleeps with Feuchtwanger and then with Huxley before going back to Bedford. Afterwards Feuchtwanger writes in his diary: 'Pretty upset about Eva.' He likes to toy with others and hates the feeling that someone is toying with him. He knows all about hurting people, though. He takes a stroll along the harbour front with Sybille one evening, but when she remains obstinately true to her own sex he tries it on with Sascha, the bored wife of the philosopher Herbert Marcuse. As soon as Eva finds out, she comes running to him and into his bed. This time she gets pregnant and has to travel to Paris for an abortion. For the time being, life in Sanary-sur-Mer is governed by physical and psychological turmoil, jealousy and passion. It seems as if the Nazi horrors are far away and everyone here is safe from them.

Mascha Kaléko's poems conjure up so many variations on love and life, transience, treachery and a stubborn belief in happiness. Yet she has written about uncertainty from a position of certainty in her loving relationship with her husband Saul, who is blindly devoted to her. She has cheated on him a few times, yes, but:

> The others are the tug of waves,
> You the harbour deep.

When they feel the stirrings of a crisis, they do what couples tend to do in a bid to rekindle their flame – they look for a new apartment. They have only just moved into a wonderful old flat in Charlottenburg's Bleibtreustrasse when Mascha senses that she is pregnant – and she knows that the father is not Saul. Maybe anticipating this moment, Saul has already written to her that she should keep any infidelities secret from him.

Yet with every passing week, as her tummy grows, it becomes harder to conceal her secret or her love for Chemjo Vinaver, the Jewish composer who cast a spell over her from the moment they met. They were sitting at neighbouring tables at the Romanisches Café when he passed her a message saying, 'I have to have a baby with you.'

Avitar Alexander is born on 28 December 1936. Mascha does not dare to tell her husband the truth, and thus begins a year of suffering. She loves her son and yet in his smile she sees only her lover. Her husband, on the other hand, proudly remarks on how much the boy resembles him.

Mascha feels utterly torn. One day in 1937, flanked by the man whose ring she wears and the man to whom her heart belongs, she comes clean. Avitar Alexander wails in his pram.

Chemjo Vinaver moves in with his lover and their son, and Saul moves out into a guesthouse. The author of a book called *Hebrew for Everyone: For Advanced Learners*, he is an absolute beginner when it comes to living alone. On 22 January 1938, Vinaver and his wife are divorced, and on 28 January he marries Mascha. She has written countless poems warning about the need for caution when wishes come true; now it's her turn. Four days after the wedding she writes in her diary in shock: 'He is so irascible, and when he shouts I think, So this is the "true love" the whole world envies us for? I left the man I didn't love to follow the man I do and to find peace, mine and my child's, with him.' Only a few weeks later she writes in an outpouring of emotion: 'For me he is the dearest man on earth. I know that he loves me very, very, very much and I believe him when he says that I am the only woman in his life who can be both his home and his love.' That October, they and their son emigrate to the United States, and Central Park West in New York City becomes their new home. Their love for one another continues, as does their yearning for Berlin. She writes:

Sure, I'm very happy
But *glücklich* I am not.

*

After Berlin and Paris, New York is the third metropolis in which Kurt Weill and Lotte Lenya have lived in the space of only five years. They have travelled light for the final stage of their emigration – a few suitcases containing clothes, sheet music and notebooks, and the last remnants of income from *The Threepenny Opera*. Now they have to start again, like all the other people who wash up here, relieved at first but then bedevilled by fears of the future.

They refuse to let themselves be lulled by the nostalgia of the other German émigrés at the Bedford Hotel, though. They want to work rather than sit around with tears in their eyes, talking about the good old days. They want to build their careers in the New World. They swot up on their English and are very successful in their respective fields; within a year of arriving in the United States, Weill has his first show on Broadway and Lenya her first American lover, a playwright by the name of Paul Green.

On 19 January 1937, they say 'I do' for the second time at a New York registry office. The process of reconciliation is complete, even though Weill knows that there will always be a few walk-on parts at this stage of their marriage. 'Twice is for life,' Lenya says when she tells her friends about their new wedding. After he moves to Hollywood for a few months, Weill reflects: 'I think we're the only married couple without any problems.' *Mazel tov*. Or, as Rilke once put it: 'Love, my God, love.'

Konrad Adenauer leaves Maria Laach abbey, his refuge since 1933. As their family home in Cologne has been seized by the Nazis, he and his wife and children move to Rhöndorf. Gussie's brother Ernst builds them a small house there, and they live on Konrad's radically reduced pension from his time as mayor of Cologne. In these quiet and desolate years, Konrad fears that his best days are behind him.

On 21 February 1937, Leni Riefenstahl tells the American reporter Padraic King how she feels when she thinks of Adolf Hitler: 'For me Hitler is the greatest man who ever lived. He is truly faultless, so down to earth and also bursting with virile strength. He radiates charisma. All the great men of Germany – Frederick the Great, Nietzsche, Bismarck – had flaws. Hitler's fellow travellers aren't perfect either. He alone is pure.'

Riefenstahl is doing what she believes she has to do. After all, Hitler personally saved her. After Goebbels spread rumours that Riefenstahl had a Jewish grandmother, Hitler called him to heel. Even though the business about the grandmother remains murky, Goebbels must show her public deference. This includes making an appearance at the June house-warming party for the property Hitler's favourite director has bought in Berlin-Dahlem, on an Aryanised piece of land that belonged to the Wertheim family before they emigrated. A small party gather on the freshly mown lawn to drink punch: Hitler, Goebbels, Leni's brother Heinz and his wife, her mother, and the lady of the house. There is another lady too, dressed identically to Leni in a white blouse and a knee-length skirt, who hovers in the background and whom Leni introduces to the gentlemen as Dr Ebersberg. Heinrich Hoffmann, Hitler's friend and photographer, has come along, so many photos exist of this balmy evening when Riefenstahl is re-embraced by the Thousand-Year Reich.

Annetta Ebersberg appears in the photos, but she will be absent from Riefenstahl's nine-hundred-page autobiography even though she has been Leni's closest friend since the mid-1930s. Hitler doesn't enquire about her, and neither does Goebbels; they accept the explanation that Dr Ebersberg is a physician. Having just cleared Riefenstahl of the nasty whiff of having a Jewish grandmother, it seems the two top Nazis would prefer to turn a blind eye to the possibility that she is bisexual. Once the big cheeses have left, Leni packs her bags and has one last drink with Annetta, her brother and her mother. She has to be off early the next morning for the Paris premiere of *Triumph of the Will*.

Hermann Hesse is still kneeling in his luxuriant garden high above Lake Lugano, pulling up weeds, an activity that has the advantage of getting him away from his wife. 'I divide my days between the studio and working in the garden, the latter furthering meditation and intellectual digestion and thus largely pursued alone.' This is what he now craves most in his marriage – to be alone. Ninon feels much the same. Two sad partners in an enormous, meticulously organised house, each of them with too much past and too few dreams. A sign hangs on their fence: *No Visitors Please*. The ringing of church bells in the little villages by the lake echoes up the valley to the garden of Casa Rossa.

In his loneliness at the military administration office in Hanover, Gottfried Benn is tempted to give matrimony another try. In order to do this, though, he must first give his two lovers their marching orders. When Elinor Büller demands a love letter from him, he sends her a laconic message: 'Love is a crisis of the organs of touch.' He adds: 'I have enlisted a little confidante in the past weeks and I wish to keep her.' He writes the same thing to Tilly Wedekind. As usual Benn finds only small words for major events in his life. And to make sure that his penfriend Oelze in Bremen doesn't expect too much, he provides a thumbnail physical description of the 'little confidante': 'Tall, slim, overbred, not pretty, protruding white teeth.' As so often, it looks as if he wants to protect the small joys of his existence by presenting them to the outside world as misfortunes.

It is fascinating and upsetting to see how the poetic energy that courses through Benn's Stadthalle poems in the summers of 1935 and 1936 flags when he meets a new woman and abandons the loneliness that he has suggested is the basis for all lyric poetry. The young lady in question is Herta von Wedemeyer, an ash-blonde noblewoman from Hanover who, he emphasises, is at least a 'perfect typist'. He is fifty-one and she thirty-one. He likes that, and he clearly views marriage to a German aristocrat as a possible shield against increasingly hostile moves by the Nazis, who are now calling his earlier writings 'degenerate' and imputing him with Jewish ancestry. Before she becomes his wife, however, he wants to know more about her financial situation. He has the effrontery to write to the Association of German Nobility to this end.

The enquiry reveals that he stands to gain very little, but Benn decides to take her to Berlin and marry her anyway, and he finds a dark ground-floor flat at Bozener Strasse 20 where they can live. As the wedding approaches, he sends his old friend and publisher Erich Reiss a detailed aperçu of the consequences of marriage from his point of view: 'For a man there is only illegality, fornication and orgasm; therefore anything resembling attachment goes against his nature. In marriage there are financial matters, dietary matters, social issues, shared interests – all of which torpedo sex.' He continues: 'Human attachment to the spouse cripples the nasty and base and criminal sensations that underpin all authentic coitus for a man. He becomes impotent, but this impotence in marriage is an ovation for the wife as a person.'

In this case his ovation goes like this: 'My wife is delicate, refined, highly degenerate and always tired, which suits me very nicely. At eight o'clock she is ready for bed.'

By 1937, Vladimir and Véra Nabokov know that it is time for them to leave Berlin with their little son, Dmitri. Those who murdered Vladimir's father are returning to the city, this time as heads of the 'mediation service' that keeps Russian émigrés under observation; to inspire even greater confidence, it is placed under Gestapo supervision. Being Russians, and Véra a Jew, the Nabokovs are subjected to intense surveillance.

Véra urges her husband to explore the possibilities of immediate emigration to Paris, but on the way there he falls in love with a woman named Irina Guadagnini. Her job sounds like a product of the writer's imagination: she is a dog groomer. Wracked with guilt towards his wife, who is waiting terrified in Berlin, Vladimir breaks out in an enormous psoriasis rash after the first few nights in bed with Irina. He writes to tempt Véra to Paris, but she refuses to come until he has established a firm financial footing for his family in exile. Their letters, which used to be so imbued with warmth and wit and poignant love, now take on an unsettling tone. Vladimir acts as if nothing has changed and writes: 'Little pussy, is it time for you to get ready to come to me?'

But Véra has got wind of Vladimir's affair, and he is too cowardly to admit to it, so their correspondence about their emigration plans is tainted with distrust, doubt and fear. On 30 March he writes to her: 'My darling, what is the matter? I have received no letter for four days.' He can guess what the matter is. Another factor is Véra's daunting task of obtaining visas for herself and little Dmitri in Berlin. She suggests England as a place of exile, then Belgium – France is contaminated for her now by Vladimir's affair. In a letter dated 6 April he writes: 'What on earth is the matter? You will probably tell me in your next letter that you will happily stay in Germany, at a Bavarian spa resort.'

Véra finally confronts him with the allegations she has heard. On 20 April, Hitler's forty-eighth birthday, Vladimir writes her a barefaced lie: 'The same rumours have reached my ears too. I shall smash in the grubby faces of those who are spreading them. When all is said and done, I couldn't give a damn about the horrible things people delight in saying about me, and nor should you.' On 27 April, after many other letters, he writes: 'I don't have the energy to carry on this game of correspondence chess. I give up.'

Somehow, despite this stalemate, the couple manage to meet up in Prague on 22 May. Vladimir takes the train from Paris, Véra and Dmitri from Berlin. After Vladimir has owned up to the affair and declared it over, Véra agrees to move to Cannes with him. Nonetheless, it will take a long time for the poison of mistrust and the pain of betrayal to dissipate. But the day will come when he writes to her: 'I love you, I am happy, everything is fine.' Their marriage will endure for fifty-two years, and the stain with the dog groomer grows out of it like hair dye.

*

Will things be fine? Nineteen thirty-seven is the brightest year of this dark decade for Klaus Mann. He has come up with an idea for a book about these years in exile: 'My next novel. A grand collage of émigré lives. *The Persecuted* or something similar. Taking parallel paths, but bound together by some hook or other ... Passport problems. Lack of money. Lack of sex. Hatred. Hope. Homesickness. Fear (and hope) of war.' Rarely have lives been described as concisely as in this outline, which later develops into *The Volcano: A Novel among Emigrants.* Klaus knows what keeps him from writing: drugs. He is so addicted that every day now his diary reads: 'Taken.' Eventually his parents and Erika manage to persuade him to go into rehab.

The Budapest sanatorium where Klaus starts his detox on 27 May has the promising name Siesta. Among the medical staff there is Dr Robert Klopstock, 'in whose arms Franz Kafka died', as Klaus writes in his diary, but under this doctor's guidance he comes back to life. Two months into his agonising withdrawal programme, Klaus writes to his worried mother in Zurich: 'I will certainly not start again in the foreseeable future – maybe some day in a long, long time.' He has a very specific reason for battling his way back towards a drug-free life.

Thomas Quinn Curtiss – 'Tomski', as Klaus affectionately calls him – is a twenty-two-year-old American with sensual lips, wavy hair and close-fitting suits who studied with the Soviet film director Sergei Eisenstein in Moscow. Now he lives in Budapest, and he visits Klaus at the clinic every day.

After a decade of love affairs, Klaus confides to his diary: 'I have set my heart on him. The "higher entity" cannot possibly grant me any greater satisfaction than this relationship has brought me.'

The summer, when the worst afflictions of withdrawal are over, is perhaps the best time of Klaus's life. As the younger man's adored elder, he takes Tomski on a whirlwind tour of the European stations of his life. They travel to Zurich to see his parents, and they visit Erika and Therese Giehse in the picturesque Swiss canton of Grisons, where they are on holiday with Annemarie

Schwarzenbach. Klaus shows him the canals of Amsterdam, and together they go to Sanary-sur-Mer, where Klaus spent a different, bygone summer. Looking back, he writes three unimaginable words: 'I was happy.'

The author Ernst Jünger manages to hide – from the Nazis and also from himself – in the Harz Mountains, and then, from 1936, in Überlingen on the shores of Lake Constance. Day after day he roams the forests, collecting beetles. He spends the evenings pinning and labelling them, delighting in their carapaces and their Latin names. His remarkable wife, Gretha, suffers alongside him. He demands that she call him 'Commander', and she agrees. She spends her life searching for a vocation; unfulfilled by her role as mother to their two boys, she begins to write and travel under her Commander's suspicious eye. Unlike her, Ernst had numerous affairs in Berlin, and emigration doesn't put a stop to his womanising. Gretha doesn't blame him, though; she blames the women who seduce him.

Ernst nevertheless treats his wife with the cool detachment he has elevated to his emotional ideal since his first book, *Storm of Steel*. Gretha can only groan at this 'new objective' treatment, as she calls it in a mixture of sarcasm and despair. To a friend she complains, 'I am tiring. This has become a horrible, untenable state of affairs for me because I feel myself being slowly drawn into his spiral of desolation, depression and utter rejection of life, just as an insect attracted to a light becomes incapable of escaping a spider's web.' Yes, Gretha had walked right into the entomologist's net and he occasionally studies her like a small, strange beetle that happens to share his habitat.

He answers this question with an astrological explanation: 'Over the course of our lifetime we constantly encounter the individual who knocks us off our fixed orbit and forces us to be sociable, whether we like it or not.' He follows up with a defence of his own affairs and a refusal to take responsibility: 'This is why fidelity is basically beyond our power. Gravitational forces have a greater effect on us than virtue.'

Alma Mahler-Werfel's temporary lover and long-term confessor, the theologian Johannes Hollnsteiner, has the opportunity to display his own confessions in an odd marriage annulment trial in Vienna. It is also worth saying that he does this out of a peculiar form of love.

Members of the Catholic Church can only enter into a new marriage if their previous marriage has been annulled; as president of Vienna's metropolitan and diocesan court, Hollnsteiner therefore wields a lot of power. The Austrian chancellor Schuschnigg, whose wife died in a road accident in 1935, comes before the court because he would like to wed Vera Gräfin von Czernin-Chudenitz. She is currently married to Count Fugger von Babenhausen, with whom she has four children.

Johannes Hollnsteiner sets to work fixing things for his chancellor. And lo and behold, the countess's first marriage is annulled because, in Hollnsteiner's view, it was a 'coerced marriage' that contravenes the Catholic Church's principles of freedom. The trial drags on and on. By the time the theologian has fought it out, Schuschnigg has been taken captive by the Nazis and Austria has been incorporated into the Third Reich in the so-called 'Anschluss'. The deposed chancellor is nevertheless permitted to marry his beloved Vera in a Gestapo jail on 1 June 1938. However, a prisoner is not allowed to attend his own wedding, so Schuschnigg is represented by his brother Artur. After the ceremony Vera joins her husband in jail and goes with him when he is moved first to Dachau concentration camp and then to the camp at Sachsenhausen.

What a reversal of fortunes! In 1937, for the first time in her life, Erika Mann experiences true unhappiness and then undergoes perhaps her sternest test. Having both acquired British husbands and therefore British passports, she and Therese Giehse attempt to transfer their Peppermill revue to America. The project fails, however, because there is no tradition of satirical political shows in the United States, nor a conception of laughter being the only remedy for particular forms of pain. In the process, Erika and Therese grow apart, despite all that they have experienced together during their exile years and their shared sense of humour. Erika strolls confidently across the international stage, but Therese struggles with the language and the different theatrical culture. Therese is horrified by how easily Erika has taken to the superficial American way of life and given up on finding an audience for the revue, while Erika accuses Therese of not trying to learn English out of sheer obstinacy.

Beset by anger and insecurity, Therese becomes obsessively jealous of Erika's flirtations, until Erika actually falls a little in love with a man – more out of spite than anything else. (Everyone has assumed that there was nothing erotic in her marriages to Gustaf Gründgens or W. H. Auden, both known to be gay.)

Now, however, at the Bedford Hotel on Fortieth Street in Manhattan, she develops feelings for the exiled Jewish author and doctor Martin Gumpert. In the words of Klaus Mann, he is 'a very peaceful man with a round Buddha-like face, a small mouth and dark, strong eyes. His gaze betrays a passion that is otherwise imperceptible from the stoical surface.' His passion is also clearly directed towards Erika, who is also being wooed by Klaus's friend Fritz Landshoff. Gumpert successfully seduces Erika, who seems eternally grateful to him for trying to use new medication to wean her brother off drugs. In any case, they sleep together and Erika gets pregnant. Gumpert dreams of getting married and living as a family, but Erika feels threatened by a tidal wave of feelings at the idea of being a wife and mother. Refusing to relinquish her independence, her 'turbulent solitude' and her freedom, she has an abortion.

In the midst of this emotional chaos, Erika's old friend Annemarie Schwarzenbach arrives in New York and tries to chart a way through the confusion by listening to the German émigrés at the hotel and trying to give useful advice. But Erika freaks out, writing to her mother that 'this delicate asylum-dweller' is pouring oil on troubled waters with her 'country-boarding-school manners'.

Nerves are obviously raw. Not long afterwards, Therese packs her bags and sails back to Europe. Annemarie goes with her, giving them a great deal of time on deck and in their cabin to ponder what makes Erika tick. Meanwhile, Erika finds solace in her parents' shadow. It threatened to swallow her brother Klaus alive, but to her it offers protection. What strange creatures we humans are.

Something poignant happens in Venice in September 1937. Two German international superstars whose fortunes are on the wane meet one morning in the perpetually sinking city; by that evening they are sinking into bed together. She plays her oldest trick by asking him for a light at Caffè Florian, and once more it works. She raises the cigarette to her lips, leans towards him and rests her pale, slender fingers on his suntanned hand. The only sound is the hiss of the match, then the burning of paper and then the deep inhalation with which Miss Dietrich draws in not only the nicotine but also the man holding the lighter.

Erich Maria Remarque, at war with writer's block. Marlene Dietrich, an actress whose latest movies have been flops and who is exhausted by her commute between Berlin and Hollywood and by her extravagant sex life. The two of them connect at first sight. 'We can read one another in total delight,' he writes to her after a few days, 'and fall into the other's traps just as quickly.' What they are experiencing is a kind of magical understanding where, to their relief, no explanations are needed.

It doesn't last long. Dietrich increasingly signals to Remarque that he is not the only person she allows into her bed. Remarque records the minor barbs and major torments of this mismatched relationship in his diary with masochistic accuracy. In any case, their meetings are always brief – in luxury suites in Paris, halfway between Porto Ronco and Hollywood – and she treats him like a maid. First he has the honour of giving long, oily massages to the woman he likes to stroke and call his 'puma'. Whenever she has to take a long-distance call from America in the middle of the night, he is allowed to be her receptionist. And in the morning he may bring her fruit to the bedroom, warm her dressing gown on the radiator and draw her a bath. He never complains, but he realises something's wrong: he, a proud man, is being reduced to a submissive servant. In a diary entry dated 27 October 1938 he reminds himself: 'Soldier! ... You cannot be a film star's sponge. That is a job for someone who doesn't work. You have work to do.' All the same, their relationship lasts for a while longer. He is simply too flattered to be the man who crosses the street in Paris or Antibes with Miss Dietrich on his arm. A lot of love between two people, Rainer Maria Rilke used to say, involves each protecting the solitude of the other.

In September 1937, Ludwig Wittgenstein again comes into conflict with his ideals. Once again the setting is the wilds of Norway, where six years earlier Marguerite Respinger tried in vain to lure him out of his reserve and inner complexes. This time it is a man who poses the challenge, during the long, bright northern nights when the air and sea are still and the stars don't seem sure if they should shine because the birds are already singing.

Francis Skinner, a shy, pretty Cambridge mathematics student, reveres the philosopher who is twice his age, but Wittgenstein is disturbed by how 'very sensual' he feels when alone with Francis. He desperately hopes that theirs will remain a 'human' relationship, from which we learn that it is sex that Wittgenstein finds inhuman. He notes in his diary: 'Have lain two or three times with him. Always with the initial feeling that there is nothing wrong, but then with shame. Have also been unfair, irritable and insincere towards him and tormenting.'

Wittgenstein is scared of his hormones, which is why he blames the infatuated Skinner. When the distraught younger man leaves Norway, Wittgenstein crawls back into his hut with the feeling that this sexual arousal has corrupted something inside him 'as in a rotten apple'.

Wittgenstein is confused and naturally chooses to overcome the problem with logic. He considers how love might be kept 'untainted' by the Fall, which for him is the moment when lust overcomes him. He thinks back over these two rare moments, in the Norwegian summers of 1931 and 1937, but finds no way out of the labyrinth of his ego. 'Yesterday evening I had more ideas about the need for purity in my conduct (I thought of Marguerite and Francis).' Twice in his life, his body sought to overcome the logic of his intellect, but eventually it has had to admit defeat.

Theodor Adorno has fled from the Nazis to England, where he has holed up inside the ancient walls of Merton College, Oxford. In 1937, as the situation becomes increasingly perilous for his fiancée, Gretel Karplus, she too manages to escape to England. He writes to Max Horkheimer, who has already emigrated to the United States, that Germany has become 'hell'. During a trip to visit the European branches of the Institute for Social Research in September 1937, Horkheimer acts as best man at Theodor and Gretel's wedding in London. Gretel knows what this wedding signifies, after their ten-year relationship. Having been heavily involved in bohemian circles in late-1920s Berlin and subsequently run a leather business, she is condemned to a life as a housewife and her husband's loyal assistant. She must also give up any notions of having children, her husband having made clear to her at an early stage that this would distract him from thinking.

In February the following year, they board an America-bound liner in Southampton and put Europe behind them; Horkheimer has arranged a position for Adorno at Princeton. As the new bride starts furnishing their first apartment outside Germany, her husband offers a glimpse of his attitude in *Minima Moralia*: 'Incidentally, Gretel is entirely absorbed in organisational matters, a task in which I most cynically refuse to get involved.'

To Gretel, however, we owe some entirely uncynical descriptions of émigré life in New York surrounded by Max Horkheimer, Kurt Weill and Lotte Lenya: 'First a small party at Max's, then we all moved on to a nice little nightclub where Lenya was performing. Yes, in fact everything is even more concentrated here than in Berlin, like a throwback to the years from '25 to '32.' (Of all of them, Lenya alone manages not only to step back in time but also to make a leap forwards; in 1963, she plays ex-KGB officer Rosa Klebb in the James Bond film *From Russia with Love*.)

That winter it is not an affair but a wedding that shakes the Nazi regime in Berlin. The widowed sixty-year-old Reich Minister of Defence and anthroposophist Werner von Blomberg falls head over heels in love with Margarethe Gruhn, a prostitute thirty-five years his junior. They require the blessing of the supreme commander of the Wehrmacht, Adolf Hitler, to get married. Blomberg tells the Führer that Gretchen is 'a simple girl of the people'. Hitler suggests himself and Göring as best men, and the lovers are pronounced man and wife at the Ministry of War on 12 January 1938. Rumours immediately abound that Hitler has given his blessing to a minister marrying this woman, and when Margarethe Gruhn's police files are seized by the Gestapo, they confirm this suspicion. Not only did she work as a prostitute, she also frequently posed for pornographic photographs.

Blomberg comes under pressure to get his marriage annulled, but he chooses his wife and resigns from his post. Their marriage is described as being very happy, but Hitler takes advantage of the debacle to radically restructure the whole war ministry and party apparatus.

Nineteen thirty-eight is the toughest year in the life of the tennis-playing baron Gottfried von Cramm. In the latter years of the Weimar Republic he was able to lead an unfettered bisexual lifestyle, frantic but elegant. In the early thirties his white tennis trousers and tight-fitting polo shirts helped to make him the global icon of a newly respectable and well-intentioned Germany. He even accepted losing the 1935 Davis Cup final when he judged that the umpire had made an error in his favour.

'Every year when Cramm walks out onto Centre Court at Wimbledon,' the BBC's Alistair Cooke declared in 1937, 'several hundred young ladies sit up a little straighter in their seats and forget their companions.' Yet in spite of his many affairs, Gottfried has never forgotten his own companion. He has sworn undying love to Lisa, his androgynous wife who is friends with the photographer Marianne Breslauer, Annemarie Schwarzenbach and Ruth Landshoff. Like her husband, she places feelings over marital fidelity. Yet in spite of their love for one another, they divorce in 1938.

The divorce proceedings declare that Lisa is 'solely to blame', partly due to her earlier fling with a French tennis player and partly because of her current relationship with Gustav Jaenecke, her husband's doubles partner at Wimbledon. In their heart of hearts, though, they both know that this divorce is a mere technicality; they have always been in love, even if Lisa has suffered dreadfully from the fact that her husband loves men more than women. When she sues for a divorce, she writes: 'I don't want to tell you that I am sad, nor do I want to write you a love letter. I just want to thank you for all you have done for me, especially in recent times. Once again you were so incredibly decent and touching towards me. You probably won't believe this, Petit, but I will never forget it. I could kill myself for every nasty thing I have done to you.'

In 1938, the Gestapo takes over the task of tormenting Gottfried von Cramm. They take him into custody on 5 March on account of his homosexuality, unmoved by his status as a world-famous tennis player and poster boy for a better Germany. This is about principles: Cramm is a bisexual, Jew-friendly critic of the regime. But he also turns out to be a tough nut for the Gestapo to crack. He admits to having had homosexual relations with Herbert Manasse until 1936 but assures the officers that he has had regular sexual intercourse with his wife, with whom he is still very much in love even if they are now divorced.

What he omits to say is that since 1937 he has been having an affair with Barbara Hutton, the world's richest woman, whom he met during a tennis tournament in Egypt.

Cramm is subjected to two weeks of interrogation at Gestapo headquarters in Prinz-Albrecht-Strasse in Berlin. His mother comes to Berlin from the family's country seat in Bodenburg to support him. She manages to visit him in his cell, where she finds him in utter despair. He is threatening to kill himself and, she writes, has 'only one concern: that his family should forgive him'. This, however, is the one thing he doesn't need to worry about. His mother sticks by him, as do his brothers and his ex-wife. All of them visit him in prison and hold his hand.

On 15 April, Barbara Hutton herself comes to Berlin with her husband, a German count, and takes up quarters at Hotel Adlon. The very next day she receives a visit from Jutta, Gottfried's mother, who presents Barbara with roses from her son. A month later, Gottfried is sentenced to a year in prison for breaching Paragraph 175, which outlaws homosexuality. The judge declares him a 'weak and unstable character' because 'he initially could not find the courage to stand up strongly to his wife and get rid of the lovers he knew she took', and this is evidence of his insufficiently 'manly attitude'. Gottfried writes to his mother: 'The more I think about Barbara, the more touched I am, slightly flattered as well. Imagine: she is married and brings her husband along to help another man in this situation! It is a minor miracle.' Maybe it is the many appeals from inside Germany and abroad that do it, maybe it is due to 'good behaviour', but in any case he is released early from jail on 16 October.

He tries to pick up his life where it was interrupted, but he is plagued by severe bouts of depression and feelings of guilt. His conviction on sex crimes then gets him excluded from Wimbledon and a major US tournament. And a year later, he is called up to the General Göring Luftwaffe regiment and forced to go to war against the Allied nations whose tennis tournaments and bohemian circles he so adores.

The Nazis arrest the songwriter Bruno Balz repeatedly for infringements of Paragraph 175. He takes his revenge by photographing himself in a ridiculous Hitler pose and sticking the picture on page 175 of a copy of *Mein Kampf*. His name no longer features on film posters or gramophone recordings of his compositions after his incarceration, but UFA cannot do without him. On 21 September 1936, Balz is forced to get married. The Gestapo has found Selma Pett, an unpretentious Pomeranian farmgirl devoted to Hitler, for this purpose. She moves into Balz's spacious apartment at Fasanen-strasse 60 in Berlin, and he brings his parents to live there too. Here, boxed between his boyfriend, his wife and his mother, Balz comes up with 'Ich brech die Herzen der stolzesten Frau'n' ('I Break Even the Proudest Women's Hearts') for Heinz Rühmann and 'Kann denn Liebe Sünde sein?' ('Can Love Ever Be a Sin?') for Zarah Leander.

On 4 May, the Nobel Peace Prize winner Carl von Ossietzky dies in a sanatorium for lung patients while in Gestapo custody as a result of being tortured and injected with tuberculosis bacteria. His wife, Maud, has been by his side during his final days. He is too weak for her to confess to him that she entrusted the 100,000 marks he received with the Nobel Prize to a conman who has run off with the money.

The Anschluss shatters the delicate trio of Alma Mahler-Werfel, Franz Werfel and Johannes Hollnsteiner. While Alma and Franz initially flee to Italy, then England and finally France, the Gestapo drag Hollnsteiner from his monastery of St Florian on suspicion of having collaborated with Schuschnigg's Austrian government – the chancellor has also been arrested. After eight weeks of interrogations and abuse, Hollnsteiner is transferred to Dachau concentration camp without trial. There, he has to work in a quarry in the scorching heat until he collapses from exhaustion. (He will not be allowed to return to his monastery until 1939.)

Although Alma and Franz Werfel's marriage was on the point of disintegration before they emigrated, the alarming political situation creates a temporary bond between them. Before they head into exile Alma writes in her diary: 'My marriage has long since ceased to be a marriage. I live unhappily alongside Werfel.' For his part he is increasingly shocked by his wife's antisemitic onslaughts against him and horrified by her support for the Nazis. She is even more confused now that the Gestapo has deported her beloved Hollnsteiner to a concentration camp while her Jewish husband is free to come and go as he pleases. She has a 'nervous breakdown', using the English term to describe her condition, and he has a minor heart attack.

The couple only relax when they reach Sanary-sur-Mer, the small port between Saint-Tropez and Marseilles that exerted such a calming influence on Thomas Mann and his family five years earlier, and even caused Bertolt Brecht to occasionally stop brooding and gaze up at the stars.

Alma and Franz find an old Saracen watchtower on the edge of a cliff, by the narrow footpath leading up from the town to Thomas Mann's former villa. Franz sets up his desk on the second floor of the tower. He may never have had a more beautiful view: he can look out over the wide sea and the hills of southern France that begin just outside the town. Below, on the windowless first floor, Alma sits and writes her diary by the dim light of a standard lamp: 'Good heavens. It is impossible to go on living like this without hope. I am done.' She is enraged at being forced to leave her dear Vienna for the sake of her Jewish husband and at finding herself, at fifty-nine, having to shop for baguettes and strange fruit in a godforsaken town on the Mediterranean coast, where she has no cleaning lady and no one recognises and curtsies to her in the street. It's hot and the place is teeming with mosquitoes and devoid of parties.

What's more, wherever she goes here, every German speaker is either a Jew or a Communist. It's vile. Alma feels as if life is playing tricks on her. Can it be that she, consort of the famous, is an émigré purely because she missed the right moment to divorce her husband? While he is upstairs, fretting about the ubiquitous Nazi spies and working away at his manuscripts, Alma is downstairs negotiating with the propaganda ministry in Berlin about the sale of the Bruckner scores from Gustav Mahler's estate.

No, Franz and Alma's marriage is in tatters and even their desperate situation in exile cannot repair the damage. Even when Sanary-sur-Mer's undisputed royalty, the Feuchtwangers, come over for dinner, the Werfels row like fishwives, with Alma screaming at Franz: 'Never forget I'm not a Jew!' She needn't worry – how could he ever forget?

Libertas and Harro Schulze-Boysen have an enemy in their bed as they ramp up their resistance to the Nazi regime by distributing leaflets and pasting illegal posters. Günther Weisenborn is an old friend of Harro's from his time at *Der Gegner* magazine. He is close to Bertolt Brecht, a former dramaturge at the Volksbühne and author of a novel called *Barbarians* that the Nazis burned in May 1933. Weisenborn joins the resistance group that meets every Thursday at Waitzstrasse 2, and he quickly wins Libertas's mind and then her body.

Initially, Libertas hopes that Günther might give her some literary tips, but in May 1938 they travel together to the island of Hiddensee, where their writing endeavours quickly fade into the background: 'In the dunes all day lying and running and playing and making love, white-hot, animal-like, climbing and swimming, Libs and me, brown. We have a wonderful bedroom: full moon, nightingale, May, the Baltic beyond the terrace, love!' This is Günther's pacy, passionate summary of their working holiday. Harro is faced with the precise situation he portrayed as his ideal to his mother the previous year: the 'adventures and obstacles' are now outside his marriage.

Libertas finds the whole business so normal that on the way back from Hiddensee she drops in on her mother at Schloss Liebenberg to introduce her lover. We do not know if she was in love, nor if she sees the affair with Günther as a kind of serendipitous compensation for the physical pleasures she has foregone by marrying a man mutilated by Nazi torturers. What is clear, however, is that not for one second does she cease to care for Harro. When she meets Thomas Mann during a trip to Zurich, she confides in him about her husband's clandestine activities and his moral fortitude. If anything should happen to him, she wants to be sure neutral countries will be aware of what he has done.

Libertas's premonitions turn out to be accurate: that month, Harro's name is included in the Reich Security Main Office's 'A-Kartei' index listing former opponents of the Nazi regime who are to be deported to Sachsenhausen in the event of a political crisis.

The final act of the drama surrounding the artist Ernst Ludwig Kirchner begins on 6 May 1938 when, high up on the Stafelalp above Davos, he receives no letters to mark his fifty-eighth birthday. He has been waiting for the postman with Erna, his loyal companion who has long been hoping for a marriage proposal from him. But the postman doesn't come.

Kirchner has had to endure the pain of being viewed as the epitome of depravity ever since he was included in the 'Degenerate Art' exhibition in Germany, and a major retrospective of his pictures at the Kunsthalle Basel closed without a single sale. As if that were not enough, 639 of his paintings, sculptures and drawings have been removed from German museums, and the Prussian Academy of Arts in Berlin has demanded that he resign his membership.

With the Anschluss, the German army is now only fifteen miles from Davos on the Schlappin Pass. The next war is apparently imminent, but his soul is still tormented every day by the last one. 'A silent tragedy', Erna will later write, 'has been playing out here for months.'

The overall picture is so desolate that Ernst sets about destroying his work and starts taking significant doses of morphine again after many years of abstinence. He injects Eukodal, dozens of empty vials of which are later found buried in the pastures around the Wildbodenhaus.

We do not know why he goes to Davos town hall on 10 June to arrange a ceremony for him and Erna. Maybe it's to ensure that she is his legal heir, or maybe it's to fulfil her dearest wish after she has devoted her life to assuaging his pain. If either or both of these hypotheses is true, then it is equally mysterious why he takes the bus to Davos town hall on 12 June to retract his marriage arrangements.

The fifteenth of June is an uncommonly cold day, with fog in the air and driving snow. Ernst injects a dose of Eukodal and slides into despair. Erna leaves the Wildbodenhaus around half past nine and heads for their nearest neighbours' house a few hundred yards away to summon a doctor by phone. In her absence Ernst stuffs into his coat pockets 8,740 francs in cash, his passport, his thirty-year-old engineering degree from Dresden University, a syringe of morphine and three full doses of Eukodal. He runs into the thick fog, tries to catch up with Erna, screams and shoots himself with his old Browning. Two shots straight into the heart. The doctor, arriving in a taxi, can only confirm the death of his most famous and most desperate patient.

Ernst is buried three days later. The wintry, foggy conditions have lifted. It is a splendid early summer's day, the wildflowers are blooming and the sky is blue. Two deer gaze down from a forest meadow as the funeral procession makes its way up from the small church to the cemetery. Erna, finally allowed to call herself Erna Kirchner, stays in the Wildbodenhaus until the war is over, and then she dies too.

In Paris, Jean-Paul Sartre and Simone de Beauvoir seem oblivious to the Nazi atrocities and the lost émigrés surrounding them. Just as in autumn 1933, when they found nothing noteworthy about streets full of marching SA troops and swastika flags as they ate cheesecake at Café Kranzler in Berlin, in 1938 they are still absorbed in their complex love lives.

Both of them have obtained posts in Paris, where they have rented separate flats, one above the other. Sartre recovers from his unsuccessful pursuit of de Beauvoir's pupil, Olga Kosakiewicz, by chasing her younger sister Wanda every day; after two years of constant courting and wooing he finally gets to sleep with her. Meanwhile, Simone begins an affair with her pupil Bianca Bienenfeld, who will later compare her teacher's incisive mind and sleek body to the 'prow of a ship ploughing through the waves'. Next, after a long hiking trip, she starts sleeping with Jacques-Laurent Bost, her pupil's fiancé, and with Olga, the previous object of Sartre's lust. In turn, Sartre starts going after his partner's young girlfriend and is able, after months of efforts, to lure Bianca Bienenfeld into a cheap hotel room and seduce her. Sartre and de Beauvoir write letters to each other with detailed accounts of their conquests.

It's hard enough for us today to keep track of things, so what must it have been like for them? To mark his emancipation from Simone and to avoid falling for her pupils, Sartre tries his luck with a young actress called Colette Gilbert. It works. No sooner is he dressed and out of the room than he sits down to pen a brief write-up for Simone, who is away with Bost: 'That is the first time I have slept with a dark-haired, actually a Black woman. She is strangely hairy with some fur on her back. A tongue like a party horn that keeps unrolling until it tickles your tonsils.' Does Simone de Beauvoir really want to know all this?

Simone tends to remain quite vague in her reports on her trysts with Bost. Sartre chides her for this and thinks she should write about herself for once – in her letters and also in her books. He argues that her life is much more interesting than her fictional characters. To which de Beauvoir replies: 'I would never dare.' And Sartre counters: 'Do dare!'

In addition, Sartre confesses that he is a little confused by all of these seductions, never entirely sure what he should do once he has finally won. Then, however, he does achieve some lasting satisfaction. After years of hesitation, Gallimard decides that it will publish his novel *Nausea* after all. On the day he gets the news he writes Simone perhaps his most impassioned letter ever: 'I feel more comfortable with this kind of happiness than with the kind that a woman's favours procure me. I think of myself with great pleasure.' What a way to sign off!

With the melancholy Erich Maria Remarque now besotted with Marlene Dietrich, Margot von Opel falls in love, out of spite, with the even more melancholy Annemarie Schwarzenbach, who has been unable to find happiness in her marriage to the French ambassador in Tehran. But Schwarzenbach spends the summer at a rehab clinic in Samedan in the Swiss Alps, while Margot is with Leni Riefenstahl on the beach on the German resort island of Sylt. Annemarie and Margot subsequently travel to the United States to look for happiness there; they won't find it.

Bertolt Brecht enjoys some wonderful weeks with Ruth Berlau in Sweden. It is summer 1938, and she is writing what will become *Any Beast Can Do It*, a book about what humans have forgotten by switching on their brains in bed. Ruth gives a witty account of why women lost their animal appetites over the centuries: because men are so often failures. Bertolt notes some of the findings of Ruth's research in his diary: 'Seventy per cent of all women are apparently frigid. Orgasm is a fluke.' However, when she starts considering whether to publish her book in the United States, Brecht is sceptical. It's not a book for men, he writes. 'Believe me, *Any Beast Can Do It* works as a book for women or not at all.' Of course, being his loyal acolyte, she believes him.

On 26 September 1938, the poet Else Lasker-Schüler is stripped of her German citizenship. The Gestapo justifies the decision in a letter to the Reichsführer SS, Heinrich Himmler: 'She was a typical example of the emancipated woman that emerged in the post-war period. In her lectures and writings she sought to pour scorn on the spiritual and moral values of German women. After the seizure of power she fled to Zurich, where she publicised her anti-German attitude by disseminating stories of atrocities.' This action also causes her Swiss residency permit to lapse. She raises money from her Swiss friends to allow her to emigrate to Palestine, and escapes the following year to Tel Aviv via Marseilles.

*

In September 1938, shocked to the core by the Munich Agreement that allows Germany to annex the Sudetenland in Czechoslovakia, Klaus Mann resolves to leave for the United States for good. In New York he takes a room at the Bedford Hotel, where he runs into lots of old acquaintances from Berlin, including Billy Wilder, Vicki Baum and Rudolph von Ripper. 'After all, this is your home,' the friendly receptionist says when Klaus is unsure which address he is supposed to use as a new immigrant.

He is soon giving lectures in New York and praising the mindset of his new home: 'People in the States have more understanding, more compassion and more respect for our lives – the lives of people who have lost their homes and their livelihoods due to their beliefs or their race – than people in Europe.'

His parents follow him across the Atlantic in the autumn of 1938. They too have lost all confidence in their security in Europe, and they are imbued with the conviction that they embody 'Germany' wherever they go. 'German culture is where I am,' Thomas Mann once said. Klaus, however, struggles with this self-image and is sceptical about how Americans will receive his father: 'He is victorious wherever he goes. Will I ever step out of his shadow? Will my energy last that long?' Before long, Klaus resumes his regular and excessive drug-taking.

Victor Klemperer looks into the past by reading his old diaries. He is surprised to discover that he suspected the 'peak of wretchedness and intolerableness' had been reached back in 1937, yet things are continuing to get worse. Eva is so depressed that she hardly gets out of bed anymore, often not emerging from her room until afternoon. As a Jew, Klemperer is no longer allowed to use a library, own a car or go to the cinema. Their money has run out. He tries desperately to find a means of emigrating to America or Palestine, but his efforts are in vain. A few years later he will have to wear the yellow star when he steps out into Dresdner Strasse, but he notes drily in his diary: 'I do not want to assert prematurely that we have reached the last circle of hell.'

*

In 1939, Louis-Ferdinand Céline receives a letter from Vienna from Cillie Pam, in which she tells him that her husband has been murdered in Dachau. On 21 February, Céline replies that this is sad news indeed, but also notes that he is being frozen out in France for his antisemitic views, and has to answer for them in court. 'You see, the Jews persecute people too.' Cillie drops the letter in horror.

Soon afterwards Cillie reads that Céline's new book, *School for Corpses*, has been published in German. It contains these lines: 'I feel very close to Hitler and all the Germans; I see them as brothers; they have good reason to be racist.' He finds Italian antisemitism 'bloodless, insufficient. I think it's dangerous. The difference between good and bad Jews? Nothing.' Céline concludes by saying that the Jews are to blame for everything. They dominate the world financial system and Hollywood, the press and international institutions, and they even dare 'to screw the most beautiful Aryan women'.

After enduring a cheerless and painful decade in Paris, Berlin and Venice during the thirties, Ruth Landshoff, the symbol of Berlin's Roaring Twenties, successfully emigrates to the United States. In January 1937, she gets divorced from Friedrich Graf Yorck von Wartenburg. In March, she boards an America-bound liner in Cherbourg. In New York she moves in with her fellow émigré and friend Francesco von Mendelssohn. Francesco gradually falls ever deeper into addiction and depression; rehab clinics become his home away from home. His sole companion is his Stradivarius cello, though his arms are far too weak to embrace it.

Afraid that Francesco is going to drag her down with him, Ruth soon moves to California and tries to make ends meet in Hollywood. No one will publish her writing, so she resorts to distributing flyers promoting speeches about her glory days. She can be booked to talk about Charlie Chaplin, the Roaring Twenties, *The Blue Angel* or Berlin around 1930. Her most interesting lecture might have been 'Greta Garbo, or Emotion without Consequences', which was about the coolness that a whole generation elevated to an axiom, led by Garbo and Marlene Dietrich.

But since no one wants to hire her to give these speeches, Ruth plans an assassination instead. She and an American friend write a short novel together: *The Man Who Killed Hitler* is about a Viennese therapist who bumps off the Führer with a bust of Hindenburg. Unfortunately, this is just a pipe dream. (Much later, when Hitler really is dead, Landshoff moves from Los Angeles back to New York, where she becomes close friends with Truman Capote and Andy Warhol and dies in 1966, at the epicentre of Pop Art.)

Rudi and Speedy Schlichter sometimes pay a visit to their old friends the Jüngers. Rudi, who first painted Ernst Jünger back in the twenties, executes a more recent painting of him, a heroic nude that now stands in his studio. As the political situation in Germany becomes ever more menacing, and even Gottfried von Cramm is jailed for homosexual acts, Ernst's heroism gives way to naked terror. He writes to Rudi, telling him that he has realised that 'such a portrait isn't really possible in this country' and politely requests that he censor it: 'I would therefore be very grateful if you would cover me with a light jacket.' His idea is that that this jacket would be the one he mentions in his new book; the painting could be titled *On the Marble Cliffs*, like the book.

Leni Riefenstahl is becoming more and more hooked on morphine. Julius Streicher, publisher of the Nazi propaganda magazine *Der Stürmer*, writes to her: 'You must immediately stop taking the drug and go to a drying-out centre. I know it will be hard, my beloved Leni, but it is the only solution, because I want you to live and be healthy.'

On 23 March, Erich Maria Remarque sets off across the Atlantic to join Marlene Dietrich. He needs to confess to her that he has remarried Jutta Zambona to protect her from persecution. Dietrich makes a scene, but she actually fancies the speedboat world champion and millionaire's wife, Joe Carstairs. Then Sternberg comes out of the woodwork again. And so Dietrich's whole entourage, including her husband and his lover, travel back with her and Remarque to Europe. Remarque hates being buffeted around like this. He has nothing but contempt for Rudi Sieber, for having made peace with his position as a cuckold. And he hates watching Dietrich's attempts to drown her troubles at the bar of the Hôtel du Cap-Eden-Roc in Antibes. The facts don't lie: no one in Hollywood wants to make a film with her anymore.

Dietrich's retinue play out a black tragicomedy on the Côte d'Azur over the summers of 1938 and 1939. There is even a bit part for a most unexpected supporting actor. Several photographs show Remarque and Dietrich next to a young John F. Kennedy on the beach of the Hôtel du Cap-Eden-Roc, his teeth the same dazzling white as his bathrobe, a brief glimpse of the future in this cataclysmic script. (A few years later, he will have a short fling with Dietrich in America, and she probably also had one with his father, Joe, in the summer of 1938.) Occasionally, Wallis Simpson and her husband, the recently abdicated King Edward VIII, come down from their nearby château to the beach and stay for dinner at the hotel. One last summer of the old European order.

Remarque's pain and loneliness as Dietrich's partner at this stage in her life move him to pen some extremely poetic entries in his diary: 'We all have so little warmth in our hearts for ourselves – we, the children of troubled times – so little confidence in ourselves – far too much bravery and far too little hope. Life's stupid little soldiers, children of troubled times with a dream, sometimes at night.'

The only thing that manages to assuage his worries in these days trapped between heaven and hell are the phone calls from his gallerist. Each new commission for a screenplay or a book is judged entirely on whether it will enable him to buy a new Cézanne watercolour with the proceeds. One extraordinary advantage of the paintings is that, unlike Dietrich, they cannot get up and leave once you bring them home.

*

On 27 March, after Thomas Quinn Curtiss has left Klaus Mann, despairing at his drug habit, Klaus writes in his diary: 'I cannot and do not want to live for very long. One day I will look for death via the fair and gruesome roundabout path of drugs ... It will not be weakness. I will wish for it.'

Very rarely in the works of the great artists is there a moment when they open wide a window onto their souls, such is the fear that a breath of wind might extinguish the inner fire. Such instances are particularly scarce in the art of Max Beckmann, who still buttons his shirt up to the top and turns up the collar of his coat around his chin. One of these precious glimpses, however, is offered by *Portrait of a Young Girl*, which he paints in 1939. This picture of a blonde woman, sitting on her small hotel balcony on the Riviera, with palm trees waving below her, her head propped dreamily on one hand and her legs drawn up on a deck chair, radiates a strange innocence.

This sunny portrait is painted during what are dark days for Beckmann. Having fled to Holland, he and his wife, Quappi, are determined to make it from there to the French Riviera. Every time he sits in his Amsterdam studio he dreams he is somewhere else – either in the past or in the future. This only burnishes the glow of the south in his imagination in the shadow of the dark, wet Dutch winter days. Back in the twenties, this tough guy and incorrigible romantic used to spend his evenings sitting under a potted plant in the station café, bidding sad farewells to the trains heading off to Nice and Marseilles.

So it is a longstanding yearning that Beckmann depicts in this 1939 picture of a girl on a summer evening with palm leaves glinting between the balcony railings. Of course, it is also a very new yearning; this young woman is most certainly a real woman, even if Beckmann will never reveal who she is. Quappi has been keeping a close eye over him throughout the thirties and is growing tired of his escapades. So what has Beckmann painted here? Why is the girl holding a letter? Is the artist conjuring up a woman dreaming of him? We'll never know.

The Jewish writer Ernst Toller, one of the central figures of German émigré literature, has escaped to America with his young wife, Christiane Grautoff. On 22 May 1939, he hangs himself in their New York hotel room. When he receives word of Toller's suicide, his friend Joseph Roth collapses in Paris and dies two days later. Roth is only forty-five, but years of drinking have left him with hardly any teeth, a liver like a sponge and a face the colour of ashes.

'It's war, sadly it's war. My comrades are dying,' Klaus Mann notes in his diary when he reads about their deaths. And Stefan Zweig, whose wife, Friderike, was with the dying Roth in Paris, writes to the French Nobel-winning novelist Romain Rolland: 'We in exile will not grow old. I loved him like a brother.'

On 13 July 1939, Henry Miller spends his final night in France before returning to America via Greece. He is staying at a small hotel in Aix-en-Provence, and Anaïs Nin does him the honour of going to bed with him one last time. There is something touching about the fact that having surpassed each other in indiscretion for years, neither of them ever breathes a word about this final night together. When they part the next morning and Miller travels on to the harbour in Marseilles, he doesn't know whether to laugh or cry. He reads Nostradamus and draws up horoscopes for himself and for Hitler. After concluding that Hitler will outlive him, he abruptly ends his interest in astrology ... and goes on to survive Hitler by thirty-five years.

In the summer of 1939, Gala and Dalí retreat to the seaside. In September, the newspapers report that Germany has invaded Poland, and the fear of an imminent war is tangible. Dalí's nerves are tingling and he can't keep still. The only thing that can calm him is painting. His mind is full of images of his encounter with Sigmund Freud the previous year. At long last he met his hero, the man who uncovered the truths of the subconscious. Since then, however, the battles his subconscious wages against him have only got worse. Freud could not have been less interested in Dalí's paranoia.

Gala and Dalí are no longer on the Mediterranean but in the small Atlantic resort of Arcachon, on the westernmost edge of Europe. They need the reassurance of being able to look out towards America in the evenings and dream of New York, the Mecca with which they align their bed. They meet up with Marcel Duchamp that summer, and Coco Chanel. Dalí fills canvas after canvas, as if obsessed, while Gala reads him books about alchemy and metaphysics. Sometimes she tickles his feet and he purrs like a cat. After dinner Dalí loves to let Gala gently brush his teeth so that he can feel clean. Before they go to bed Gala lays tarot cards, but however much she shuffles them, the same ones keep coming out on top: Judgement, the horned Devil, and Death as a skeleton.

After she is at last wed to Gustav Jaenecke – he has delayed the ceremony again and again – Lisa Jaenecke writes to her ex-husband (and Gustav's ex-doubles partner), Gottfried von Cramm, who has now been released from imprisonment: 'Petit, do you sometimes think about our marriage? In my memories it seems it was ideal. You are still the only person to whom I can tell everything. Unfortunately we were silly, spoilt children who needed to be punished.'

Cramm holds this letter in his hand for a very long time, reading it over and over again. Then he goes out with a spring in his step to the tennis court in Bodenburg where ten years earlier he sealed victory over Lisa, on his first match point. The evening sunlight comes slanting down through the tall beech trees. His white tennis shoes crunch as they draw circles on the red cinders, one of which is shaped a little like a heart.

Gottfried Benn is withdrawing from the world. By day he studies files in his position as a military doctor at the Bendlerblock military headquarters in central Berlin; in the evenings he returns to the dark ground-floor flat in Bozener Strasse, where his tired young wife, Hertha von Wedemeyer, has already gone to bed. He writes in a poem: 'He who restrains himself leaves a perfect mark.' Benn opens a bottle of lager and stares out for hours at the laundry drying in the back courtyard. It is 13 August 1939. In the stifling heat of the apartment, he takes out his fountain pen and writes to Oelze in Bremen: 'A conscious mind, in summer, in a city, aged fifty, without achievements, notices the geranium pots. Coming to terms with it, with this ending all his own, with this one late dream. That is individual consciousness. Now it will fade. That is the autumn, but it doesn't break our heart, it broke our consciousness – and that is more.'

That same scorching summer of 1939, Marlene Dietrich is living in Antibes, still with her husband and his girlfriend, her daughter, her mother, her former lover Sternberg and her current lover Remarque, enjoying lazy weeks of sunbathing, drinking and suffering at the Hôtel du Cap-Eden-Roc.

On 14 August, Dietrich leaves Antibes. For the first time in many years she has been offered a small role in a film and she intends to take the ship home to America. On the station platform Rudi says that he would like her to treat him with more respect next time. Dietrich merely waves, and her white sleeve billows in the wind as she departs. Goodbye, Europe. That autumn she plays the barmaid Frenchy in the western *Destry Rides Again*. The songs she sings in the saloon in a smoky, melancholy voice that lacks any trace of a future and ignores the present are by Friedrich Hollaender, who has also found refuge in Hollywood. However, the way she acts and sings, more down to earth and flirtatious than ever before, suggests that she has learned her lesson and is now capable of presenting herself as the poster girl of the Wild West. As if in reward for this performance, Marlene Dietrich is confirmed as a citizen of the United States.

And so Dietrich ends the thirties in much the same way as she rang them in with *The Blue Angel* – as a lascivious woman of the world who turns the head of every man who passes her. This time, however, she has an affair not with the director but with the leading man, Jimmy Stewart.

Erich Maria Remarque leaves behind Europe and his wife, who showers him with accusations and blame, and sets out to be close to Dietrich. When he arrives in Hollywood and she imperiously ignores him – she has no need of her hangdog Old World lover just now – he shouts at her, 'Love me!' For a moment she is completely silent, but then she starts singing the song of her life, the one that Friedrich Hollaender crafted especially for her in 1932: 'I Don't Know Who I Belong To'. He slams the door and leaves.

Even in Santa Monica and Beverly Hills, all Klaus Mann does is dream of the Europe he has left behind – and he's not the only one. As he sips cocktails with Aldous Huxley and Ludwig Marcuse, they remember the hot summer of 1933 in Sanary-sur-Mer. By Vicki Baum's pool, on Ruth Landshoff's sofa, during an afternoon on the beach with Christopher Isherwood or an evening in a bar with Billy Wilder and Fritz Lang, he talks at great length about 1920s Berlin, which starts to take on a golden halo.

Yet when Klaus finds himself alone in his room with the neon light glowing and drugs winking at him, he is gripped by tristesse: 'This terrible weeping again, these tears of fatigue and hopelessness. Oh, they do not comfort me.' He is tormented by thoughts of the Nazi regime, by exile, and by the end of his relationship with Thomas Quinn Curtiss.

Curtiss also feels the occasional pang of his past love, but this August he decided to put an end to things. Klaus seeks solace with naïve toy boys, though he quickly tires of them and dreads the prospect of having to spend a whole weekend with any of them. Instead, he dreams his way back into the good old days, flicking through magazines like *Die Fackel*, *Der Querschnitt*, *Die Dame* and *Die Weltbühne* in the journalist Rolf Nürnberg's library. In a November 1932 issue he comes across one of his own articles: 'Sexual Pathology and National Socialism'. His own prophecy consoles him somewhat, as does a letter from his father praising his new novel. Soon enough, though, the searing Californian sun has consumed all his positive energy. Hearing about the suicide of a desperate exiled friend, his mind goes back to all those who have died in the past few years – Joseph Roth, Ernst Toller, Ricki Hallgarten – and he wonders if Annemarie Schwarzenbach is still alive. 'Memories, on and on,' he writes on 21 August 1939, then, peering into the abyss: 'The horrible ending they all meet. Thoughts of my own demise. May it happen before I see the passing of everyone I have known and loved.'

Durs Grünbein has written a poem about 23 August 1939. It ends thus:

> Think back to the day, a summer's day,
> the last time people in the cities of Europe
> sat in their cafés without restriction,
> almost unsuspecting, laughing and chatting,
> with the hectic gestures, the shy glances
> of people in the fast-forward of archive footage,
> the blue haze of cigarettes hanging above the pavement.
> Think of the Surrealists' picnic,
> the grown-up games on the shores
> of the Côte d'Azur, Timmendorf, the Crimea,
> the great, retarding moment
> before, on the Spanish border,
> the last of the humanists
> died wretchedly in a dry riverbed.

The last of the humanists, Walter Benjamin, is moved to a French internment camp a few days later, after the German invasion of Poland, along with all the other German émigrés in Sanary-sur-Mer and Paris. He is taken first to the huge Stade de Colombes football ground on the edge of Paris and then to the Château de Vernuche. Everyone who sees or talks to him there is worried by his unnaturally calm state. At night Benjamin's sheets are cold with fear, but he dreams of the past and writes delightful letters to Hélène Léger, the Parisian prostitute who has won his heart.

Benjamin tells her how intensely he thinks about the hours they spent together: 'How can one replace these memories which are often the things that count most in life?' Soon afterwards he writes his essay 'On the Concept of History'. Entrusted to Hannah Arendt and Heinrich Blücher, it contains his reflections on Paul Klee's *Angelus Novus*. 'An angel is depicted there who looks as if he is about to distance himself from something which he is staring at ... The Angel of History must look just so. His face is turned towards the past. Where *we* see the appearance of a chain of events, *he* sees one single catastrophe, which unceasingly piles rubble on top of rubble and hurls it before his feet.' Here, in a nutshell, is the tragedy of the thirties, of Benjamin and all Jewish émigrés.

As the translator of Marcel Proust's *Remembrance of Things Past*, Benjamin has learned that modern thought is naïvely forward-facing, even though salvation can actually only be found in the past. Memory is more important than present perception or utopias: that is Proust's great legacy and his reassuring promise. Benjamin puts this lesson into practice with his memoirs, *Berlin Childhood around 1900*, and with his praise of the Angel of History, which does its best to be his guardian one last time in 1939. The angel can already see the disaster ahead, however, and Benjamin knows it.

Every time he senses a world war approaching, Heinrich Mann feels a strong desire to get married. He always waits too long, though, until bureaucratic problems arise that result in strange shotgun weddings after the outbreak of hostilities. That was the case with his first wife, Mimi, twenty-five years ago, and the same thing is now being repeated with Nelly Kröger, when he is sixty-eight. In exile she has increasingly abandoned herself to drugs and alcohol – her way of fleeing reality, escaping from the other émigrés' intellectual conversations and from the snobbish Mann family, who all despise her.

When Thea Sternheim visited the couple in Nice, she called Nelly a 'simultaneously fat and attractive Thusnelda'.* Only Heinrich achieves the feat of thinking only of Nelly's 'beautiful body. That thought always makes me restless', as he writes in every letter to her. When Nelly returns from rehab at the Villa Constance clinic yet again, he hopes that he will be able to formalise this restlessness by wedding her.

And thus on 9 September, eight days after the war starts and just before all the Germans in France are taken to internment camps, a registrar in Nice performs the official ceremony. Nelly's neurologist is their witness. Since Heinrich has become the owner of a Czechoslovak passport after being stripped of his German citizenship, his north German wife also takes on his new nationality. Heinrich's wedding present to her is a French edition of his book *Hatred,* with a dedication that is 'a testimony to ten years together, full of suffering and happiness'. The next day, Nelly Mann starts knitting warm underwear for Czechoslovakian soldiers stationed in France. And the day after that she starts drinking litre upon litre of French wine again.

Otto Dix, painter of war and the city, has retired to the furthest extremity of the Reich – first to his sister-in-law's family castle in Randegg and now to Hemmenhofen on Lake Constance, where he paints one landscape after another in the style of the Old Masters. Rather than prostitutes and soldiers, there is now the occasional Mary and Joseph. Dix has emigrated into the landscape and also into religion and history. His turn to tradition proves a fountain of premonitory pictures. For example, Dresden is visible in the background of *Lot and His Daughters*, the canvas showing the city burning as it will five years later.

Even after being dismissed from the Dresden Academy of Fine Arts, Otto regularly makes the long train journey there to see his

---

*Thusnelda, a Germanic noblewoman, was captured in 15 CE by the Roman general Germanicus during his invasion of Germania.

lover Käthe König. His wife has no option but to tolerate this long-distance relationship, and their children never find out about it. By the summer of 1939, however, his double life can no longer be concealed; he and König have a baby of their own.

This is not the only example of how Otto's life is falling apart around him. Following the failed attempt on Hitler's life at Munich's Bürgerbräukeller, detectives turn up in Hemmenhofen and knock on his door. He is held in custody for two weeks under suspicion of being in on the plot. It is Käthe who succeeds in making some compromising material vanish from an agency in Dresden, leaving the Gestapo no choice but to release Otto and let him go home to Martha.

In a letter, Simone de Beauvoir explains her love life to her lover, Jacques-Laurent Bost: 'I have only one sensual life, and that is with you.' But she must set something straight, embarrassing though this is for her: 'I have a physical relationship with Sartre too, but it is not very important. It is essentially tender and – I don't quite know how to express this – I do not feel involved because he isn't either.' After this confession, Sartre, de Beauvoir and Bost spend a few relaxing summer days together in Marseilles. When they are alone again, Bost asks her to burn his letters. He will do the same with hers. He might want to marry his fiancée Olga after all. This brings Simone to tears. She seeks comfort from Jean-Paul, but all Sartre wants is to give her a blow-by-blow account of how he seduced Olga's sister Wanda.

Next thing, Bost and Sartre are called up and must report for duty on 31 August. De Beauvoir's heart is almost breaking as she accompanies Sartre to the station, but he only notes phlegmatically: 'Everyone wants the other person to love him without being clear about what it means to want to be loved – or that if he wants the other person to love him, all he wants is for the other person to want to be loved; which is what causes lovers' permanent insecurity.' And Simone? Now that her two men have gone to war, this permanently insecure lover moves into the Hôtel du Danemark in

Rue Vavin with Olga and Wanda – Sartre's lover and her lover's fiancée.

On the evening of 31 August, the day Sartre reports for duty, Harro Schulze-Boysen sails out over the Wannsee in his boat *Haizuru*, on which he met his wife five years earlier. He has invited Günther Weisenborn, the friend who has been having an intense affair with Libertas for the past year, to have a confidential conversation out on the water. During their evening sail, Harro persuades his friend to bring the relationship to an end. Unfortunately, something else is about to begin the next morning: 'the largest war in history', as Harro puts it.

That night Günther makes a note about Harro in his diary: 'Slim, handsome and clear was his profile silhouetted against the evening sky over Lake Wannsee. A German, a man like a flame, a friend on the eve of war.' Weisenborn has promised not to compete for Libertas's affections any longer. He has noticed anyway that her love for Harro, regardless of erotic attraction, is far greater than her love for him. A few minutes before their simultaneous executions in Plötzensee on 22 December 1942, after the uncovering of their 'Red Chapel' resistance cell, Libertas will write to Harro: 'We will never have to part again. How great and beautiful that is.'

Claus Graf von Stauffenberg, who posed as the prototype of the German soldier for a monument in 1934, invades Poland in the first days of September 1939 with the 9,935 men of his 1st Light Motorised Division. Before they marched out of Wuppertal he bought a few works of classical philosophy for the journey from his local bookshop.

Two anxious letters from his wife reach him on the Polish front. He writes back to Nina at their home in Bamberg that she doesn't need to worry, even though the fighting 'brought more casualties than necessary'. His fellow officers are unfortunately very inexperienced and the Poles very brave, he writes, adding that the countryside he and his tanks are conquering is not at all to his liking, full of 'never-ending poverty and dilapidation'. Once he and the Wehrmacht have mopped up, as he sees it, causing countless deaths and bringing devastation on the country in a matter of days, he returns triumphantly to his barracks in Germany.

Claus is still a German soldier devoted to his Führer and also an intellectual snob. He is annoyed, he tells Nina in a letter, to have lost his sturdy rubber coat during the Polish campaign. Oh, and by the way, some of the castles they plundered contained some very nice Empire furniture.

When Hitler orders the Wehrmacht to attack Poland, he rings up Leni Riefenstahl and asks her if she fancies shooting a few films on the frontline. She accepts without a second thought. She goes to a tailor on the Kurfürstendamm, who invents a uniform for her, complete with insignia and epaulettes. Then she puts together her crew: her current lover, the sound engineer Hermann Storr, and two other film technicians. She sets off for the front, taking the train north-east from Berlin's Stettiner Bahnhof.

The Riefenstahl Special Film Unit enjoys the Führer's personal protection, but frontline soldiers find this eccentric woman filmmaker a pain in the neck. It is hard to stay calm when she adorns her make-believe uniform with a pistol under the belt on her left hip and a dagger inside her boot. War is raging, and this amateur Amazon barges onto the battlefield, all in the Führer's name. However, when she witnesses twenty-two Jews being shot in Końskie, 'our visitor left the field in shock', reports General von Manstein, chief of staff to Gerd von Rundstedt, commander of Army Group South.

Meanwhile, in Hollywood, Marlene Dietrich and Erich Maria Remarque are tearing each other to pieces. He slaps her, she bites his hand, and then he walks out. The next morning, only a few drops of blood on Dietrich's cold marble staircase testify to his visit. Remarque looks at the ruins of the relationship and jots down in his diary an order to withdraw his emotional troops: 'Resolution: get out!'

Hannah Arendt's husband, Heinrich Blücher, is interned at the Stade de Colombes when war breaks out, like every other German émigré in France. He puts a brave face on the situation, reads Kant and Descartes, and writes a rather philosophical declaration of love to Arendt: 'My darling, I am happy when I think that you are mine. And I am doing a lot of thinking.' Then, however, his feelings get the better of him and the right half of his brain takes control: 'My beautiful one, my stroke of luck is to have a feeling that I feel so strongly that it will last a lifetime and never change, or only increase even more.' Heinrich will be proved right. And his letters to Hannah will be his only surviving writings.

In early September, reality has also taken hold of that small seaside haven for German émigrés, Sanary-sur-Mer. Both Lion Feuchtwanger's wife, Marta, and his main lover, Eva Herrmann, urge the Jewish author to leave Europe without delay, but he waits for too long.

On 16 September, he writes: 'Slept terribly. Summoned by the police. Along with the other Germans who are still here. Tomorrow I have to go to a concentration camp. A sign at the police station: *Bienvenue à tous.*'

On 23 September, Feuchtwanger is transferred to Les Milles internment camp south of Aix-en-Provence, but a week later the famous writer is free. Marta can only stare in disbelief when he is suddenly standing right there in front of her at Villa Valmer, asking her if she wants to go for a swim in the sea. One last time they go down the steps, one last time they enter the warm water of the Mediterranean, one last time they take comfort from the sight of the red sun sinking into the sea. And yet the large grey warships sailing out from nearby Toulon's naval harbour are a sign that their exile under the palm trees is at an end. They are completely silent as the menacing ships loom larger. After drying themselves in deathly silence and near paralysis, they climb back up to their villa. Both of them sense this will not be their home for much longer.

Having recently completed his book *On the Marble Cliffs*, Ernst Jünger is given the rank of captain and posted to a barracks in Celle in Lower Saxony. When he goes home to bid farewell to his family, he complains to his wife that he is stressed by the weeping women at the barracks as they wave their husbands off to war. It troubled him greatly during the First World War, too. Gretha entirely agrees with him: 'The blazing force of affection should find an expression other than weakness. Men are going to war as they have done for centuries, and we should not stay behind in powerless sorrow and sap their strength with melancholy letters or laments.'

Eighteen-year-old Sophie Scholl is in love with a twenty-two-year-old officer cadet called Fritz Hartnagel whom she met at a dance two years ago. He has a soldier's short-cropped hair, she a tousled bob with two recalcitrant strands that she keeps having to blow out of her eyes. They could not be more different, but they are both religious. Once she asks him, 'Don't you think that sex could be overcome by the mind?' But neither of them is cut out for monastic life.

In summer 1939, they go on holiday together to northern Germany and sleep together, although Sophie is reticent, as her Christian beliefs only allow sex after marriage. First she keeps Fritz at a distance, then she entices him to come closer, and so the ballet continues. Very soon, though, she buys a pair of cheap rings and they check into the northern hotels as a married couple. She has too great an appetite for life to settle for the ascetic lifestyle she demands of herself.

Sophie is a young German woman, torn between her pretensions and her desires. She loves wine and driving cars, and yet she is still full of rage. A leader of the League of German Girls, the female equivalent of the Hitler Youth, she nonetheless hates the Nazis. Fritz talks a lot about love and as much about the Fatherland.

So they spend this last summer of peace on holiday. First they travel to Heiligenhafen on the Baltic coast and through the fenlands around Worpswede, where they lie in the grass. The weather in the Fatherland is hot and fine, and they dream a little of the future. Then Fritz is called up. Sophie writes to him immediately after the outbreak of war: 'I cannot understand how people are now continually putting other people's lives in danger. I cannot understand it and it disgusts me.' Fritz replies: 'You cause me great conflict by asking about the point of all this bloodshed.' Sophie will opt for active resistance and distribute leaflets that say: 'Rip off the cloak of indifference you have cast around your hearts!' But what about Fritz, the man whose heart she opened? He will serve as a loyal officer of the Nazi regime. Their stances could not be more different, but they are in love. He suffers serious wounds at Stalingrad; she joins the resistance and is sentenced to death for her actions in 1943. Sophie's execution turns him against the regime, and he surrenders to the Americans. After the war he becomes a judge and fights against re-armament and joins the peace movement. He also marries Sophie's sister, Elisabeth, remaining close to his great love even beyond the grave.

On the orders of Joseph Goebbels, Bruno Balz is released from the Gestapo jail at Prinz-Albrecht-Strasse 8 for twenty-four hours. He has been tortured on a daily basis, but UFA studios has made it clear to Goebbels that it will be impossible to finish filming Zarah Leander's new movie without his songs. The film's working title? *The Great Love.*

Balz is whisked out to Babelsberg as day breaks. As Gestapo officers sit and watch, he composes in those twenty-four hours two of his greatest songs: 'I Know Some Day a Miracle Will Happen' and 'This Will Not End the World'. Neither of these predictions will prove to be accurate.

BIBLIOGRAPHY

General literature on the period 1929–1939

Peter Ackroyd, *Charlie Chaplin* (London, Chatto & Windus, 2014).

Anni Albers: Fabrics, Ann Coxon (ed.) (London, Tate Publishing, 2018).

Jane Alison and Coralie Malissard, *Modern Couples. Art, Intimacy and the Avant-Garde* (London, Prestel, 2018).

Roland Barthes, *A Lover's Discourse: Fragments*, tr. Richard Howard (New York, Hill and Wang, 1978, 2010).

Vicki Baum, *Grand Hotel*, tr. Basil Creighton & Margot Bettauer Dembo (New York, NYRB, 2016).

Vicki Baum, *It Was All Quite Different* (New York, Funk & Wagnalls, 1964).

Sybille Bedford, *Jigsaw: An Unsentimental Education* (London, Penguin, 1990).

Sybille Bedford, *Quicksands: A Memoir* (London, Penguin, 2006).

Carel Blotkamp, *The End: Artists' Late and Last Works* (London, Reaktion Books, 2019).

R. J. B. Bosworth, *Claretta: Mussolini's Last Lover* (New Haven, Yale University Press, 2017).

Brassaï, *Paris nocturne*, tr. Quentin Bajac (London, Thames & Hudson, 2013).

Marianne Breslauer, *Photography 1927–1936* (Winterthur, Switzerland, Fotostiftung Schweiz, 2010).

Luis Buñuel, *My Last Breath: An Autobiography* (London, Flamingo, 1983).

Louis-Ferdinand Céline, *Letters to Elizabeth*, tr. Alphonse C. Juilland (Stanford, Montparnasse, 1990).

Nancy Cunard, *Negro: An Anthology* (London, Wishart, 1934).

Charles Darwent, *Josef Albers: Life and Work* (London, Thames & Hudson, 2018).

Mary V. Dearborn, *Mistress of Modernism: The Life of Peggy Guggenheim* (Boston, Houghton Mifflin, 2004).

Wolfram Eilenberger, *Fire of Freedom: The Salvation of Philosophy, 1933–1943*, tr. Shaun Whiteside (London, Allen Lane, 2023).

Andrew Field, *The Life and Times of Djuna Barnes* (London, Secker & Warburg, 1983).

Dan Franck, *Bohemians: The Birth of Modern Art*, tr. Cynthia Liebow (London, Weidenfeld & Nicolson, 2001).

André Gide, *Journals: 1889–1949*, tr. Justin O'Brien (London, Secker & Warburg, 1947–1951).

Nina Gladitz, *Leni Riefenstahl: Karriere einer Täterin* [*Leni Riefenstahl: Career of a Perpetrator*] (Zurich, Orell Füssli, 2020).

Joseph Goebbels, *Die Tagebücher 1924–1945*, 5 vols (Munich , K.G. Saur, 1987).

Margaret L. Goldsmith, *Patience geht vorüber* [*Patience Passes*] (Berlin, Kindt & Bucher, 1931).

Heike B. Görtemaker, *Eva Braun: Life with Hitler*, tr. Damion Searls (London, Penguin, 2012).

George Grosz, *A Little Yes and a Big No: The Autobiography of George Grosz*, tr. Lola Sachs Dorin (New York, Dial Press, 1946).

Gusti Hecht and Georg Greko, *»Muss man sich gleich scheiden lassen?«* [*"Is Divorce Really Necessary?"*] (Berlin, R. Mosse, 1932).

Hermine, Princess of Prussia, *An Empress in Exile: My Days in Doorn* (New York, J. H. Sears, 1928).

Franz Hessel, *Walking in Berlin: A Flaneur in the Capital*, tr. Amanda DeMarco (Cambridge, MA, MIT Press, 2013).

Franz Hessel, *In Berlin: Day and Night in 1929*, tr. Amanda DeMarco (Berlin, Readux Books, 2013).

Karoline Hille, *Gefährliche Musen: Frauen um Max Ernst* [*Dangerous Muses: The Women around Max Ernst*] (Berlin, Ebersbach, 2007).

Peter Hoffmann, *Stauffenberg: A Family History, 1905–1922* (Montreal, McGill-Queen's University Press, 2008).

Eva Illouz, *The End of Love: A Sociology of Negative Relations* (Cambridge, Polity Press, 2021).

Eva Illouz, *Why Love Hurts: A Sociological Explanation* (Cambridge, Polity Press, 2012).

Don James, *Surfing San Onofre to Point Dume: 1936–1942* (San Francisco, Chronicle Books, 1998).

Peter Jelavich, *Berlin Alexanderplatz: Radio, Film and the Death of Weimar Culture* (Berkeley, University of California Press, 2006).

Hans Keilson, *There Stands My House: A Memoir*, tr. Elena Lappin (Brunswick, Scribe, 2012).

John F. Kennedy, *Unter Deutschen: Reisetagebücher und Briefe 1937–1945* [*Among the Germans: Travel Journals and Letters 1937–1945*] (Berlin, Aufbau, 2013).

Bibliography

Count Harry Kessler, *The Diaries of a Cosmopolitan 1918–1937*, tr. and ed. Charles Kessler (London, Weidenfeld & Nicolson, 1971).

Irmgard Keun, *The Artificial Silk Girl*, tr. Kathie von Ankum (London, Penguin, 2019).

Wolfgang Koeppen, *A Sad Affair*, tr. Michael Hofmann (London, Granta, 2004).

Klaus Kreimeier, *The UFA Story: A History of Germany's Greatest Film Company, 1918–1945*, tr. Rita Kimber and Robert Kimber (New York, Hill & Wang, 1996).

Brian Ladd, *The Ghosts of Berlin. Confronting German History in the Urban Landscape* (Chicago, University of Chicago Press, 1997).

Gustav Landauer and Gabriel Kuhn, *Revolution and Other Writings: A Political Reader*, tr. Richard J. F. Day (Oakland, CA, PM Press, 2010).

Jacques-Henri Lartigue: Collection Renée Perle, 2 vols (Paris, Tajan, 2000 and 2001).

Lotte Laserstein: Face to Face, Alexander Eiling and Elena Schroll (eds.), exhibition catalogue, Städel Museum, Frankfurt am Main, in collaboration with Berlinische Galerie, Munich, Prestel, 2018.

Norman Lebrecht, *Genius and Anxiety: How Jews Changed the World, 1847–1947* (London, Oneworld, 2019).

Bernard Lebrun et al., *Robert Capa: The Paris Years, 1933–1954* (New York, Abrams, 2012).

Helmut Lethen, *Cool Conduct: The Culture of Distance in Weimar Germany* (Berkeley, University of California Press, 2002).

Thomas Levenson, *Einstein in Berlin* (New York, Bantam Books, 2003).

Peter Longerich, *Goebbels: A Biography*, tr. Alan Bance, Jeremy Noakes and Lesley Sharpe (New York, Random House, 2015).

Oliver Lubrich, *Travels in the Reich, 1933–1945: Foreign Authors Report from Germany* (Chicago, University of Chicago Press, 2009).

Fiona MacCarthy, *Walter Gropius: The Man Who Built the Bauhaus* (Cambridge, Mass., Harvard University Press, 2019).

Curzio Malaparte, *Coup d'État: The Technique of Revolution*, tr. Sylvia Saunders (New York, E.P. Dutton, 1932).

Curzio Malaparte, *Diary of a Foreigner in Paris*, tr. Stephen Twilley (New York, NYRB, 2020).

Patrick Marnham, *Dreaming with His Eyes Open: A Life of Diego Rivera* (New York, Knopf, 1998).

Charles Marsh, *Strange Glory: A Life of Dietrich Bonhoeffer* (New York, Knopf, 2014).

Bibliography

Reinhard Mehring, *Carl Schmitt: A Biography*, tr. Daniel Steuer (Cambridge, Polity Press, 2022).

Simon Sebag Montefiore, *Stalin: The Court of the Red Tsar* (London, Weidenfeld & Nicolson, 2003).

Kevin D. Moore, *Jacques-Henri Lartigue: The Invention of an Artist* (Princeton, Princeton University Press, 2004).

Melissa Müller, *Anne Frank: The Biography*, tr. Rita Kimber and Robert Kimber (New York, Metropolitan Books, 2013).

Ulrike Müller et al., *Bauhaus Women: Art, Handicraft, Design* (London, Thames & Hudson, 2009).

Stefan Müller-Doohm, *Adorno: A Biography*, tr. Rodney Livingstone (Cambridge, Polity Press, 2009).

Robert E. Norton, *Secret Germany: Stefan George and His Circle* (Ithaca, Cornell University Press, 2002).

Meret Oppenheim, *My Album [From Childhood to 1943]*, ed. Lisa Wenger and Martina Corgnati (Zurich, Scheidegger & Spiess, 2022).

Robert Payne, *The Great Garbo* (London, W. H. Allen, 1976).

Olaf Peters, *Otto Dix* (Munich, Prestel, 2010).

Leni Riefenstahl, *A Memoir* (New York, St Martin's Press, 1999).

David Robinson, *Chaplin: His Life and Art* (London, Grafton, 1983).

Rowohlt-Almanach 1908–1962, Mara Hintermeier and Fritz J. Raddatz (eds), 3 vols (Reinbek, Germany, Rowohlt, 1962).

Rudolf Schlichter 1890–1955: Watercolours and Drawings, introduction by Godfrey Pilkington (London, Piccadilly Gallery, 1986).

Max Schmeling, *An Autobiography*, tr. George von der Lippe (Chicago, Bonus Books, 1998).

Hans-Peter Schwarz, *Konrad Adenauer: A German Politician and Statesman in a Period of War, Revolution, and Reconstruction*, vol. 1: *From the German Empire to the Federal Republic, 1876–1952*, tr. Louise Willmot (Providence, RI, Berghahn, 1995).

Anna Maria Sigmund, *Women of the Third Reich* (Richmond Hill, Ontario, NDE Publishing, 2000).

Jörg Später, *Kracauer. A Biography*, tr. Daniel Steuer (Cambridge, Polity Press, 2020).

Oswald Spengler, *The Decline of the West*, tr. Charles F. Atkinson (London, Allen & Unwin, 1932).

Oswald Spengler, *The Hour of Decision*, tr. Charles F. Atkinson (London, Allen & Unwin 1934).

Gunta Stölzl, *Bauhaus Master*, Monika Stadler and Yael Aloni (eds) (New York, Museum of Modern Art, 2009).

Gabriele Tergit, *Käsebier Takes Berlin*, tr. Sophie Duvernoy (London, Pushkin Press, 2020).

Calvin Tomkins, *Duchamp: A Biography* (New York, Museum of Modern Art, 2014).

Bernard Toulier, *Jacques-Henri Lartigue: Un dandy à la plage* [*Jacques-Henri Lartigue: A Dandy at the Beach*] (Paris, La Découverte, 2016).

Amanda Vaill, *Hotel Florida: Truth, Love, and Death in the Spanish Civil War* (New York, Farrar, Straus and Giroux, 2014).

Hugo Vickers, *Loving Garbo: The Story of Greta Garbo, Cecil Beaton and Mercedes de Acosta* (New York, Random House, 1994).

Tony Villecco, *Pola Negri: The Hollywood Years* (Port Crane, NY, self-published, 2017).

Wallis and Edward, Letters 1931–1937: The Intimate Correspondence of the Duke and Duchess of Windsor (London, Weidenfeld & Nicolson, 1986).

Peter Walther, *Darkness Falling: The Strange Death of the Weimar Republic, 1930–1933*, tr. Peter Lewis (London, Head of Zeus, 2021).

Andrea Winklbauer, *Lady Bluetooth: Hedy Lamarr*, tr. Nick Somers (Vienna, Jüdisches Museum, 2019).

[Ruth (Landshoff) Yorck, with D. S. Jennings and D. Malcolmson], *The Man Who Killed Hitler* (Hollywood, George Palmer Putnam, 1939).

Sibylle Zehle, *Max Reinhardt: Life as a Festival* (Vienna, Brandstätter, 2020).

Selected reading on the main characters in the book

Hannah Arendt

Hannah Arendt, *Rahel Varnhagen: The Life of a Jewish Woman*, tr. Clara Winston and Richard Winston (New York, Harcourt Brace Jovanovich, 1974).

Hannah Arendt and Heinrich Blücher, *Within Four Walls: The Correspondence between Hannah Arendt and Heinrich Blücher, 1936–1968*, Lotte Kohler (ed.), tr. Peter Constantine (New York, Harcourt, 2000).

Antonia Grunenberg, *Hannah Arendt and Martin Heidegger: History of a Love*, tr. Peg Birmingham, Kristina Lebedeva and Elizabeth von Witzke Birmingham (Bloomington, Indiana University Press, 2017).

Hildegard E. Keller, *Was wir scheinen* [*How We Appear*] (Cologne, Eichborn, 2022).

Elisabeth Young-Bruehl, *Hannah Arendt: For Love of the World* (New Haven, Yale University Press, 1982).

Bibliography

Simone de Beauvoir

Simone de Beauvoir, *Memoirs of a Dutiful Daughter*, tr. James Kirkup (London, Penguin, 1963).

Annie Cohen-Solal, *Jean-Paul Sartre: A Life*, Norman MacAfee (ed.) (London, Heinemann, 1987).

Christiane Zehl Romero, *Simone de Beauvoir* (Reinbek, Germany, Rowohlt, 2001).

Hazel Rowley, *Tête-à-Tête: The Tumultuous Lives of Simone de Beauvoir and Jean-Paul Sartre* (New York, Harper Collins, 2006).

Max Beckmann

Mathilde Beckmann, *Mein Leben mit Max Beckmann* [*My Life with Max Beckmann*] (Munich, Piper, 1983).

Sabine Rewald, *Max Beckmann in New York*, Emily Walter (ed.) (New York, The Metropolitan Museum of Art, 2016).

Walter Benjamin

Walter Benjamin, *Das Adressbuch des Exils, 1933–1940: 'Wie überall hin die Leute verstreut sind'* [*The Address Book of Exile, 1933–1940: 'How people are scattered everywhere'*] (Leipzig, Koehler & Amelang, 2006).

Walter Benjamin, *Begegnungen mit Benjamin* [*Encounters with Benjamin*], Erdmut Wizisla (ed.) (Leipzig, Lehmstedt, 2015).

Walter Benjamin, *Berlin Childhood around 1900*, tr. Carl Skoggard (Cambridge, Mass., Harvard University Press, 2006).

Walter Benjamin, *One-Way Street and Other Writings*, tr. E. F. N. Jephcott and Kingsley Shorter (London, Verso, 1979).

Walter Benjamin, 'On the Concept of History', tr. Dennis Redmond (Frankfurt am Main, Suhrkamp Verlag, 1974).

Walter Benjamin and Gretel Adorno, *Correspondence 1930–1940*, tr. Wieland Hoban (Cambridge, Polity Press, 2008).

Lorenz Jäger, *Walter Benjamin: Das Leben eines Unvollendeten* [*Walter Benjamin: The Life of an Incomplete Man*] (Berlin, Rowohlt, 2017).

Vicente Valero, *Experiencia y pobreza: Walter Benjamin en Ibiza* [*Experience and Poverty: Walter Benjamin in Ibiza*] (Barcelona, Periférica, 2001).

Gottfried Benn

Gottfried Benn, *Impromptus*, tr. Michael Hofmann (London, Faber, 2014).

Gottfried Benn, *Selected Poems and Prose*, tr. David Palsey (Oxford, Carcanet, 2013).

Bibliography

Gottfried Benn and Friedrich Wilhelm Oelze, *Briefwechsel 1932–1956* [*Correspondence 1932–1956*], 3 vols (Stuttgart, Klett-Cotta, 2016).

Martin Travers, *The Hour That Breaks: Gottfried Benn – A Biography* (Lausanne, Peter Lang, 2015).

Bertolt Brecht

Bertolt Brecht, *Journals 1934–1955*, tr. Hugh Rorrison, ed. John Willett (London, Routledge, 1993).

Bertolt Brecht, *Letters 1913–1956*, tr. Ralph Manheim (Abingdon, Routledge, 1990).

Bertolt Brecht, *Poems 1913–1956*, tr. Ralph Manheim, John Willett et al. (London, Eyre Methuen, 1976).

Bertolt Brecht, *Threepenny Novel*, tr. Desmond I. Vesey and Christopher Isherwood (New York, Grove, 1956).

Bertolt Brecht and Helene Weigel, *'Ich lerne: gläser und tassen spülen': Briefe 1923–1956* [*'I'm Learning to Wash Glasses and Cups': Letters 1923–1956*] (Berlin, Suhrkamp, 2012).

Stephen Parker, *Brecht: A Literary Life* (London, Bloomsbury, 2014).

Gottfried von Cramm

Jens Nordalm, *Der schöne Deutsche: Das Leben des Gottfried von Cramm* [*The Handsome German: The Life of Gottfried von Cramm*] (Hamburg, Rowohlt, 2021).

Alfred Döblin

Alfred Döblin: 1878–1978. Eine Ausstellung des Deutschen Literaturarchivs im Schiller-Nationalmuseum [*Alfred Döblin: 1878–1978. An Exhibition at the German Literary Archive ...*], Marbach, German Literary Archive, 1978.

Eckhardt Köhn, *Yolla Niclas und Alfred Döblin* (Engelrod, Germany, Luchs, 2017).

Salvador Dalí

Dominique Bona, *Gala* (Paris, Flammarion, 1993).

Mary Ann Caws, Salvador Dalí (London, Reaktion Books, 2008).

Tim McGirk, *Wicked Lady: Salvador Dali's Muse* (London, Hutchinson, 1990).

Marlene Dietrich

Edgar Rai, *Im Licht der Zeit* [*In the Light of Time*] (Munich, Piper, 2019).

Bibliography

Donald Spoto, *Dietrich* (London, Bantam Press, 1992).

Karin Wieland, *Dietrich & Riefenstahl: Hollywood, Berlin, and a Century in Two Lives*, tr. Shelley Frisch (New York, Liveright, 2015).

Zelda and F. Scott Fitzgerald

Pietro Citati, *La morte della farfalla: Zelda e Francis Scott Fitzgerald* [*The Death of the Butterfly: Zelda and Francis Scott Fitzgerald*] (Milan, Adelphi, 2016).

F. Scott Fitzgerald, *The Letters of F. Scott Fitzgerald*, Andrew Turbull (ed.) (New York, Scribner, 1963).

F. Scott Fitzgerald, *Tender Is the Night* (New York, Scribner, 1934).

F. Scott Fitzgerald and Zelda Fitzgerald, *Dear Scott, Dearest Zelda: The Love Letters of F. Scott and Zelda Fitzgerald*, Jackson R. Bryer and Cathy W. Barks (eds) (New York, St Martin's Press, 2002).

Zelda Fitzgerald, *Save Me the Waltz* (New York, Scribner, 1932).

Andrew Turnbull, *Scott Fitzgerald* (London, Bodley Head, 1962).

Ernest Hemingway

Ernest Hemingway, *A Moveable Feast* (New York, Scribner, 1964).

Ernest Hemingway, *The Letters of Ernest Hemingway, 1932–1934*, Sandra W. Spanier and Robert W. Trogdon (eds) (Cambridge, Cambridge University Press, 2011).

Ernest Hemingway, *Selected Letters 1917–1961*, Carlos Baker (ed.) (New York, Scribner, 2003).

Kenneth S. Lynn, *Hemingway* (Cambridge, Mass., Harvard University Press, 1995).

Hermann Hesse

Gunnar Decker, *Hesse: The Wanderer and His Shadow*, tr. Peter Lewis (Cambridge, Mass., Harvard University Press, 2018).

Volker Michels, *Hesse: A Pictorial Biography*, tr. Yetta Ziolkowski (New York, Farrar, Straus and Giroux, 2013).

Bärbel Reetz, *Hesses Frauen* [*Hesse's Women*] (Berlin, Insel, 2012).

Theodore Ziolkowski, *Soul of the Age: Selected Letters of Hermann Hesse, 1891–1962* (New York, Farrar, Straus and Giroux, 1991).

Christopher Isherwood

Christopher Isherwood, *Berlin Stories* [includes *Mr Norris Changes Trains* and *Goodbye to Berlin*] (London, Chatto & Windus, 1945).

Christopher Isherwood, *Christopher and His Kind* (London, Methuen, 1976).

Ernst Jünger
Ernst Jünger, *The Adventurous Heart: Figurines and Capriccios*, tr. Russell A. Berman (Candor, NY, Telos, 2012).
Ernst Jünger, *Gärten und Strassen: Aus den Tagebüchern 1939 und 1940* [*Gardens and Streets: From the Diaries 1939 and 1940*] (Berlin, E. S. Mittler & Sohn, 1942).
Ernst Jünger, *On the Marble Cliffs*, tr. Tess Lewis (New York, NYRB, 2023).
Helmuth Kiesel, *Ernst Jünger: Die Biographie* (Munich, Siedler, 2007).
Ingeborg Villinger, *Gretha Jünger: Die unsichtbare Frau* [*Gretha Jünger: The Invisible Woman*] (Stuttgart, Klett-Cotta, 2020).

Mascha Kaléko
Mascha Kaléko, *Das lyrische Stenogrammheft* [*The Lyrical Shorthand Pad*] (Berlin, Rowohlt, 1933).
Andreas Nolte, *The Poems of Mascha Kaléko* (Burlington, VT, Fomite, 2010).
Jutta Rosenkranz, *Mascha Kaléko: Biografie* (Munich, dtv, 2007).

Erich Kästner
Sven Hanuschek, *'Keiner blickt dir hinter das Gesicht': Das Leben Erich Kästners* [*'No One Sees Behind Your Face'. The Life of Erich Kästner*] (Munich, Hanser, 1999).
Erich Kästner, *Going to the Dogs: The Story of a Moralist*, tr. Rodney Livingstone et al. (New York, NYRB, 2013).

Ernst Ludwig Kirchner
Eberhard W. Kornfeld, *Ernst Ludwig Kirchner: A Chronology* (Davos, Kirchner Museum, 1990).
Eberhard W. Kornfeld, 'Zu Ernst Ludwig Kirchners Suizid am 15. Juni 1938' ['On Ernst Ludwig Kirchner's Suicide on 15 June 1938'] in: *Schriften zu Ernst Ludwig Kirchner*, vol. 4 (Bern, Galerie Kornfeld, 2021).

Victor Klemperer
Victor Klemperer, *I Shall Bear Witness: A Diary of the Nazi Years, 1933–1941*, tr. Martin Chalmers (New York, Random House, 1998).
Victor Klemperer, *The Language of the Third Reich: LTI, Lingua Tertii Imperii: A Philologist's Notebook*, tr. Martin Brady (London, Athlone, 2000).

Bibliography

Victor Klemperer, *Licht und Schatten: Kinotagebuch 1929–1945* [*Light and Shadow: Cinema Diaries 1929–1945*] (Berlin, Aufbau, 2020).

Ruth Landshoff

Thomas Blubacher, *Die vielen Leben der Ruth Landshoff-Yorck* [*The Many Lives of Ruth Landshoff-Yorck*] (Frankfurt, Insel, 2015).

Jan Bürger, *Im Schattenreich der wilden Zwanziger: Fotografien aus dem Nachlass von Ruth Landshoff-Yorck* [*In the Shadows of the Roaring Twenties: Photographs from the Estate of Ruth Landshoff-Yorck*] (Marbach, Deutsche Schiller-gesellschaft, 2017).

Ruth Landshoff, *Roman einer Tänzerin* [*Novel of a Dancer*], Walter Fähnders (ed.) (Berlin, AvivA, 2002).

Ruth Landshoff, *Die Vielen und der Eine* [*The Many and the One*] (Berlin, Rowohlt, 1930).

Tamara de Lempicka

Laura Claridge, *Tamara de Lempicka: A Life of Deco and Decadence* (London, Bloomsbury, 2000).

Baroness Kizette de Lempicka-Foxhall, *Passion by Design: The Art and Times of Tamara de Lempicka* (New York, Abbeville, 1987).

Lotte Lenya and Kurt Weill

Jens Rosteck, *Zwei auf einer Insel: Lotte Lenya und Kurt Weill* [*Two on an Island: Lotte Lenya and Kurt Weill*] (Berlin, Propyläen, 1999).

Donald Spoto, *Lenya: A Life* (New York, Ballantine, 1989).

Alma Mahler-Werfel

Friedrich Buchmayr, *Der Priester in Almas Salon: Johannes Hollnsteiners Weg von der Elite des Ständestaats zum NS-Bibliothekar* [*The Priest at Alma's Salon. Johannes Hollnsteiner's Path from the Austrian Elite to Nazi Librarian*] (Weitra, Austria, Bibliothek der Provinz, 2003).

Oliver Hilmes, *Malevolent Muse: The Life of Alma Mahler*, tr. Donald Arthur (Boston, Northeastern University Press, 2015).

Man Ray

Emmanuelle de l'Ecotais, *Man Ray, 1890–1976* (Cologne, Taschen, 2004).

Man Ray, *Self-Portrait* (New York, McGraw-Hill, 1963).

Arturo Schwarz, *Man Ray: The Rigour of Imagination* (London, Thames & Hudson, 1977).

Bibliography

Erika Mann

Erika Mann, *The Lights Go Down*, tr. Maurice Samuel (New York, Farrar & Rinehart, 1940).

Erika Mann and Klaus Mann, *Escape to Life* (Cambridge, Mass., Houghton Miffin Riverside Press, 1939).

Armin Strohmeyr, *Dichterkinder: Liebe, Verrat und Drama – der Kreis um Klaus und Erika Mann* [*A Novelist's Children: Love, Betrayal and Drama – Klaus and Erika Mann's Circle*] (Munich, Piper, 2020).

Gunna Wendt, *Erika und Therese: Erika Mann und Therese Giehse – eine Liebe zwischen Kunst und Krieg* [*Erika Mann and Therese Giehse – A Love Between Art and War*] (Munich, Piper, 2018).

Heinrich Mann

Manfred Flügge, *Heinrich Mann: Eine Biographie* (Reinbek, Germany, Rowohlt, 2006).

Manfred Flügge, *Traumland und Zuflucht: Heinrich Mann in Frankreich* [*Dreamland and Refuge: Heinrich Mann in France*] (Berlin, Insel, 2013).

Willi Jaspers, *Die Jagd nach Liebe: Heinrich Mann und die Frauen* [*Hunting for Love: Heinrich Mann and His Women*] (Frankfurt, S. Fischer, 2007).

Kirsten Jüngling, *Nelly Mann: 'Ich bin doch nicht nur schlecht': Eine Biographie* [*Nelly Mann: 'I'm not all bad' – A Biography*] (Berlin, Propyläen, 2008).

Heinrich Mann, *Der Hass: Deutsche Zeitgeschichte* [*Hatred: Contemporary German History*] (Amsterdam, Querido, 1933).

Klaus Mann

Renate Berger, *Tanz auf dem Vulkan: Gustaf Gründgens und Klaus Mann* [*Dancing on the Volcano: Gustaf Gründgens and Klaus Mann*] (Darmstadt, Lambert Schneider, 2016).

Klaus Mann, *Briefe* [*Letters*] (Berlin and Weimar, Aufbau, 1988).

Klaus Mann, *Briefe und Antworten, 1922–1947* [*Letters and Replies, 1922–1947*], Martin Gregor-Dellin (ed.) (Munich, Ellermann, 1987).

Klaus Mann, *The Fifth Child*, tr. Lambert A. Shears (New York, Boni & Liveright, 1927).

Klaus Mann, *Mephisto*, tr. Robin Smyth (New York, Penguin, 1977).

Klaus Mann, *Speed: Erzählungen aus dem Exil* [*Speed: Stories from Exile*] (Reinbek, Germany, Rowohlt, 1990).

Klaus Mann, *Tagebücher 1931–1949* [*Diaries 1931–1949*], Joachim Heimannsberg, Peter Laemmle and Wilfried F. Schoeller (eds), 6 vols (Munich, Spangenberg, 1987–1991).

Bibliography

Klaus Mann, *Der Vulkan: Roman unter Emigranten* [*The Volcano: A Novel among Emigrants*] (Reinbek, Germany, Rowohlt, 1999).

Frederic Spotts, *Cursed Legacy: The Tragic Life of Klaus Mann* (New Haven, Yale University Press, 2016).

Thomas Mann

Thomas Mann, *Diaries 1918–1939*, tr. Hermann Kesten (New York, Abrams, 1982).

Thomas Mann, 'Disorder and Early Sorrow' in *Stories of a Lifetime: The Collected Stories*, vol. 2 (New York, Mercury Books, 1961).

Thomas Mann, '"Alles ist wertlos." Thomas Mann in Nidden', Thomas Sprecher (ed.), *Marbacher Magazin*, 89 (special issue, 2000).

Henry Miller

Mary Dearborn, *The Happiest Man Alive: A Biography of Henry Miller* (New York, Simon & Schuster, 1991).

Robert Ferguson, *Henry Miller: A Life* (New York, W. W. Norton, 1991).

Henry Miller, *Quiet Days in Clichy* (Paris, Olympia Press, 1956).

Henry Miller, *Tropic of Cancer* (Paris, Obelisk Press, 1934).

Lee Miller

Carolyn Burke, *Lee Miller: On Both Sides of the Camera* (London, Bloomsbury, 2005).

Lee Miller, Walter Moser and Klaus Albrecht Scröder (eds), catalogue of the exhibition at the Albertina Museum, Vienna, 2015.

Antony Penrose, *Surrealist Lee Miller* (Muddles Green, East Sussex, UK, Lee Miller Archives, 2019).

Vladimir Nabokov

Brian Boyd, *Vladimir Nabokov: The Russian Years, 1899–1940* (London, Chatto & Windus, 1990).

Michael Maar, *Speak, Nabokov*, tr. Ross Benjamin (London, Verso, 2009).

Vladimir Nabokov, *King, Queen, Knave*, tr. Dmitri Nabokov (New York, McGraw-Hill, 1968).

Vladimir Nabokov, *Letters to Véra*, tr. Olga Voronina and Brian Boyd (London, Penguin, 2014).

Thomas Urban, *Vladimir Nabokov: Blaue Abende in Berlin* [*Vladimir Nabokov: Blue Nights in Berlin*] (Berlin, Propyläen, 1999).

Dieter E. Zimmer, *Nabokovs Berlin* (Berlin, Nicolai, 2001).

Anaïs Nin
Deirdre Bair, *Anaïs Nin: A Biography* (New York, Putnam, 1995).
Anaïs Nin, *D. H. Lawrence: An Unprofessional Study*, tr. A. Swallow
    (London, Spearman, 1961).
Anaïs Nin, *The Diary of Anaïs Nin*, 7 vols (New York, Harcourt Brace
    Jovanovich, 1966–1980).
Anaïs Nin, *Henry and June. From A Journal of Love: The Unexpurgated Diary
    of Anaïs Nin, 1931–1932* (San Diego, Harcourt Brace & Co., 1991).
Anaïs Nin, *Incest. From A Journal of Love: The Unexpurgated Diary of Anaïs
    Nin* (New York, Harcourt Brace Jovanovich, 1992).

Pablo Picasso
Mary Ann Caws, *Picasso's Weeping Woman: The Life and Art of Dora Maar*
    (Boston, Bulfinch Press, 2000).
*Pablo Picasso und Marie-Thérèse Walter: Zwischen Klassizismus und
    Surrealismus* [*Pablo Picasso and Marie-Thérèse Walter: Between
    Classicism and Surrealism*] (Bielefeld, Kerber, 2004).
John Richardson, *A Life of Picasso. The Triumphant Years, 1917–1932*, vol. 3
    (New York, Knopf, 2007).

Erich Maria Remarque
Gabriele Katz, *Liebe mich! Erich Maria Remarque und die Frauen* [*Love Me!
    Erich Maria Remarque and Women*] (Berlin, ebersbach & simon, 2018).
Erich Maria Remarque, *The Road Back*, tr. A.W. Wheen (New York, Little,
    Brown, 1931).
Wilhelm von Sternburg, *Erich Maria Remarque. 'Als wäre alles das letzte
    Mal': Eine Biographie* [*Erich Maria Remarque. 'As if it were the last time':
    A Biography*] (Cologne, Kiepenheuer & Witsch, 1998).

Joseph Roth
David Bronsen, *Joseph Roth: Eine Biographie* (Cologne, Kiepenheuer &
    Witsch, 1974).
Gabriele Kreis, *'Was man glaubt, gibt es': Das Leben der Irmgard Keun*
    [*'Believe and it exists': The Life of Irmgard Keun*] (Zurich, Arche, 1991).
Joseph Roth, *'Ich zeichne das Gesicht der Zeit': Essays, Reportagen, Feuilletons*
    [*'I Draw the Face of Time': Essays, Reports, Features*] (Zurich, Diogenes,
    2019).
Wilhelm von Sternburg, *Joseph Roth: Eine Biographie* (Cologne,
    Kiepenheuer & Witsch, 2009).
Volker Weidermann, *Ostend, 1936: Stefan Zweig, Joseph Roth, and the*

Summer Before the Dark, tr. Carol Brown Janeway (London, Pushkin Press, 2016).

Harro and Libertas Schulze-Boysen
Wolfgang Benz, *Im Widerstand: Grösse und Scheitern der Opposition gegen Hitler* [*Resistance: The Grandeur and Failure of Opposition to Hitler*] (Munich, C. H. Beck, 2019).
Hans Coppi, *Harro Schulze-Boysen: Wege in den Widerstand* [*Harro Schulze-Boysen: Paths to Resistance*] (Koblenz, Föhlbach, 1995).
Silke Kettelhake, '*Erzähl allen, allen von mir!': Das schöne kurze Leben der Libertas Schulze-Boysen* [*'Tell everyone about me. Everyone!' The Beautiful Brief Life of Libertas Schulze-Boysen*] (Munich, Buch & Media, 2008).
Norman Ohler, *The Bohemians: The Lovers Who Led Germany's Resistance Against the Nazis*, tr. Tim Mohr and Marshall Yarbrough (Boston, Houghton Mifflin Harcourt, 2020).

Annemarie Schwarzenbach
Annemarie Schwarzenbach, *All the Roads Are Open: The Afghan Journey*, tr. Isabel Fargo Cole (London, Seagull Books, 2020).
Annemarie Schwarzenbach, *Lyric Novella*, tr. Lucy Renner Jones (London, Seagull Books, 2011).

Kurt Tucholsky
Lisa Matthias, *Ich war Tucholskys Lottchen* [*I Was Tucholsky's 'Lottchen'*] (Hamburg, V. Schröder, 1962).
Kurt Tucholsky, *Castle Gripsholm*, tr. Michael Hofmann (New York, NYRB, 2019).
Kurt Tucholsky, *Gesamtausgabe: Texte und Briefe* [*Complete Works: Essays and Letters*], Antje Bonitz, Dirk Grathoff, Michael Hepp & Gerhard Kraiker (eds), 22 vols (Reinbek, Germany, Rowohlt, 1996–).

Karl Vollmoeller
Klaus Konrad Dillmann, *Karl Gustav Vollmoeller: Eine Zeitreise durch ein bewegtes Leben* [*Karl Gustav Vollmoeller: A Journey Back in Time Through a Tumultuous Life*] (Heidelberg, Ginkgo Medien, 2009).
Karl Vollmoeller, *Aufsätze zu Leben und Werk* [*Essays on Life and Work*] (Berlin, epubli, 2017).

Bibliography

Ludwig Wittgenstein

Manfred Geier, *Die Liebe der Philosophen: Von Sokrates bis Foucault* [*Philosophers and Love: From Socrates to Foucault*] (Hamburg, Rowohlt, 2020).

James C. Klagge and Alfred Nordmann (eds), *Ludwig Wittgenstein: Public and Private Occasions* (Lanham, Md., Rowman & Littlefield, 2003).

Charlotte Wolff

Charlotte Wolff, *The Hand in Psychological Diagnosis* (Abingdon, Routledge, 2015).

Charlotte Wolff, *On the Way to Myself: Communications to a Friend* (Abingdon, Routledge, 2015).

Kurt and Helen Wolff

Barbara Weidle, *Kurt Wolff: Ein Literat und Gentleman* [*Kurt Wolff: A Man of Letters and a Gentleman*] (Bonn, Weidle, 2007).

Helen Wolff, *Hintergrund für Liebe* [*Background to Love*] (Bonn, Weidle, 2020).

Kurt Wolff and Michael Ermarth, *Kurt Wolff: A Portrait in Essays and Letters* (Chicago, University of Chicago Press, 1991).

ACKNOWLEDGEMENTS

This book relies on previous work by a large number of wonderful authors whose books have traced the lives of my protagonists through the twenties and the thirties. The bibliography therefore lists the many works that served me well while writing.

I would also like to thank all the people who offered me precious insights and ideas while I was preparing and writing this book: Mayen Beckmann, Jörg Bong, Jan Bürger, Marion Detjen, Marcus Gaertner, Durs Grünbein, Nikola Herweg, Holger Hof, Eberhard W. Kornfeld, Helmut Lethen, Ursula März, Christoph Müller, Jens Nordalm, Maria Piwowarski, Adam Soboczynski, Christoph Stölzl, Benjamin von Stuckrad-Barre and Michael Töteberg.

I am particularly grateful to four people for reading the manuscript with a keen and critical eye: Erhard Schütz (who brought so much to *1913* as that book's first professional reader), Michael Maar, Eva Menasse and Uwe Naumann.

For their steadfast support and many valuable suggestions regarding the contents I would like to thank Siv Bublitz, my publisher at S. Fischer Verlag, my editor Yelenah Frahm and my agent Matthias Landwehr.

TRANSLATOR'S NOTE

It has been both a challenge and a pleasure to work on Florian Illies's *Love in a Time of Hate*, which has expanded my reading and forged countless fruitful connections in my mind. I would like to thank Florian for entertaining my many queries, and I am also grateful to Nick Humphrey at Profile and Rebecca Saletan at Riverhead for their wonderful editing.

The bibliography has been adapted to include some useful references in English. I hope that the fascinating panorama Florian Illies paints of German and European literary culture in the face of growing Nazi terror will inspire readers to explore the riches available in translation.

Many thanks to Karen Leeder for sharing her translation in progress of Durs Grünbein's poem '23rd August 1939'. With the exception of two lines from Scott Horton's translation of Hugo von Hofmannsthal's poem 'Manche freilich ...', published in the 10 November 2007 issue of *Harper's* magazine, all the poetry translations in the book are my own. Equally, I am responsible for all the footnotes.

INDEX

Index

Index